MODI AND THE REINVENTION OF INDIAN FOREIGN POLICY

Ian Hall

BRISTOL
UNIVERSITY
PRESS

For Renée

First published in Great Britain in 2019 by

Bristol University Press
University of Bristol
1-9 Old Park Hill
Bristol
BS2 8BB
UK
t: +44 (0)117 954 5940
www.bristoluniversitypress.co.uk

North America office:
Bristol University Press
c/o The University of Chicago Press
1427 East 60th Street
Chicago, IL 60637, USA
t: +1 773 702 7700
f: +1 773-702-9756
sales@press.uchicago.edu
www.press.uchicago.edu

British Library Cataloguing in Publication Data
A catalogue record for this book is available from the British Library

Library of Congress Cataloging-in-Publication Data
A catalog record for this book has been requested

ISBN 978-1-5292-0460-5 hardcover
ISBN 978-1-5292-0462-9 paperback
ISBN 978-1-5292-0463-6 ePub
ISBN 978-1-5292-0461-2 ePdf

Cover design by blu inc, Bristol
Front cover image: Raj K. Raj/*Hindustan Times* via Getty Images
Printed and bound in Great Britain by CMP, Poole
Bristol University Press uses environmentally responsible print partners

Contents

Abbreviations

ABVP	Akhil Bharatiya Vidyarthi Parishad [All India Student Council]
ASEAN	Association of Southeast Asian Nations
BJP	Bharatiya Janata Party [Indian People's Party)
BJS	Bharatiya Jana Sangh [Indian People's Association]
BMS	Bharatiya Mazdoor Sangh [Indian Workers' Union]
BRI	Belt and Road Initiative
BRICS	Brazil, Russia, India, China and South Africa
CPEC	China–Pakistan Economic Corridor
FDI	Foreign Direct Investment
GST	Goods and Services Tax
IAS	Indian Administrative Service
IB	Intelligence Bureau
IFS	Indian Foreign Service
IPS	Indian Police Service
MEA	Ministry of External Affairs
MoD	Ministry of Defence
MOIA	Ministry of Overseas Indian Affairs
NRI	Non-Resident Indian
PDD	Public Diplomacy Division
PLA	[Chinese] People's Liberation Army
PMO	Prime Minister's Office
PRC	People's Republic of China
RAW	Research and Analysis Wing
RCEP	Regional Comprehensive Economic Partnership
RSS	Rashtriya Swayamsevak Sangh [National Volunteer Association]
SAARC	South Asian Association for Regional Cooperation
SAGAR	Security and Growth for All in the Region
SJM	Swadeshi Jagran Manch
SPMRF	Dr. Syama Prasad Mookerjee Research Foundation
UNSC	United Nations Security Council
UPA	United Progressive Alliance
VIF	Vivekananda International Foundation
VHP	Vishva Hindu Parishad

Glossary

acche din	good days
ahimsa	non-violence
asmita	sense of self/identity
Bharat	India
dharma rajya	government guided by right or religion
Hindutva	'Hindu-ness'/Hindu nationalism
Lok Sabha	lower house of Indian parliament
Moditva	'Modi-ness'
pracharak	preacher/organiser
Rajya Sabha	upper house of Indian parliament
Rashtra	polity
samman	respect/honour/national pride
samriddhi	prosperity
samvad	cooperation
Sangh	the 'family' of Hindu nationalist organisations
sanatana dharma	'true religion'
Sarsanghchalak	leader of the RSS
sahayog	cooperation
suraksha	security
swadeshi	self-reliance
vasudhaiva kutumbakam	'the world is one family'

Notes on the Author

Ian Hall is a Professor at Griffith University, Queensland, Australia. He is the Deputy Director (Research) of the Griffith Asia Institute, an Academic Fellow of the Australia India Institute at the University of Melbourne, and a co-editor (with Sara E. Davies) of the *Australian Journal of International Affairs*. His most recent books include *Dilemmas of Decline: British Intellectuals and World Politics* (University of California Press, 2012) and, as editor, *The Engagement of India: Strategies and Responses* (Georgetown University Press, 2014). He regularly commentates on Indian foreign policy and Indo-Pacific affairs. His Twitter account is *@DrIanHall*.

Acknowledgements

I am very grateful to a host of people for giving up their time to talk to me about Modi and Indian foreign policy. They include Aakriti Bachhawat, Kanti Bajpai, Nicolas Blarel, Kartik Bommakanti, David Brewster, Priya Chacko, Shibashis Chatterjee, Sreeram Chaulia, Deep Datta-Ray, Sandra Destradi, Sumit Ganguly, Surupa Gupta, Dhruva Jaishankar, Robin Jeffrey, Yogesh Joshi, Andrew B. Kennedy, Sumitha Narayanan Kutty, Diego Maiorano, Rory Medcalf, Sylvia Mishra, C. Raja Mohan, Anit Mukherjee, Rani Mullen, Amitendu Palit, Parama Sinha Palit, Harsh V. Pant, Manjeet Singh Pardesi, Rajesh Rajagopalan, Abhijnan Rej, Abhijit Singh, Bhubindar Singh, Sinderpal Singh and Constantino Xavier. My apologies to anyone I have forgotten along the way. I have also benefited in immeasurable ways from conversations with officials from Australia, India, Japan, New Zealand, the UK and the US. I am grateful for both their time and their insights into the subject of this book. I should note, of course, that none should be held responsible for the arguments or judgements advanced in what follows.

Special thanks must go to Devesh Kapur for his kind invitation to present on a related topic at a seminar at the Center for the Advanced Study of India that he used to run, to Manjari Chatterjee Miller and Kate Sullivan for involving me in the workshops in Boston and Oxford that resulted in a special issue of *International Affairs* on Modi and Indian foreign policy, and to Surupa Gupta and Rani Mullen for asking me to contribute to a special section published in *International Studies Perspectives*. I am also grateful to Venkat Iyer for inviting me to reflect on Modi's foreign policy for *The Round Table: The Commonwealth Journal of International Affairs*.

Elements of this book were presented at the International Studies Association conferences in Atlanta, Hong Kong and San Francisco, at Jawaharlal Nehru University, at the Institute of Advanced Study at Warwick University, at a meeting of the Henry Jackson Society, at Chatham House, at the New Zealand Foreign Policy School, Otago University, and at both the Institute of South Asian Studies and the S. Rajaratnam School of International Studies in Singapore. Thanks are due to everyone who participated at all of those events for their comments, queries and suggestions. I would also like to express my gratitude to the International Institute for Strategic Studies for an invitation to the 2018 Shangri-La Dialogue, at which Prime Minister Narendra Modi was the keynote speaker. And I must thank all those individuals and organisations that periodically give me public platforms to comment on Indian foreign policy. They include Katharine Adeney and the team that publishes *Asia Dialogue*, and Daniel Flitton at the Lowy Institute's *The Interpreter*.

I am fortunate to work in a community of talented scholars and professional staff at Griffith. For various insights, thoughts, and criticisms on this project, I would particularly like to thank Luis Cabrera, Sara Davies, Kai He, Michael Heazle, Huiyun Feng, Lee Morgenbesser, Nikolay Murashkin, Andrew O'Neil, David Schak, Pat Weller, Wes Widmaier and Xu Yi-Chong. I am especially grateful to the team at the Griffith Asia Institute, led by Caitlin Byrne – to Kathy Bailey, Kahlia Bartley, Meegan Thorley and Natasha Vary – for all the work they do supporting the Institute's research and policy dialogues. Griffith University permitted me to take research leave to finish the manuscript, while the S. Rajaratnam School of International Studies at Nanyang Technological University supported the visiting fellowship that allowed me to complete this book. I cannot thank Rajesh Basrur, Anit Mukherjee, Sumitha Narayanan Kutty, Sinderpal Singh, and the wider RSIS community enough for their conviviality and hospitality. Last but not least, I must thank my PhD student, Teesta Prakash, for her swift proofreading of the manuscript and her helpful comments along the way.

The research that led to this book was funded by an Australian Research Council Discovery grant (DP150102471). In parallel, the Ministry of Foreign Affairs of Japan, via the Consulate General in Brisbane, generously funded two trilateral conferences that involved invaluable in-depth interactions with Indian as well as Australian and Japanese analysts and diplomats.

I must add a special word of thanks for Stephen Wenham at Bristol University Press. It cannot be easy to coax books from authors, but in this case Stephen did so with exactly the right mix of grit and tolerance. I am grateful to the readers of the proposal and manuscript for their comments and suggestions, and to Laura Greaves for her skilful copy-editing.

Sadie, Scarlett, Eddy and Millie provided much-needed distractions throughout the time it took to write this book. But my biggest debt is owed to Renée, to whom this book is dedicated, with love.

Preface

From the beginning, independent India was 'the subject of a particular, very deliberate act of invention' (Corbridge and Harriss, 2000, p. xvii). Its political system, constitution, economic system and society were self-consciously moulded by a postcolonial political elite. India's inventors were the leaders of the Indian National Congress (INC), a mostly upper-caste, well-educated, English-speaking group that had struggled for independence for more than a generation and that inherited government after the British relinquished control of the country on 15 August 1947. Despite the haste in which power was transferred, the widespread violence that accompanied Partition, and the enormity of the governing such a large, complex, overwhelmingly poor country, this group seized with alacrity their extraordinary opportunity to imagine and craft a new Indian state, and with it, Indian society. They were not, of course, wholly united in their 'ideas of India', but with energy and purpose they set about the task of constructing a new state, putting in place institutions and processes to manage their disagreements, and reforming society.[1] Within five years, they had determined that India should have a democratic political system, that federalism was the best means of managing its diversity, that the state should not privilege one religion over another, and that government ought to play a major role in modernising its economy and society. They agreed an ambitious constitution, held a general election, launched a Five-Year Plan to develop the economy, and engaged in a remarkable bout of diplomatic activism in support of decolonisation, disarmament and the peaceful resolution of disputes.

This postcolonial, ideological 'invention of India' (Tharoor, 2003), led by the Congress Party, and the country's first Prime Minister, Jawaharlal Nehru, did not of course please all. Already dismayed by the Partition of India, Hindu nationalists in particular criticised the Nehru government's commitments to secularism and socialism, and its desire to modernise India following Western models. They wanted an India that advanced the interests and values of the Hindu majority and that was governed in ways more closely aligned with what they perceived as authentically Indian thought and practice.

These views did not find widespread support until the latter half of the 1980s and early 1990s. By then, it was readily apparent that the Nehruvian model had not delivered all that it had promised. Corruption, graft, political violence, economic malaise, social unrest, separatism and communal tensions all beset India. New Delhi's relations with significant parts of the world, including much of East Asia and the West, were attenuated and often testy. In response, India's Congress-led government of Rahul Gandhi, Nehru's grandson, and especially P.V. Narasimha Rao embarked on programmes of economic reform, attempting to remove or at least limit state intervention and regulation.

These reforms were an attempt to 'reinvent' India, Corbridge and Harriss famously argued, aiming to set aside the state-led model of modernisation that Nehru and the Congress Party had put in place after 1947 (2000, p. xix). Although not without problems, or indeed critics, the reforms were successful in delivering higher rates of economic growth through the 1990s and into the new century. They transformed the Indian economy, changed Indian society, and provided a platform, as we will see, for a more confident foreign policy. They did not constitute, however, the only attempt at reinventing India that emerged during the 1980s and 1990s. These economic reforms ran in parallel to – and at times intersected and came into conflict with – another effort, one arising from Hindu nationalist forces then gathering strength in the country. This movement aimed at displacing key features of the postcolonial political settlement, especially the principles that the state should not interfere in religious matters, including the laws applicable in issues like divorce, and that the state should not favour one religious community over others. It also aimed at dismantling the quasi-socialist system of state-led economic management institutionalised by Nehru and extended by his successors, despite divisions within the Hindu nationalist movement about what ought to replace it.

These concerns came to fore between 1998 and 2004, when the Hindu nationalist Bharatiya Janata Party (BJP) led a coalition government under Atal Bihari Vajpayee. Hardliners within and outside the BJP pushed for a 'uniform civil code' applicable to all religious groups, for the construction of Hindu temples, including one at the controversial site of Ayodhya in Uttar Pradesh, where a mosque had been torn down by Hindu nationalists in 1992, and for sweeping changes to school curricula. They also called for the repeal of Article 370 of the Constitution, which gave special status to Jammu and Kashmir. In the main, however, the BJP-led government confined itself to an agenda of economic liberalisation at home and pragmatic engagement abroad, especially with the US, as it was unable to persuade its coalition partners to pursue a thorough reinvention of domestic and foreign policy, and of India itself.[2]

Among Hindu nationalists, the desire to erase the India that Congress invented after 1947 and to replace it with something different did not, however, dissipate or disappear. Although the BJP lost the 2004 election and spent a decade in opposition, it continued to be a significant political force, and the vision of India the BJP championed continued to appeal to many voters. When Narendra Modi came to power at the head of a resurgent BJP in May 2014, that vision returned to the fore. Before and after becoming Prime Minister, Modi himself made no secret of his disdain for Nehru's idea of India and the political legacy of the postcolonial Congress Party (Mantri and Gupta, 2013). He offered a 'New India' in its place, one grounded on different principles to those of Nehru and his allies, who pursued secularism and socialism at home, and non-alignment and activism abroad. He claimed a 'mandate for change' and for a transformation of 'mindsets' not just in domestic policy, but also in India's international relations (MEA, 2017a). And in contrast to Vajpayee's government, Modi commanded an outright majority in the Lok Sabha, the lower house of parliament, giving him greater means – at least in principle – to realise a reinvention.

This book explores what Modi did with that unprecedented power in the area of foreign policy during his first term in office, from 2014 to 2019. It lays out the agenda Modi and his allies had for reinventing Indian foreign policy and traces its origins in Hindu nationalist thinking about international relations. It pushes back against the portrayal of Modi as a pragmatist or realist in foreign policy, arguing that he has acted in that area – as in others – as a self-consciously transformational leader with a clearly ideological agenda that has structured priorities and shaped approaches to key issues.[3] Finally, it assesses whether Modi's attempted reinvention succeeded or failed, and what its track record tells us about who makes and implements foreign policy in India, and why they do it in the way that they do.

Ian Hall
School of Government and International Relations
Griffith University
May 2019

1

Introduction

In late May 2019, Narendra Modi defied political gravity, and the expectations of many analysts, by emerging from a keenly contested election campaign with an even bigger majority than he had had before. His victory was hailed in the Indian media as a 'TsuNaMo' – an allusion to both the 'Modi wave' that had carried him into office in May 2014, and one of the Prime Minister's popular nicknames, 'NaMo' (Kohli, 2019). It confirmed Modi as the dominant political force of contemporary India, a figure lauded by millions and feared by many. His crushing win demonstrated not just his capacity to craft narratives of mass appeal, but also the success of his effort to re-craft his image since first coming to power – to make himself more than a mere politician, using foreign policy as one of the means to that end.

The general election that originally swept Modi and his Hindu nationalist Bharatiya Janata Party (Indian People's Party or BJP) into office in May 2014 was one of the most extraordinary episodes in Indian political history. Never before had so many Indians – over 814 million – been eligible to vote, and so many gone to the polls, on a turnout of just over 66 per cent. Never before had so much money been spent in the campaign – more than US$5 billion,[1] according to one credible estimate (Kapur and Vaishnav, 2018, p. 4). And never before had the BJP won an outright majority in the Lok Sabha, the lower house of parliament, let alone the 336 seats out of 543 that it, along with its coalition partners, came to control.[2] The Congress Party – which had dominated India's politics in the postcolonial era – was outpaced and outspent, and left with just 44 members of parliament (MPs).[3]

At the centre of the election was Narendra Modi, the BJP's designated candidate for the post of Prime Minister, and one of the most successful and controversial figures in contemporary India. Born in 1950 into a relatively poor family, Modi rose to prominence through the ranks of the equally controversial Hindu nationalist movement, the Rashtriya

Swayamsevak Sangh (loosely, the National Volunteer Association – the RSS) and then, in the 1980s and 1990s, through those of the BJP, for which he worked as a fixer, strategist and spokesperson. In October 2001 he entered into political office for the first time, becoming Chief Minister of his home state of Gujarat. Five months later he faced a defining crisis that brought him to national and international attention. On 27 February 2002, a train full of Hindu nationalist activists stopped in the town of Godhra. It was then set on fire – accidently or deliberately – during a confrontation between the passengers and local Muslims. Fifty-nine people died, and in response, communal rioting spread across Gujarat, a state with a long history of such violence (Shani, 2007). Between one and two thousand more people were killed, and many more injured, robbed, and displaced.[4]

Modi's leadership during these events was widely criticised, even within the BJP, tarnishing his reputation for years to follow. He was accused of doing too little to stop the rioting and to protect Muslim communities in particular. Some even suggested that his government had ordered the police not to intervene during the violence and not to investigate crimes in its aftermath. Modi was criticised for stirring and exploiting communal tensions for political advantage before and after the violence, especially in the election campaign that took place in late 2002 (see especially Nussbaum, 2007). A few went so far as to label him a 'fascist' (Nandy, 2002), or even – in the words of Congress Party leader Sonia Gandhi, speaking during the Gujarat state election campaign in 2007 – a *maut ka saudagar* ('merchant of death') (*Times of India*, 2007). Western governments deemed him off-limits for diplomats and after pressure was exerted on the State Department by American legislators, he was refused a visa to visit the US (see Verma, 2014, pp. 357–62).

Modi's supporters, of course, cast him in a very different light. They dismissed suggestions that he had been negligent or complicit in the communal violence of 2002. At the same time, they celebrated his declared commitment to defend Hindu communities and interests, as well as Gujarat's reputation. Hard-line Hindu nationalists praised him as the *Hindu Hriday Samrat*, or 'King of Hindu Hearts' (Jaffrelot, 2016). Proud Gujaratis appreciated his efforts to rebuff accusations made elsewhere in India, and abroad, that the state was a hotbed of communal violence. They liked Modi's efforts to promote and protect their distinct *asmita* or (loosely) 'self', and appreciated his appeals to the wisdom of great Gujaratis of the past, including Mohandas K. Gandhi and Sardar Vallabhbhai Patel. Over time, as Modi won successive elections in Gujarat, others – especially in the growing middle class, the business community and in the Gujarati diaspora abroad – emphasised what they saw as his commitment to good governance and economic development, and his apparent success in delivering them. They began to perceive and portray Modi as a very different kind of Indian politician from the usual variety – as an energetic, 'can-do', technologically savvy, business-friendly, corruption-free, transformational leader.[5]

Modi's ability to appeal to these various constituencies – to cultural nationalists, to businesspeople, and to the actual and aspiring middle class – as well as his exceptional skills as a strategist and orator helped him secure the BJP's nomination for the post of Prime Minister prior to the 2014 election (Nag, 2014, pp. 219–25). The belief that he could rescue India from economic torpor and widespread corruption, together with the hope that – as one of his campaign slogans put it, '*acche din aane wale hain*' ('good days are coming') – propelled him and the BJP into power. Casting himself as a '*vikas purush*' (loosely, 'development man') untainted by scandal and scams, Modi aided the BJP's mission of breaking out beyond its traditional heartlands in the north and west of India, surging into new areas in the northeast, south, and the east of the country. Employing messaging carefully crafted to appeal to different constituencies in India's diverse society – a strategy honed by the BJP in Gujarat – they attracted new voters in large numbers (Jha, 2017). And despite Modi being twenty years older than his principal opponent, Rahul Gandhi, then 44 years old, they gained the support of large numbers of younger voters, partly due to a campaign that made extensive use of technology, from targeted messaging to mobile phones and social media to holographic projections of Modi's speeches (see especially Basu and Misra, 2015, and Price, 2015).

Foreign policy in motion

The extraordinary campaign that paved the way for the BJP's victory in 2014 left, however, some important questions unanswered. One was how the new government was going to handle India's relations with the rest of the world. On that topic, neither the Modi nor the other principal BJP leaders had given much away in the months leading up to the election. Understandably, they, like Modi's main opponent, Rahul Gandhi, had focused on the issues that mattered most to voters: economic development and combating corruption (Singh, T., 2013). Foreign policy – something more distant from the everyday experiences and aspirations of the *aam aadmi*, the ubiquitous 'common man' of Indian political discourse – was rarely discussed in the hundreds of speeches Modi and his opponent delivered on the campaign trail. In one or two, there were hints of positions that might be taken – particularly in an address given in Chennai in October 2013 (see Panda, 2013) – but little else. What was written on foreign policy in the BJP's election manifesto, covering barely three pages out of a total of fifty-two, was couched mostly in high-flown generalities (BJP, 2014a, pp. 39–41).[6]

This lack of detail inevitably led to much speculation – some well grounded and some less so – and generated considerable anxiety in India and abroad (Pal, 2014). Some worried that Modi's erstwhile reputation as a nationalist firebrand might lead him to a precipitous confrontation with Pakistan and perhaps also China. The distinguished writer William Dalrymple, for example, recalled Modi's infamous comments during the 1999 Kargil Crisis, when just months after both countries had tested nuclear weapons, Indian and Pakistani troops fought for control of the Siachen Glacier in the disputed region of Kashmir. Dalrymple observed that when asked on television how he thought India ought to respond to the infiltration of Pakistani forces into the area, Modi, then a BJP national spokesperson, had responded: '*Chicken biryani nahi, bullet ka jawab bomb se diya jayega*' ('We won't give them chicken biryani; we will respond to a bullet with a [nuclear] bomb') (Dalrymple, 2014). Others observed Modi's equally robust comments about the People's Republic, made in disputed state of Arunachal Pradesh, which Beijing claims as 'South Tibet', while he was on the campaign trail. China has a 'mindset of expansion', he declared, and that it ought to abandon it in favour of a commitment to development. 'I swear in the name of this soil', he told the rally, 'that I will never allow the state [Arunachal Pradesh] to disappear ... and to bow down' to Beijing (Karmakar, 2014).

Other analysts were more sanguine. A few suggested that Modi's relative inexperience in foreign policy and diplomacy would likely mean that it would take him some time before he did anything dramatic or consequential in the area (Lucas, 2014). Many argued that Modi's reputation as a hardliner might perhaps give him the latitude unavailable to recent Congress leaders to improve relations with Pakistan – for him to act as a kind of Indian Nixon to Pakistan's China (Mohan, 2015a, pp. 68–70). Some worried that ties with the US might cool, and progress in advancing the relationship might slow. They noted that Washington had earlier banned Modi from entering the country over his handling of communal violence in Gujarat and that US and European diplomats in India had avoided contact with the Chief Minister for a time.[7] But they also noted that Modi would most likely focus on economic diplomacy, and try to put foreign policy at the service of domestic development, which, they concluded, would in the long term improve the US-India partnership (Ganguly, 2014). They expressed the hope that his government might try to further open up India's economy to trade and investment, and make substantive progress on connectivity in South Asia, the world's least integrated region. Finally, some observed Modi's apparent interest in building India's so-called soft power, using its cultural heritage and inheritance, as well as its diaspora, to influence the region and the world (Schaffer and Schaffer, 2013). But given the reticence shown by both Modi and the BJP in laying out a clear platform, and given the scale of the domestic challenges they would face, few thought that foreign policy would be an early priority for his government.

Once in office, however, Modi sprang an immediate surprise on both outside observers and the Ministry of External Affairs (MEA). In an unprecedented move, he had officials issue invitations to all South Asian leaders and the New Delhi-based diplomatic community to attend a ceremony in front of the Rashtrapati Bhavan, the official residence of the President of India, and witness his swearing-in as Prime Minister. Partly, this was characteristic showmanship, but it was also an attempt to reset relations with India's neighbours, including Pakistan – whose Prime Minister, Nawaz Sharif, was photographed congratulating Modi with a cordial handshake and a smile.[8] A clear message was conveyed: under the new government, New Delhi would put the 'neighbourhood first' – as the policy soon became known – and put new energy into building and maintaining strong ties with the smaller states of South Asia.[9] And at the same time, another less conciliatory missive was directed at China. On the guest list for Modi's 'inauguration' were both the head of the Tibetan government-in-exile, Lobsang Sangay, and Taiwan's representative in New Delhi, Chung Kwang Tien. The subtext was clear: this government was not going to have its relationships with any part of the region circumscribed by Beijing (Gokhale, 2017a, p. 5).

True to the expectations of some analysts, but faster than anticipated, Modi also moved to make economic diplomacy a bigger focus of the MEA and India's overseas missions. A few weeks after the election, in June 2014, he gave a speech to new entrants into the Indian Foreign Service (IFS), telling them to concentrate on boosting trade and investment to aid the domestic economy (Roy, 2014a). In late September 2014, a little over four months after coming to power, Modi then launched his 'Make in India' initiative at a grand jamboree in Mumbai. Aiming to bring overseas capital into the country to boost 25 areas of manufacturing, the policy promised – in a departure from past practice – to permit 100 per cent foreign ownership in the majority of those sectors. Thereafter, his foreign visits included meetings with investors and manufacturing business leaders to sell the scheme (Chaulia, 2016, pp. 90–3). In parallel, Modi worked to secure more reliable access to energy resources, concluding – among other agreements – a deal to import uranium from Australia during Prime Minister Tony Abbott's visit in September 2014 (Palit, 2015, p. 19). Last but not least, his government worked to soften India's intransigent stance in long-running multilateral trade talks (Narlikar, 2017, p. 106).

Soon after his swearing-in, Modi also embarked on a series of high-profile foreign visits, each symbolic, and all carefully stage-managed. In keeping with the notion of 'neighbourhood first' and resetting relations with other South Asian states, he went first to Bhutan, in mid-June 2014, and sent his foreign minister to Bangladesh (Mohan, 2015a, p. 46). He roamed more widely in the second half of the year, heading to Brazil, Japan, the US, Australia and Fiji, as well as making a series of visits closer to home, to Nepal (twice) and to Myanmar. He attended four major multilateral meetings: the BRICS (Brazil, Russia, India, China and South Africa) summit, the East Asia Summit, the G20, and the South Asian Association for Regional Cooperation (SAARC) summit. Throughout, Modi put on an elaborate show. In Australia and the US, alongside his formal diplomatic commitments, there were major public events, complete with music and dancing, that allowed Modi to mingle with members of the Indian diaspora, to thank them for their support during the election campaign and to bask in their approval, which they delivered with alacrity. At both the Melbourne Cricket Ground and Madison Square Gardens the attendees chanted Modi's name. At the Australian Parliament in Canberra, in mid-November, he was greeted by MPs and the public like he was a 'rock star' (Ireland, 2014).

In these early months much effort was also devoted to rebranding foreign policy and reordering priorities – at least on paper. In Modi's first Independence Day speech, on 15 August 2014, and then at the United Nations (UN), he declared once more his government's desire to improve relations with India's neighbours and to work together with them to eradicate poverty, putting the 'neighbourhood first' (Modi, 2014a, 2014b; cf. Muni, 2017). Moved by a concern that New Delhi had done too little to engage the states of what India thinks of as West Asia, despite the presence in the Middle East of large numbers of Indian workers and India's rising demand for the region's oil, Modi announced that his government would implement a new 'Link West' policy to parallel India's venerable 'Look East' approach, dating back to the mid-1990s (Mohan, 2014a). Then, at the ASEAN–India Summit held in Myanmar immediately after Modi's state visits to Australia and Fiji, and the G20 in Brisbane, Modi declared that 'Look East' itself would be revivified and renamed 'Act East' (Rajendram, 2014).

There was drama too about Modi's high-level summitry in these early months of his government, especially in his bilateral meetings with other leaders. During a five-day long state visit to Japan in late August and early September 2014, he and Prime Minister Shinzō Abe elevated bilateral ties to the new level of a Special Strategic and Global Partnership, and agreed a 'Vision 2025' to guide its future development. A few days later, in mid-September, Modi welcomed President Xi Jinping to India. The Chinese leader was taken to Gujarat for talks and photo shoots, including a notable piece of theatre in which the two men sat together and talked, while the cameras clicked, on an elaborate gilded swing. Amidst the agreements signed and investment deals promised, there were also departures from the usual script for Sino-Indian meetings, as Modi used a joint press conference to bluntly state New Delhi's 'serious concern' about incursions by the People's Liberation Army across their disputed border, including one that occurred just prior to Xi's arrival (Bajpai, 2017, p. 81). Then, a few days after that, Modi arrived in the US to address the United Nations General Assembly (UNGA) and meet President Barack Obama.

In New York, Modi spoke in Hindi, as his BJP predecessor, Atal Bihari Vajpayee, had done. Characteristically effusive and sweeping, he recalled India's 'ancient wisdom' and expressed the desire to tackle climate change, terrorism and poverty in 'genuine international partnership'. He called for an 'International Yoga Day' to recognise that 'invaluable gift of our ancient tradition' (Modi, 2014b). A couple of weeks later, this latter wish was granted by the UNGA. Outside the UN, Modi was acclaimed at Madison Square Gardens and even made a cameo appearance at the Global Citizen Festival in Central Park, alongside the actor Hugh Jackman. At well-publicised events in New York, he met bankers and business leaders to assure them that his new government was friendly to their interests, both at home and overseas, and to encourage them to invest in India.

The state visit that followed was more about fence building than about the future. It was intended on both sides to signal that both Obama and Modi were willing to continue to do business and to maintain the strategic partnership forged in the mid-2000s by their predecessors, George W. Bush and Manmohan Singh, despite past American misgivings about the new Prime Minister and the visa ban imposed on him after the 2002 riots. But in the event, the meeting went better than planned, as the two leaders built some personal rapport and made a show of their supposed friendliness. Obama took Modi for an apparently unscheduled visit at the Martin Luther King memorial in his presidential limousine. The two published an editorial in *The Washington Post* lauding a 'partnership' that 'is robust, reliable and enduring' – and, importantly, 'expanding'. 'Forward together we go – *chalein saath saath*', the article ended, signalling a mutual desire to keep US-India relations on an even keel and moving in the right direction (Modi and Obama, 2014).

Substantive progress soon followed in strengthening ties between the two countries. In November, Modi tweeted an invitation to Obama to become the first US president to be the guest of honour at India's Republic Day parade on 26 January 2015.[10] It was accepted. During the visit, New Delhi agreed to renew the landmark ten-year Defence Framework Agreement first agreed by Bush and Singh, which was due to expire in 2015. Together, the US and India also launched a so-called Joint Strategic Vision Statement, outlining their preferred regional order (MEA, 2015a). Along with the bear hug Modi inflicted on Obama when he landed in New Delhi, these were further clear signs that the Indian Prime Minister was content to let bygones be bygones, and that his administration was committed to the strategic partnership, unlike its predecessor, which had wavered, especially toward the end of its term. At this moment, Modi also shook up his foreign policy team, bringing in Subrahmanyam (conventionally, 'S.') Jaishankar – then ambassador to Washington, and former ambassador to Beijing – as his new Foreign Secretary, to head the MEA (Haidar, 2015).

Once in post, Jaishankar moved swiftly to craft a new understanding of India's role in the world, supplying a narrative intended to make sense of Modi's energetic personal diplomacy in the first few months of his government and set the course for future action. In reported comments at a think tank dialogue in March 2015, he suggested that the major challenge facing India was China's surging economic and military power and welcomed recent moves to strengthen the strategic partnership with the US (Roggenveen, 2015). Jaishankar's clearest statements about how the Modi government conceived of the aims of Indian foreign policy came, however, in July, at a book launch in New Delhi (MEA, 2015b) and then in a Fullerton Lecture delivered for the International Institute for Strategic Studies in Singapore (MEA, 2015c). In both, he argued that India now aspired to become a 'leading power' in a 'multi-polar world', taking principled positions and shouldering burdens. At the same time, he claimed, Indian diplomacy was being reformed to play a key 'role in our national development', making 'full use of personal chemistry, narratives, culture, and our diaspora' (MEA, 2015b).[11]

In parallel, the BJP and its supporters also began to articulate a new narrative about the Modi government's approach to foreign policy. In early April 2015, the Party's National Executive met in Bengaluru (formerly Bangalore) to discuss various issues, including international relations and India's role in the world. It concluded with an endorsement of a lengthy resolution of close to four thousand words drafted by Ram Madhav – like Modi, a RSS leader turned functionary and politician – who had been appointed a BJP General Secretary in 2014. The resolution noted the 'great pride' the party had in Modi's 'dynamic and visionary leadership' in foreign policy, the government's near unprecedented 'speed and resolve', and the way that it had boosted 'global interest and confidence' in India and 'optimism' about its prospects. In ten months, it observed, the Prime Minister and External Affairs Minister, Sushma Swaraj, had 'engaged with' 94 countries in one way or another. The resolution also laid out the set of principles that informed that approach, which it termed the *Panchamrit*, borrowing a term from Hindu devotional practice that refers to five foods mixed as an offering.[12] The five 'pillars' of this foreign policy *Panchamrit* were, according to the resolution: '*Samman* – dignity and honour; *Samvad* – greater engagement and dialogue; *Samriddhi* – shared prosperity; *Suraksha* – regional and global security; and *Sanskriti evam Sabhyata* – cultural and civilizational linkages' [capitalisation in original] (BJP, 2015).

The resolution made clear the BJP's understanding of the government's foreign policy priorities. Above all was India's economic development, which required 'access to capital, technology, resources, energy and skills' and the maintenance of global confidence in the country. Moreover, it demanded 'a secure environment, a peaceful neighbourhood and an open and stable global trading system'. Second was the aim of ensuring that India – or Bharat, to use the term in the resolution, one preferred by some Hindu nationalists – is acknowledged and respected in the world. A foreign policy 'rooted in our inheritance of a timeless tradition of intellectual and economic engagement through peaceful co-existence' was not merely in line with the right values; it was also best fitted to ensure that 'Bharat…enjoys enhanced international stature'. In less than a year, the resolution concluded, Modi's government had succeeded in establishing these two overarching priorities, to be pursued with the *Panchamrit*, and had thus 'transformed foreign policy into a major instrument to realize our national ambition of Bharat's rise as a strong and respected world power' (BJP, 2015).

Despite the very different idioms in which they were expressed, and contrasting emphases, Jaishankar and Madhav's understandings of Modi's approach, laid out after the first year of his term in office, chimed with each other in a number of places. Under Modi, they both argued, foreign policy was being put to the service of development, first and foremost; resetting relationships in South Asia was a priority; 'soft power' was seen as an essential instrument, and one that India possessed due to its cultural and civilizational inheritance and its long history of interactions with societies across the Indo-Pacific; and New Delhi had aspirations to act as a major player. Just as important, in outlining Modi's supposed approach, were the language and concepts both Jaishankar and Madhav avoided.

The words 'nonalignment' and 'strategic autonomy' – long synonymous with Indian foreign policy – appeared nowhere in their texts, nor almost all of the Prime Minister's speeches after 2014 (Ganguly, 2017, p. 132).

Some have interpreted these omissions as heralding a shift from older ideological understandings of how best to conduct India's international relations to a more pragmatic, even 'realist' approach.[13] In this book, I question that argument. I posit that Modi's track record in foreign policy between 2014 and 2019 did not merely involve injecting energy into Indian diplomacy and shedding inherited ideological baggage in favour of mere pragmatism, as many argue. Modi and his allies tried to go further than that. In foreign policy as in domestic policy, I argue, Modi sought to be a 'transformational leader', not simply a 'transactional' one.[14] He aimed at more than merely delivering the spoils of government to his backers, instead seeking a broader transformation of Indian society – and, I argue, India's international relations – underpinned by an ideologically inspired 'vision' (Chhibber and Verma, 2018, p. 135). Modi sought to reinvent Indian foreign policy by replacing an older vision with a new approach grounded not in pragmatism or even realism, but in Hindu nationalist ideology. To use his words, he aimed at a foreign policy 'shaped by [India's] civilizational ethos' (MEA, 2017a). This vision, this book argues, set the Modi government's foreign policy priorities. Moreover, understanding it helps explain his government's devotion to building and leveraging India's 'soft power', its failure to open up the country's economy in the ways in which many outsiders imagined it might, and its patchy record on bolstering India's hard power, despite its posturing during significant crises, like those that erupted at Doklam in mid-2017 and in Kashmir in early 2019.[15]

Making Indian foreign policy

Grasping the nature and extent of Modi's attempted reinvention of Indian foreign policy requires, of course, some prior sense of how it is made and who makes it, and how foreign policy making has evolved in India over time. For scholars, at least, the answers to these questions used to be relatively settled.[16] They pointed to the institutional arrangements put in place after 1947. The leaders of post-independence India chose a parliamentary system with a president with powers similar to a constitutional monarch, making foreign policy making and implementation the responsibility of the core executive, subject to oversight from the legislative branch of government, from the lower house, the Lok Sabha (House of the People), and the upper house, the Rajya Sabha (Council of States) (Bandyopadhyaya, 1991, pp. 159–91). Formally, all are bounded by the Constitution, which aside from the normal limitations set out in such documents, also lays out a set of 'Directive Principles of State Policy' that address foreign affairs as well as a number of other areas. In language intentionally reminiscent of the United Nations Charter, Article 51 directs government to 'endeavour' to 'promote international peace and security', 'maintain just and honourable relations between nations', 'foster respect for international law and treaty obligations', and encourage the settlement of disputes 'by arbitration' (Constitution of India, 1950).[17]

In this system, the Prime Minister, together with the External Affairs Minister and others with relevant portfolios, such as finance, defence, and home affairs, are deemed responsible for formulating foreign policy, subject to approval by Cabinet and to parliamentary oversight. The MEA, headed by the Foreign Secretary, is charged with advising the Prime Minister and relevant Cabinet ministers, and is the lead agency in its implementation.

In practice, however, soon after 1947 foreign policy making became highly centralised in the hands of the Prime Minister and the Prime Minister's Office (PMO), rarely subject to sustained scrutiny by parliament, and produced with varying levels of input from the MEA (Andersen, 1983). Whether the outcomes were consistent with the Directive Principles became a moot point.

For better or worse, India's first Prime Minister, Jawaharlal Nehru, who served from 1947 until his death in 1964, dominated the foreign policy-making process during his time in office. He did so partly because he simply had more interest and expertise in international relations than his peers (see Power, 1964 and Ganguly, 1994), but also because he entrenched himself, in institutional terms, in that area. Throughout his time as Prime Minister, Nehru also held on to the post of External Affairs Minister. Although formal Cabinet conventions were followed, and moves made during his time in office to institutionalise collective decision making, such as the creation of a Cabinet Standing Committee on Foreign Affairs in 1957, while he was in power Nehru behaved as both the principal architect of policy and India's lead diplomat (Appadorai, 1969, pp. 205–7). Early in his tenure, he strongly influenced the selection of IFS officers in the early years and the key ambassadors (Mehta, 2010, pp. 32–3). Throughout, he supplied most of the ideas and strategy that underpinned policy. At least until the disastrous Sino-Indian border war in October 1962, his voice was heard most loudly in parliamentary debate on foreign policy, despite spirited opposition from a few MPs with interest in the topic, like the young Atal Bihari Vajpayee, later an External Affairs Minister himself and later still, the BJP's first Prime Minister (Nag, 2017, pp. 38–9).[18] In the background, the Consultative Committee on External Affairs in parliament became, in effect, a mechanism for communicating decisions made by the executive to MPs, rather than a deliberative body (Bandyopadhyaya, 1991, p. 163).[19]

After Nehru, foreign policy making remained highly centralised and largely isolated from influences external to the PMO and MEA. Eight of his successors held the job of External Affairs Minister at the same time as the prime ministership – though in contrast with Nehru's practice, they did so normally for relatively short periods.[20] Most if not all set the direction of foreign policy, guided as much by advisors within the PMO, rather than allowing the EAM and MEA to take the lead. In the late 1960s and early 1970s, for example, Indira Gandhi, Nehru's daughter, who ruled from 1966 to 1977, and then from 1980 to 1984, relied heavily on the advice of her Principal Secretary in the PMO, the former IFS officer, Parmeshwar Narayan (conventionally, P.N.) Haksar (Dixit, 2004, pp. 166–8).[21] Rarely, moreover, have Indian Prime Ministers since Nehru suffered much parliamentary oversight of their approach. Long after his death in 1964, crucial and consequential foreign and security policy decisions – such as the conclusion of a Treaty of Peace and Friendship with the Soviet Union in 1971, or the intervention in East Pakistan the same year – were made without formal consultation with MPs (Bandyopadhyaya, 1991, p. 166). When India tested nuclear devices in 1974 and 1998, parliamentarians were not informed prior to the events, and nor, in the second case, was the full Cabinet trusted to debate the decision before it was made.

All of this said, it must also be observed that foreign policy has long been an issue of contention between India's political parties, despite relatively low levels of interest among voters in the subject.[22] Even before the 1962 war, Nehru's handling of China was robustly criticised by his opponents in and outside parliament. Since then, his management of Sino-Indian relations has served as a means of attacking the Congress Party more broadly, especially over the past two decades, over its supposed incompetence in foreign policy.[23] Indira Gandhi's approach to the crisis in East Pakistan in 1971 became a party political dispute, providing an opportunity for her critics to attack her government before she took the decision to intervene, and a chance to consolidate her grip on power in the aftermath (see Raghavan, 2013). More recently, a series of foreign policy issues have also generated arguments between the major parties or been used as tools with which to undermine governments. The most obvious is the US-India nuclear deal, which led both to the withdrawal of the socialist-leaning Left Front from Manmohan Singh's ruling coalition and to sustained criticism from the BJP, which saw an opening to exploit, and which almost brought down the government (see especially Mistry, 2014). That issue also highlighted the importance of coalition politics in some areas of foreign policy, notably where ideologically driven (as in the case of the Left Front) or regional partners (such as Tamil parties concerned with Sri Lanka) have a particular interest.[24]

Over time, of course, the institutional context in which foreign policy is made has also grown more complex, with more actors vying for influence and more requiring a degree of consideration by the Prime Minister, the PMO and the MEA. First, the size and structure of the bureaucracy has changed.[25] The IFS has grown to around 1,000 individuals, including both 'A'- and 'B'-ranked officers, but remains very small by global standards, with staffing roughly equivalent to New Zealand's Ministry of Foreign Affairs and Trade, which serves country of only 4.8 million people. As a consequence, the MEA is still widely considered to lack capacity in many areas, including in strategic planning.[26]

The partial opening-up of the Indian economy and the conclusion or negotiation of trade deals, as well as a greater focus on economic diplomacy, has also elevated the importance of the Ministries of Finance, Commerce and Industry, and Petroleum and Natural Gas as actors in foreign policy, alongside the MEA and the Ministry of Defence (MoD). Second, other significant agencies have emerged – notably India's external intelligence service, the Research and Analysis Wing (RAW), created in 1968 to supplement the internally focused Intelligence Bureau (IB), and said to dabble in foreign relations, especially in India's neighbourhood. The post of National Security Advisor was established in 1998, with an attendant bureaucracy and a broad remit, directly reporting to the Prime Minister.[27] And while it lasted, from 2004 until 2016, when it was merged into the MEA, the Ministry of Overseas Indian Affairs (MOIA), charged with engaging India's huge diaspora, also played a significant role in foreign affairs.

These central government ministries also have to contend with a range of other actors within and beyond New Delhi, some new and some not. These include the governments of the 29 states and seven union territories, especially those bordering neighbouring states or having extensive economic, ethnic or diaspora links with other countries. These can and have affected foreign policy, most clearly concerning ties with Bangladesh and Sri Lanka, and with Middle Eastern states where large numbers of Indian migrant workers reside.[28] Moreover, some of these states now routinely practise what has become known as 'paradiplomacy', with Chief Ministers and other representatives travelling abroad to negotiate investment and other deals with foreign partners.[29] Modi, when he was governing Gujarat, was involved in these activities, becoming a prominent 'paradiplomat' long before he came to power in New Delhi, and embarking on various foreign official visits, including several to Beijing.

Beyond the states are a series of other players that can have influence on foreign policy making and implementation. Public opinion, the media and experts or commentators located in universities, think tanks and in government research and scientific establishments all matter in India – albeit in varying degrees depending on the salience and importance of the issue and the degree of knowledge of it beyond government – and must somehow be managed.[30] Prime Ministers can, of course, also avail themselves of the skills and capacities of outsiders drawn from the media or research centres, who can become significant players. In Manmohan Singh's first term, for example, the journalist Sanjaya Baru became a key advisor, as well as spokesperson (see Baru, 2015).

Beyond these areas, agricultural producers, unions and business communities are all also important – if fractured – constituencies, especially with regard to relations with neighbouring states and to trade and investment agreements. Since roughly half of India's workforce is employed in farming, the impact of foreign economic policy on their livelihoods has long been a major concern – and the principal reason why New Delhi has dragged its feet in world trade talks for two decades (Hopewell, 2016, pp. 147–75). Elsewhere, however, the opening up of India's economy has been complicated by the interests of some of the large industrial corporations that dominated key sectors of the economy, which are often protected by long-standing tariff and regulatory regimes.[31] In sum, then, the foreign policy-making process is widely thought to have become more complex and fragmented, at least in terms of the proliferation of different institutions and interest groups, though it remains concentrated in the hands of the core executive.

The Modi government and foreign policy making

After 2014, if anything, foreign policy making became more centralised – or, at least, more driven by the Prime Minister, through the PMO. In no small part, this was a function of Modi's dominant position vis-à-vis the rest of the BJP leadership – a position greatly reinforced by the scale of his election victory and his key role in delivering that success. Modi did, however, avoid the temptation of being his own foreign minister, as Nehru and many other predecessors had done. Instead, he gave the job of External Affairs Minister to one of his main rivals within the BJP, Sushma Swaraj. A lawyer from Haryana in northern India whose father was once an RSS leader, Swaraj had served as Information and then Health Minister in the Vajpayee government, and as Leader of the Opposition in the Lok Sabha during Manmohan Singh's second term. Over time, however, it became clear that Modi and Swaraj's respective responsibilities were quite different, with the former directing high-level policy and making key decisions, and the latter spending a great deal of time on foreign visits and essentially consular work, ensuring the welfare of India's diaspora, especially migrant workers in the Middle East (*The Economist*, 2015; Varadarajan, 2015). Alongside Swaraj, Modi also appointed Vijay Kumar Singh, former General and Chief of the Army Staff, as Minister of State in the MEA. For a few months, until November 2014, Singh also had special responsibility for the northeast of the country, the relatively poor and contested areas bordering Bangladesh, Bhutan, China and Myanmar.

Modi found it harder to fill the post of *Raksha Mantri* or Defence Minister. Initially Arun Jaitley, the Finance Minister, served in the role for six months, but it was clear that this was only a temporary arrangement, as the PM searched for a suitable candidate from outside parliament. It then went to Manohar Parrikar, the sitting BJP Chief Minister of Goa, who was elevated to a seat in the upper house of parliament, the Rajya Sabha, and held the post from November 2014 until March 2017. Parrikar then returned to Goa to once again head its state government. After another brief period in Jaitley's care, in September 2017 Modi reshuffled his erstwhile Minister of Commerce and Industry, Nirmala Sitaraman, an economist originally from Tamil Nadu, into the position. She remained in post until the 2019 election.

Beyond the MEA and the MoD, the other senior ministers holding portfolios that affecting foreign policy were Jaitley, who served as Finance Minister throughout Modi's government, and Rajnath Singh, the Home Minister. A highly experienced politician and an accomplished lawyer, Jaitley had earlier held various senior posts in the Vajpayee government between 1998 and 2004. More of a party builder within the BJP, Singh was a different kind of politician, but had extensive experience, having served as Chief Minister of Uttar Pradesh from 2000 to 2002 and Minister of Agriculture in the final year of Vajpayee's tenure. Between 2005 and 2009, and again from 2013 to 2014, he had also been the BJP's National President, crucial to the selection of Modi as the Party's prime ministerial candidate. Outside the Cabinet, Modi made Ajit Doval, the founding director of the Vivekananda International Foundation (VIF) think tank, former Indian Police Service (IPS) officer, and erstwhile head of the IB – an intelligence officer with a larger-than-life reputation – his National Security Advisor.[32] Doval was not the first person from the IPS to become National Security Advisor, but three of the last four post-holders since it was created in 1998 were from the rival IFS, and so his appointment was perceived by many as a deliberate attempt to ensure that Modi received advice from voices beyond the MEA. It was a signal too that his government considered internal security, as well as external security, to be a pressing issue (Pant, 2014).

Modi's consolidation of control over foreign policy was completed in the early months of his government with his appointment of Jaishankar as Foreign Secretary, the chief official in the MEA. The circumstances of that move were, however, controversial. When Modi came to office, the incumbent, the experienced diplomat Sujatha Singh, still had some 15 months to run in the position, according to convention. Her tenure was cut almost eight months short when she was replaced by Jaishankar. Formerly ambassador to Washington and before that to Beijing and Singapore, he was one of the diplomats who negotiated the US-India Nuclear Deal and a Defence Framework Agreement with the US as Joint Secretary (Americas). Jaishankar remained as Foreign Secretary for three years – having gained an extension to the normal two-year term – until he retired. In January 2018, he was replaced by Vijay Keshav (conventionally, V.K.) Gokhale, also a former ambassador to China, as well as to Germany and Indonesia, and an arguably more conventional diplomat than his predecessor.

Modi's position was reinforced in three further ways. First, his government benefited from having reputedly strong Cabinet Secretaries, as the heads of the Indian Administrative Service are known. Ajit Seth, inherited from the Manmohan Singh's period in office, stepped down in June 2015 to be replaced by Pradeep Kumar Sinha, who remained in post, with two extensions to his term, until the 2019 general election. Second, Modi brought bureaucrats from Gujarat into the PMO, individuals who had served with him when he was Chief Minister whom he trusted and relied on, and who understood his agenda. These include officials like Pramod Kumar Misra, Modi's Additional Principal Secretary, formerly Principal Secretary in the Gujarat government, who chaired the powerful appointments committee for civil servants, and spearheaded a number of the Modi's key policies, including the introduction of the goods and services tax (GST). And last but not least, Modi's dominance in foreign policy was extended through his use of the BJP party apparatus, including affiliated think tanks, to reach out to their counterparts in other countries, including China, and to exercise influence among the Indian diaspora in key states, including the US. As we shall see, BJP officials like Ram Madhav, an ideologue, organiser and unofficial emissary, aided the formulation and implementation of policy, in parallel to the bureaucracy.

Reinventing Indian foreign policy

This book argues that as part of Modi's wider project of building a 'New India', his government attempted to reground key elements of Indian foreign policy in Hindu nationalist ideology, to recast the language of international relations in its distinctive idiom, and redirect Indian diplomacy in ways that better fitted its political agenda.[33] From May 2014 onwards – indeed, from the early hours of his government – I contend that Modi and his political allies made a deliberate and concerted effort to displace inherited understandings of India's place in the world and how it ought to operate. In their stead, as new groundings for policy making, they tried to put alternative ways of thinking derived in large part from the Hindu nationalist tradition. They did this, I suggest, partly because they believed that these alternatives would produce superior policies and better serve India's national interests, but also because they believed that public perceptions of success in foreign policy would boost and sustain Modi's position as a leader, consolidate his dominant position in government, and produce payoffs at the polls. His reinvention of foreign policy was in part an attempt to improve his standing in domestic politics and that of the BJP – an intriguing move to make, given generally low levels of knowledge about, and interest in, international relations in the Indian electorate.[34]

I do not maintain, however, that the reinvention succeeded, whether in terms of displacing inherited ways of thinking about and conducting foreign policy, in terms of furthering India's national interests, or even in terms of delivering votes, although the result of the 2019 election suggests that it might. Along with a number of other scholars, I argue that Modi's government did less to change the direction of Indian foreign policy, its foundational assumptions and key practices, than might be suggested by all the drama and noise it generated.[35] Like those other analysts, I think the evidence shows that, as Rajesh Basrur (2017) puts it, the 'trajectory' of policy remained largely 'unchanged', with continuity clearly evident in the positions taken and approaches used by Modi's administration and the earlier governments of Atal Bihari Vajpayee and Manmohan Singh. Under Modi, the core elements of India's strategy established in the early 2000s remained largely the same as they did under his predecessors: New Delhi continued to prioritise domestic economic and social development; try to strike a difficult balance between protectionism and liberalisation; to build partnerships with other major powers without overt alignment; to remain the dominant player in South Asia; to pursue status as well as economic and military power; and to seek and to use 'soft power'.

Acknowledging these continuities should not however lead us to neglect the intent and substance of the Modi government's attempt at reinventing the ideological foundations of Indian foreign policy, the consequences of the exercise, which are significant, or indeed the investment involved. Modi and allies went to considerable lengths – as we shall see – to try to supply a Hindu nationalist vision of foreign policy and to displace inherited understandings of India's place in the world and role it should play. They treated this exercise as a key element in the delivery of a 'New India', arguing that 'India's choices at home and our international priorities form part of a seamless continuum' (MEA, 2017a). Exploring this vision, I argue, tells us much about Hindu nationalist understandings of the world and of India's place and role within it, about Modi's transformational style of leadership and that of similar cultural nationalist populists, and about his government's policy making and implementation. To explain what his government did in foreign policy, I argue, demands the examination of what Modi and allies purported to believe. Its emphasis on soft power and cultural influence, its reticence about opening up India's economy, despite professed prime ministerial enthusiasm for 'globalisation', and its ambivalence about building hard power fit with a vision of the world long influential on the Hindu Right.

To make this case, this book proceeds a little differently from the norm for studies of Indian foreign policy. It does not lay out in turn New Delhi's conduct of relations with key states or geographical areas. Nor does it focus on particular crises or episodes of crisis management – though I do not deny their significance for understanding the Modi government's approach. Rather, it focuses the philosophies of international relations that I argue inform policy makers, and with the rise of a Hindu nationalist alternative to inherited, largely Nehruvian, understandings of the world, what India should be, and how it ought to behave. It draws on classic texts and contemporary statements, especially speeches by key players, including Modi himself, but also powerful allies like the RSS chief Mohan Bhagwat, as well as on policy documents, media reports and contemporary analyses by journalists, think tankers and scholars. Its interpretation of these sources is leavened by conversations with officials and other observers, but I do not draw directly on those discussions.

The first half of this book explores the background to the Modi government's attempted reinvention. Chapter 2 traces the evolution of Indian foreign policy in the post-Cold War era, the approaches that have been employed by successive Congress-led and BJP-led governments, in particular, and the ideas that informed them. Chapter 3 looks at Hindu nationalist thinking about international relations and the alternative approaches to foreign policy advanced by the major thinkers in that tradition which, I argue, informed the Modi's government's approach. Chapter 4 turns to Modi himself, to his personal background and what we know of what we might call his political thought. It also explores his style of governance, which some have termed – to contrast with the concept of *Hindutva* (loosely, 'Hindu-ness') at the heart of the Hindu nationalist tradition – *Moditva* (or 'Modi-ness').

The second half examines the nature and consequences of the reinvention, using Madhav's idea of the *Panchamrit*, and other concepts drawn from Hindu nationalist thinking. Chapter 5 looks at the Modi government's attempt to render India into a 'world guru' (*vishwa guru*), using the soft power of its cultural and religious inheritance to achieve its foreign policy objectives. It argues that the idea of India as a world guru is deep-seated in Hindu nationalist ideology, and its pursuit by the Modi government consistent with those beliefs, as well as connected to the conviction that India needs to recover its national pride or dignity (*samman*) and ensure that others recognise and respect its civilisational heritage and historical influence (what Madhav termed its *sanskriti evam sabhyata*). It observes too the investment the Modi government made in dialogue (*samvad*), in religious and cultural diplomacy in multiple official and unofficial settings. Chapter 6 focuses on the Modi government's promise to bring 'inclusive development' (*samriddhi*) not just to India, but also to South Asia as a whole. It argues that hostility towards liberalisation and ambivalence about connectivity hampered this element of its reinvention of foreign policy, as well as pressure exerted by China's so-called Belt and Road Initiative. Chapter 7 turns to security (*suraksha*) and the reimagining of India's role in regional and international security. It argues that in this area, as the Modi government pursued stronger strategic partnerships with the US and Japan, tried to hold China at bay, and responded to Pakistani provocations, it struggled both to articulate a consistent Hindu nationalist agenda and to advance India's position.

In the Conclusion, I return to the reasons why Modi and his allies wanted to reinvent Indian foreign policy, what they thought they would achieve by doing so, what they achieved, what this tells us about the strength (or otherwise) of Hindu nationalist thinking in this area, and what it tells us about how foreign policy is made and implemented in India. In particular, I argue that the failure of the Modi government to make wholesale changes to India's core strategy should not distract attention from the effort that it put in during his first term in office to trying to reinvent it along ideological lines. Nor should it distract us from one of the key aims of this attempted reinvention, made plain during the 2019 general election campaign: consolidating Modi's dominant position in the political life of contemporary India.

2

Nonalignment to Multialignment

Modi and his allies believed a reinvention of foreign policy was needed after 2014 not simply because they thought that India's international relations had been mismanaged by the previous government. They were also convinced that foreign policy had been conducted poorly – and according to the wrong principles – for most of independent India's history. For them, as veteran politician Murli Manohar Joshi put it in the preface to the Bharatiya Janata Party's (BJP) 2014 election manifesto, India's leaders have failed abroad, as they have at home, because they followed 'western models'. Instead, they should have set themselves the task of 'creating a socio-economic and political paradigm of governance drawn from the civilizational consciousness of India' (BJP, 2014a, p. 2). What was needed, to use Ram Madhav's words, was a new foreign policy rooted in India's 'age-old cherished cultural and civilizational values' (BJP, 2015).

Understanding why Modi's government pursued their reinvention thus demands some exploration of how its predecessors conducted India's international relations and the beliefs and logics that drove their foreign policies. To that end, this chapter sketches the approaches employed since independence, beginning, of course, with Nehru and nonalignment. The first half outlines Nehru's approach and his direction of foreign policy, as well as its unravelling in the early 1960s, under pressure from the Mao Zedong's China, from Pakistan, and the circumstances of the Cold War. The middle sections look at how India's governments managed the country's international relations in the latter half of the Cold War and into the 1990s, as the country's economy faltered and its principal backer among the major powers, the Soviet Union, disintegrated and disappeared. The third part turns to the contemporary period, in which India began to embrace a more pragmatic approach – or at least shed some of its inherited ideological baggage – and its position in the world began to improve, largely because of renewed economic growth and changed geopolitical circumstances.[1] The conclusion lays out points of continuity and change in Modi's foreign policy, prefiguring longer discussions of the key elements of his approach in the rest of the book.

Nehru and nonalignment

Nehru was the principal architect of India's foreign policy after independence, and his conception of the country's interests and values, and the ways in which it ought to pursue them and engage with the world all continue to exercise significant influence.[2] He was able to occupy this commanding position because he was one of the few politicians in New Delhi who had any understanding of international relations, because of the sheer power of his intellect, personal charisma and energy, and because of the unusual circumstances in which he found himself in 1947. For 17 years, especially after the death of the Gujarati lawyer and deputy Prime Minister Sardar Vallabhbhai Patel in 1950, Nehru set priorities, used his speeches to articulate his vision, micro-managed his ambassadors, and conducted diplomacy with his fellow leaders. His approach was not unopposed – alternatives were voiced before and after independence (Sagar and Panda, 2015) – but it did, for a number of reasons, prevail.

By 1955, one Western analyst observed, Nehru had established himself as perhaps 'the only Foreign Minister' in the world 'whose policy virtually no one opposes' (Zinkin, 1955, p. 180).[3] It helped that he was able to take a lead role in recruiting for the nascent Indian Foreign Service, personally interviewing candidates at times during his early years in power (Mehta, 2010, p. 32).[4] To make up for the lack of experienced diplomats, he also recruited both relatives (such as his sister Vijaya Laksmi Pandit, who was variously ambassador to London, Moscow, Washington and the UN) and friends (such as the historian K.M. Panikkar or – more notoriously – the anticolonial activist, V.K. Krishna Menon).[5] All of this had the effect of ensuring that these representatives were loyal not just to the state, but also to Nehru's vision of foreign policy.[6]

Nehru benefited too because on assuming power he was faced with something close to a tabula rasa when it came foreign policy. Although he had a set of daunting domestic and international challenges to tackle, he was not hemmed in by precedent or past practice. Given postcolonial India's much diminished resources – and given that Partition had drawn new borders – New Delhi could not adopt the British approach to managing India's relations with the rest of the world. Given the onset of the Cold War, and the competition intensifying between the US and Soviet Union, there was also a risk that another devastating conflict might break out, affecting India whether or not it was directly involved (Brecher, 2011, p. 558). At the same time, Nehru was convinced – for reasons discussed in the next chapter – that newly independent India should not be passive, nor should it behave as he perceived Western powers did. Instead, he believed that it ought to set an example that others might emulate, especially among the soon-to-be or newly decolonised states in Asia and Africa. He believed too that those states could and would feel strong ties of solidarity and a need to conduct their relations with each other is a different way to the ways in which Western states behaved towards their peers and non-Western societies (see especially Das, 1961).[7]

The strategy that Nehru constructed – nonalignment[8] – was intended to keep India from becoming entangled in Cold War confrontations; give it as much of a free hand as possible to negotiate for what it needed with the superpowers, as well as with other possible partners; allow it to focus on addressing its domestic challenges, especially economic development; and permit it to articulate a new way of conducting international relations. It complemented his government's attempt to modernise through central planning, knowledge and technology transfer, and ambitious infrastructure projects, which aimed to make India as economically independent as it could be (Brecher, 2011, p. 559). For Nehru as for many in the Congress party, *swadeshi* ('self-reliance') was the best way forward, allowing India to develop in a way that minimised the vulnerability inherent in dependence on foreign capital and know-how.

Nonalignment also provided a platform from which Nehru and his representatives could engage in diplomatic activism. At the UN, in particular, they advocated vocally for causes in which they believed, including decolonisation, anti-racism and disarmament, often to the annoyance of the Western powers (Bhagavan, 2013). They championed the UN itself, seeing it as a guarantor of the security of weaker states like India, a useful platform for public diplomacy, and a stepping stone to some sort of world government (Kennedy, 2015, pp. 93–6). And they played active roles in various crises and conflicts of the 1950s and early 1960s, as intermediaries, brokers or aspirant peacemakers, from the Korean War to the Congo (Schaffer and Schaffer, 2016, p. 15).

Nehru's approach to foreign policy led his government to take a series of distinctive positions on crucial issues and in bilateral relationships important to India. It kept the US at arm's length, welcoming aid and technical assistance, but rebuffing Washington's overtures to join with it to resist the advance of Soviet and Chinese communism (Chaudhuri, R., 2014, pp. 13–77). It did much the same with the USSR, despite the pro-Moscow leanings of some of Nehru's leading ambassadors, like Krishna Menon, and despite the significant aid and diplomatic support provided by the Soviets, notably during the forcible incorporation into India of the Portuguese colony of Goa, in December 1961 (McGarr, 2013, pp. 132–7). It maintained cordial relations with the UK, recognising its economic importance to India and its value as a supplier of military equipment, but did not stint in its criticism of its behaviour in what remained of its Empire or its deceitful conduct during the Suez Crisis in 1956. Over time, however, ties frayed, as India's vocal stands on colonialism and apartheid irritated London (McGarr, 2013, pp. 98–103). With Pakistan, India tried to use the UN as a means of resolving the dispute over Kashmir, and when that approach failed, relied on bilateral diplomacy rather than threats (Brown, 2003, pp. 266–7). A settlement proved elusive, however, and the relationship remained fraught and competitive (Ganguly, 2002).

With People's Republic of China (PRC), perhaps most fatefully, Nehru's government struggled.[9] When the communists finally consolidated power in 1949, Nehru took the view that engagement was preferable to hostility, and India became the first non-communist state to recognise the new regime, on 1 January 1950. It also advocated for the People's Republic to take China's seat on the United Nations Security Council (UNSC). These gestures, Nehru's critics have long argued, did India few favours. In October 1950, Mao Zedong sent the People's Liberation Army (PLA) into Tibet, effectively incorporating into the PRC what had long been a buffer state between China and India. This act surprised Nehru's government, and Panikkar, the Indian ambassador in Peking (now Beijing), who had been assured of Mao's peaceful intentions. It also exposed as hollow India's pledges of support to the Tibetans. Shaken by China's behaviour, Nehru nonetheless persisted with his policy of 'good neighbourliness' (Nehru, 1961, pp. 306–7) and the promotion of 'Hindi-Chini-bhai-bhai' (Indian-Chinese brotherhood), including his push for wider diplomatic recognition of the PRC. He remained convinced that China had a legitimate claim to 'suzerainty' over Tibet (Nehru, 1961, p. 303). In May 1954, however, Nehru went further, effectively recognising Chinese sovereignty over the country in what became known as the Panchsheel agreement.

The thinking underlying that agreement is explored further in the next chapter, but it is worth recounting in this context what it entailed in terms of Nehru's approach to managing the relationship with the PRC. The Panchsheel involved the commitment on both sides to interact on the basis of mutual respect for sovereignty and territorial integrity, non-aggression, non-interference, equality and mutual benefit, and peaceful coexistence. They did not, however, help to resolve the other outstanding issue between the two: the demarcation of the border to the West of Nepal and to the East of Bhutan, where China claims all of what is now the state of Arunachal Pradesh as 'South Tibet'. This territorial dispute flared in 1957 as it became clear that China was in the process of building a road connecting Tibet with Xinjiang through the strategically significant and disputed area of Aksai Chin (Garver, 2001, p. 90). In late 1958, New Delhi lodged an official protest, leading to an exchange of letters between Nehru and Chinese Premier Zhou Enlai. India also began to push troops closer to the so-called McMahon Line in the East, leading to clashes with the PLA. When in 1959 unrest in Tibet festered into armed rebellion against Beijing's rule, moreover, India did little to restrain flows of fighters and arms into the country (see especially Maxwell, 2015).

When it came, Beijing's response was devastating. In October 1962, as the rest of the world was distracted by the Cuban Missile Crisis, Mao ordered the PLA to attack India's positions and drive far into its territory in a punitive strike. India's armed forces were routed and Nehru himself humiliated. To the Prime Minister's dismay the UNSC failed to condemn China's attack and no major power provided military support to India beyond the supply of arms and ammunition (Schaffer and Schaffer, 2016, pp. 26–7).[10] To his critics, the border war exposed fundamental weaknesses of his China policy and the strategic risks arising from nonalignment.

Nonalignment after Nehru

Although Nehru's conduct of foreign policy was rarely challenged in any sustained or significant way for much of his time in office, and in broad terms nonalignment was supported by most of the political elite (Singh, 1965, pp. 131–3), his approach to China was one of the issues that was criticised, both within the Congress Party and by their political opponents. In 1950, after the Chinese invasion of Tibet, it famously provoked a lengthy critique – discussed in the next chapter from his erstwhile deputy, Sardar Patel.[11] Thereafter, throughout the 1950s, Nehru was challenged within and outside parliament, about this management of relations with Beijing, about the *Panchsheel*, the recognition of China's suzerainty over Tibet, and India's support for the Dalai Lama and his government.[12] The criticisms came from the Right, from within Congress, and from Gandhi socialists like J.B. Kripalani, who lamented the fact that India had 'allowed the annihilation of the buffer kingdom of Tibet without a protest' and argued against New Delhi legitimising China's control, which he termed 'acquiescence in injustice' (Kripalani, 1959, pp. 49–50). Nehru, he worried, unconsciously echoing Patel's earlier charge, failed to grasp the nature of 'the new Communist imperialism' (Kripalani, 1959, p. 59).

Most significantly, in terms of this book, Nehru's China policy allowed the Hindu Right to establish a distinct position on India's national security and international relations beyond the issue of Kashmir (Ogden, 2014, p. 59). Through the 1950s, Deendayal Upadhyaya, the leader of the Bharatiya Jana Sangh, the forerunner of the BJP, castigated Nehru's naiveté, arguing that they had long warned the government of the 'dragon's designs' and the 'imminent danger' China posed (Upadhyaya, 1968, p. 49). He argued that it done too little to bolster India's defences, not appreciating that one cannot secure a country 'simply by [the] clever manipulation of foreign policy' (Upadhyaya, 1968, p. 51). India needed to change course and stop indulging China and advancing its interests, cut diplomatic relations with Beijing, withdraw recognition of its 'suzerainty' over Tibet, treat the Dalai Lama's court as an 'émigré Government', and materially aid the liberation of that country (Upadhyaya, 1968, pp. 52–3). Upadhyaya counselled, moreover, that nonalignment risked becoming a 'fetish', that 'new alignments have been forged' in the world since Nehru formulated the concept that demanded that India respond in kind, and that India needed friends on which it could depend (Upadhyaya, 1968, p. 52).

New Delhi did not heed this advice in its entirety, but it did begin to recalibrate its strategy. India's leaders realised that, in times of emergency, the UN system was unlikely to function as it was designed and that one or other superpower was unlikely to come to the country's aid, in the absence of a formal alliance or some other kind of security guarantee. Moreover, it was widely recognised that India needed to invest in building military power. New Delhi continued to pursue economic self-reliance and to advocate for change in the international system, but it took a more robust approach to national security that involved some compromises to nonalignment, especially after the 1965 war with Pakistan (Mitra, 2009, pp. 25–8). India prevailed in that conflict, which Islamabad initiated, restoring credibility and pride to the armed forces. Its relations with Washington, however, became attenuated as a result of the latter's decision to cease arms transfers to both sides, which implied both India and Pakistan were equally to blame for the war. Moscow, by contrast, played a more positive role, helping to broker a peace agreement at Tashkent that ended hostilities (Schaffer and Schaffer, 2016, p. 32). Thereafter, New Delhi became increasingly critical of US policy – including, to the White House's acute annoyance, its behaviour in Vietnam – and began to tilt more clearly towards the Soviet Union.

In the latter half of the 1960s and through the 1970s, India invested in its armed forces, pursued a nuclear weapons programme – leading to a bomb test in 1974, but not to the development of a deterrent – and forged a close economic and security partnership with the Soviets, signing a Treaty of Peace, Friendship and Cooperation in 1971 (Mansingh, 2015). It also became more interventionist in its region, using its forces to split Pakistan in two in 1971 and then, sometime later, to intercede in political crises and civil conflicts in the Maldives and – fatefully – in Sri Lanka. In so doing, and by investing in its navy, in particular, India sought to establish a kind of the Monroe Doctrine for South Asia and the Indian Ocean (Hagerty, 1991). And New Delhi grew more vocal in its criticism of US policy, and in a bid to regain some leadership in the postcolonial world, strongly backed the formalised Non Aligned Movement, founded in 1961. It also became a prominent advocate of a so-called New International Economic Order, calling for a redistribution of wealth and market power from global North to global South (Schaffer and Schaffer, 2016, pp. 36–7).[13]

In the latter half of the Cold War, India thus remained formally unaligned and without treaty allies, in particular. But its semi-dependence on the Soviet Union in trade and arms, as well as its active promotion of 'Third World-ism' meant that its ties with the West became attenuated. The US and India, in particular, ended up 'estranged', despite an attempt to reset relations during the 1980s, under Indira and then, more purposefully, Rajiv Gandhi (see especially Kux, 1992).

Rao and reform

Two events at either end of 1991 – the First Gulf War in January and February of that year, and then the collapse of the Soviet Union in December – threw India's strategy into disarray. The first caused a dramatic spike in oil prices and caused a balance of payments crisis, as well as a dire humanitarian predicament for Indian workers in Iraq and Kuwait, who needed to be repatriated quickly, to get them out of harm's way, and at significant expense (Malik, 1991). The second stripped New Delhi of a diplomatic ally, economic partner and supplier of military materiel. Domestically, during this period, India's politics were also in flux, with some arguing that the country faced a looming 'crisis of governability' (Kohli, 1990), and its economy was faltering, weighed down by the red-tape of the so-called License Raj and by rampant official corruption. In May 1991, in an episode that illustrated the extent of its woes, New Delhi's balance of payments situation became so acute that it was forced to devalue its currency and borrow from the International Monetary Fund on humiliating terms, which involved depositing some of its gold reserves in Europe as collateral.[14]

The general election that followed, which took place in late May and June 1991, delivered a more stable Congress-led coalition, headed by P.V. Narasimha Rao, than the two short-lived governments that preceded it.[15] Although a Nehruvian and a socialist, Rao grasped that swift action was necessary if India was to weather the crisis. His Finance Minister, Manmohan Singh, implemented a series of important measures to deregulate and stimulate the economy, cutting bureaucracy, deregulating key sectors, beginning the process of privatising state-owned enterprises, and attempting to curb corruption. The results were positive. Having grown at about 5.5 per cent in the decade between 1981 and 1990, India's gross domestic product (GDP) expanded by close to 6.5 per cent between 1992 and 1999, and then by around 6.7 per cent from 2001 to 2005 (World Bank, 2018).[16] Over time, this economic success improved both India's confidence and security, and changed foreign perceptions.[17]

In parallel, New Delhi began a new process of diplomatic outreach. The Soviet Union's demise at the end of 1991 robbed India of a friend in international relations and especially in key institutions, including the UNSC, an economic partner willing to trade on favourable terms, and a reliable supplier of military equipment. In the 1990s Russia continued to provide arms, but its own woes rendered it steadily less useful to India as the decade wore on. Partly to compensate, especially economically, Rao's government sought to revitalise relations with a series of states in East Asia, a region undergoing a rapid transformation, as Southeast Asia, South Korea, and, of course, China emulated Japan's post-war economic miracle. In September 1993, Rao visited Beijing, concluding a landmark agreement on managing the border dispute with the People's Republic, and then Seoul, where he tried to convince Korean businesses to invest in the Indian market (Sitapati, 2016, pp. 266–7). The Prime Minister also went to Thailand (in 1993) and Singapore (in 1994), focusing again on economic diplomacy, laying the groundwork for what became the 'Look East' policy (Gordon and Henningham, 1995).[18]

'Look East' was intended to boost both foreign direct investment (FDI) flows into India from East Asia and trade, as well as to reconnect with the local Indian diaspora and draw on their economic know-how. From the start, however, it also had a significant strategic component, as New Delhi sought to diversify its diplomatic and security relationships to help manage some of the challenges posed by a rapidly rising China (Singh, 1995). In both areas, despite past differences with some East Asian states dating back to the Cold War, India was welcomed with open arms. FDI began to flow, as did other forms of assistance. Notably, Japan began to direct substantial amounts of Overseas Development Assistance (ODA) to India, so that by the 1995–96 financial year, fully 40 per cent of its

ODA budget was committed to the country (Envall, 2014, p. 43). At the same time, Southeast Asian states drew India into regional institutional arrangements, making it a member of the security-focused Association of Southeast Asian Nations (ASEAN) Regional Forum in 1996, for example (Acharya, 2015, pp. 461–3).

Alongside the domestic reforms and 'Look East', Rao's government also moved to make one last highly controversial change to India's approach to its foreign relations and security challenges. Under growing pressure from powerful international actors – including the US – that were keen to make progress on nuclear disarmament, arms control, and non-proliferation, New Delhi found itself faced with a difficult choice: should it relinquish its nuclear programme, in train since the 1960s, and trust in other means of upholding its national security? Or should it defy those powerful actors, risk provoking sanctions, and arm itself with a nuclear deterrent? In the event, Rao and his key advisors took the view that India's circumstances were not sufficiently benign to abandon the prospect of a deterrent. In December 1995, he ordered a weapons test that would have signalled India's intent to become a de facto nuclear weapons state. Unfortunately, however, a US satellite observed preparations for the test and Washington conveyed its disapproval. Rao decided to back down, and never got another opportunity to test, as he was voted out of office in May 1996 (Sitapati, 2016, pp. 279–95). It was left to a successor, the Hindu nationalist Atal Bihari Vajpayee, to cross the nuclear threshold, which his government did soon after coming to power two years later, in May 1998.

Rao's domestic reforms, which dismantled many state controls and partially opened India's economy to trade and investment, his Look East policy, and his decision to test a nuclear weapons, albeit rescinded, were significant departures from earlier approaches to managing India's international relations. They challenged the notion that *swadeshi* or semi-autarkic self-reliance was the best path to economic and social development, as Nehru had argued. They repaired some relationships with key East Asian states – especially Japan and Singapore – that had earlier been alienated by New Delhi's hostility to the US playing a role in Asia and its support for the communist regime in Vietnam. They signalled a shift too in India's attitude to regional institutions, historically treated with suspicion and scepticism as putative alliances or unnecessary alternatives to UN-based multilateralism (Mohan, 2013, pp. 31–5). To adapt a metaphor from C. Raja Mohan's iconic book (2003), Rao built the bridge that allowed Vajpayee's BJP-led government to 'cross the Rubicon' after 1998 and embrace a more pragmatic and less overtly ideological approach.

In May 1996, however, Rao lost the general election and relinquished the leadership of Congress. Three Prime Ministers followed in quick succession: Vajpayee for a mere 13 days, H.D. Deve Gowda for almost 11 months, and then I.K. Gujral for almost a year. Of these, only the last left an enduring mark in foreign policy. First as Deve Gowda's EAM, and then, between April 1997 and May 1998, combining that role with the prime ministership, Gujral articulated a distinct doctrine that recalled aspects of Nehru's thinking, but also prefigured the strategies of later governments, including elements of Modi's.

The Gujral Doctrine had five parts. First, it held that India should recognise that given the disparity in size and power between it and its neighbours, it should not hanker for reciprocity in relations, but instead should be magnanimous. Second, agreements with the neighbours should be on the basis of equality, with smaller state interests duly recognised and, if possible, accommodated. Third, India should take care not to over-inflate perceptions of threats from its neighbours, including those arising from their relations with third parties, like China. Fourth, as one prominent commentator put it, 'India should rid itself of the congenital psychopathology of obsession with regard to Pakistan', which distracts it from bigger issues. And last, to quote the same observer, 'India should break out of the claustrophobic confines of South Asia, a region with no strategic resources, overburdened with poverty and population, and still a victim of the fault-lines of the British empire' (Gupta, 1997, p. 309).[19]

The Gujral Doctrine captured both the major strategic challenges faced by India and its aspiration to play a bigger role as a global power. It recognised that India's relationships with its immediate neighbours had deteriorated as a consequence of thirty or so years of heavy-handed behaviour. It disavowed the tacit assertion, made most obviously by Indira Gandhi, that South Asia was India's sphere of influence and the implicit right to interfere in its neighbours' affairs. Finally, it acknowledged that India needed to devote a significant proportion of its scarce diplomatic resources to improving ties with the major powers if it was to defend and extend its interests, and realise any wider ambitions (Mohan, 2003, pp. 237–47). In these ways it set the scene for the approaches taken later by the Vajpayee, Singh, and Modi governments.

Pragmatism beyond the Rubicon

Although condemned by the US, China, Japan and other significant players, the nuclear weapons tests conducted at Pokhran in Rajasthan's Thar Desert on 11 and 13 May 1998 focused their attention on India and, in time, opened a crucial space for diplomatic engagement (Mohan, 2003, p. 25). In the short term, the acquisition of a deterrent addressed – even if it could not lay to rest – security concerns that loomed large in New Delhi since the end of the Cold War. These concerns that revolved around several issues: Pakistan's own nuclear programme; China's fast-growing power; and indeed Western interventionism and the potential cost of acquiring the conventional weapons needed to deter it or defend against it. The tests signalled that India would not accept the nuclear order that evolved after the signing of the Nuclear Non-Proliferation Treaty (NPT), which came into force in 1970, which the US and its European allies had tried to extend and deepen after 1991, mostly notably with the 1995 Comprehensive Test Ban Treaty (CTBT). New Delhi had long seen this order as lop-sided and unjust (see especially Singh, 1998). It pointed out that unlike many other non-nuclear weapons states, such as the UK or Japan, which were both US treaty allies, it was not sheltered by one of the major powers' 'nuclear umbrellas', which extended deterrence beyond their borders (see especially Kennedy, 2011). It chafed too at the limits placed by the nuclear regime on India's ability to establish a civilian nuclear industry, brought about by its refusal to sign the NPT.[20]

International criticism and sanctions followed the tests, but so did diplomacy. In their aftermath, Washington agreed to a confidential dialogue between Vajpayee's EAM, Jaswant Singh, and the US Deputy Secretary of State, Strobe Talbott, mainly with the aim of persuading India to sign the CTBT (Schaffer and Schaffer, 2016, pp. 52–3). Singh refused to take that step, but the talks continued, and the two sides came to realise that they had a number of shared interests.[21] Beyond this dialogue, a series of other diplomatic gestures also built trust and helped the two sides to overcome inherited – and in part ideological – baggage. Washington's unequivocal condemnation of Pakistan's rash behaviour at Kargil in the Himalayas, where its forces seized territory and provoked a brief border war between with India in mid-1999, pleased the Indian government. President Bill Clinton then made a long state visit to India in March 2000, and the two countries published a joint 'vision' statement (Talbott, 2004, p. 194). A few months later, in September, Vajpayee gave a speech in New York in which he surprised the audience by referring to the US and India as 'natural allies' (Parthasarathy, 2000). And in the aftermath of September 11, 2001, New Delhi made a broad offer to aid the US in its fight against al Qaeda and its backers (Paliwal, 2017, p. 162).

Substantive progress in improving US-India ties followed. The George W. Bush administration's decision to embrace 'dehyphenation' – treating India and Pakistan as separate entities, and not shaping US relations with one in terms of relations with the other – laid the groundwork

(Tellis, 2008). Bush's personal goodwill toward India, which he perceived as a putative like-minded partner largely because it was democratic, was also helpful. Both smoothed the way to a landmark ten-year defence cooperation deal and the '123 Agreement', announced in 2005, which provided a means by which India could obtain civilian nuclear technology outside the NPT, and without it being a party to the CTBT, as Washington had earlier insisted.[22] The first made the US India's 'partner of choice' in military modernisation, helping it to reduce its dependence on Russia (Twining, 2014, p. 24). The second paved the way for India to be recognised as a de facto nuclear weapons state (Sasikumar, 2007).

In parallel, New Delhi made progress on managing its long-term strategic challenge – China – and the security threats posed by Pakistan. When the two countries went to war in 1962, India was wealthier and significantly better positioned in the world, as an active and largely respected member of the UN. By 1991, however, China's GDP was roughly twice India's – $906 billion versus $471 billion[23] (World Bank, 2018). By 2001, the gap between them had widened further, with China posting a figure of $2.4 trillion and India only $841 billion. This enabled Beijing not just to raise living standards, but also to modernise its military and exercise greater influence abroad, taking advantage of the stronger international position in which it found itself. Having taken China's UNSC seat from Taiwan and secured formal recognition from major Western powers in the 1970s, the PRC was then integrated into a series of international institutions during the 1980s and 1990s, and ushered into the World Trade Organization (WTO) in 2001 (see Johnston, 2008). This newfound centrality to both the global economy and international institutions allowed Beijing both to weather and to ward off criticisms of its behaviour towards its citizens, most notably in the aftermath of the massacre of students by the PLA in Tiananmen Square in 1989, and towards neighbouring states.

China's growing weight and the relative success of its development model posed – and continue to pose – a complex set of evolving challenges to New Delhi. Formal diplomatic relations, cut in 1962, were restored in 1979, but it was not until the late 1980s that any substantive progress was made in repairing the damage done, despite several rounds of talks about the border. In 1988, however, Rajiv Gandhi travelled to Beijing to meet Deng Xiaoping, and the two sides agreed to a range of measures, including allowing direct flights, some bilateral science and cultural diplomacy, and regular ministerial meetings. Gandhi also acknowledged that some exiled Tibetans in India were working to undermine PRC rule in that area, and affirmed India's official recognition of Chinese sovereignty. This gave some impetus to ongoing talks on the border, which continued through the 1990s with some effort made to establish confidence-building measures and dialogue mechanisms between deployed troops. But this progress was 'glacial', as Ganguly observes, even after the conclusion of a 'peace and tranquillity agreement' during Rao's visit to Beijing in 1993, which called on both sides to respect the Line of Actual Control (LAC) and to eschew military manoeuvres in its vicinity (Ganguly, 2004, p. 123).

Moreover, India's concerns about other issues related to China were not assuaged by whatever improvements occurred regarding the management of the LAC. The biggest, of course, was the issue of Beijing's ties to Islamabad – and Rawalpindi. Beginning with material support for Pakistan's military in the aftermath of its failed attempt to seize Kashmir in 1965, by the 1990s the bilateral relationship had deepened and broadened into an important security partnership.[24] Of particular worry to New Delhi was the support given by the PRC to Pakistan's nuclear weapon and ballistic missile programmes, which had both advanced quickly during the 1980s, thanks in no small part to China's assistance (Perkovich, 2004, pp. 199–203; cf. Singh, 2007, pp. 114–15). India's 1998 nuclear test was intended in part to address these concerns, pre-empting a Pakistani move across the same threshold, as well as to diminish the risk that China might use its deterrent to try to coerce New Delhi. For all these reasons, China was increasingly perceived in some circles, as India's Defence Minister, George Fernandes, stated somewhat undiplomatically a week prior to the tests, as 'potential enemy no. 1' (Burns, 1998).

Strategic autonomy and multialignment

Together, partial economic liberalisation and opening up, the Look East policy, the Gujral Doctrine, the acquisition of nuclear weapons, and the improvement of relations with Washington, shifted India away from the overtly ideological and reflexively anti-Western approach it had taken in the latter half of the Cold War toward a more pragmatic approach. It did not imply, however, a complete rejection of Nehru's legacy, nor of the ideal of nonalignment. Indeed, it could be interpreted as a return to what some think to be its essence, if nonalignment is understood as a strategy that aimed at putting India's economic and social development first and employed a flexible foreign policy to keep the country from getting entangled in others' quarrels. Under the Manmohan Singh government (2004–14), in particular, the pursuit of what became known as 'strategic autonomy' bore strong similarities to that interpretation of nonalignment, with some contemporary twists.[25]

The 'Singh doctrine', as Mohan (2005) and others have described it, had six elements. Above all, it asserted that, in Sanjaya Baru's words, 'India's relations with the world...would be shaped by its own developmental priorities' (Baru, 2015, p. 165). Second, it maintained that India's prosperity depended on further integration into the global economy, not a return to semi-autarkic *swadeshi*, with excessive government control. Third, it recognised that India's relationships with the great powers were 'shaped by economic factors', including access to energy resources, and that foreign policy needed to be attentive to this reality. Fourth, it held that deeper economic integration was needed in South Asia and that India should take the lead in bringing it about. Fifth, it suggested, somewhat tentatively, that lessons learned from India's democratic and development experience should be passed on to others. And last, it held that India ought to play a bigger role in helping other states transition to democratic politics and open economic systems (Baru, 2015, pp. 165–6). The Singh doctrine put economic development first, in other words, and measured India's engagement with the global economy, the major powers, and the region by how far it could deliver it, but held too that New Delhi still had a role to play as a 'normative power', bringing about positive change in other states and international relations (Hall, 2015b).

To realise these objectives, Singh's government continued with Look East and sustained New Delhi's engagement of Washington, concluding the defence and nuclear deals signed in 2005, but also worked to build a diverse range of so-called strategic partnerships with other states, some inherited from Vajpayee's time in office, and some new.[26] By the end of Singh's administration in 2014, India had assembled about 30 partnership arrangements, most formalised in joint statements after summits. Vajpayee agreed six, with the US, above all, but also with France, Germany, Iran, Japan and Russia. To these, Singh added deals with a series of Indo-Pacific states, including Afghanistan, Australia, China, Indonesia, Malaysia, South Korea and Vietnam, with the ASEAN groupings as a whole, and with some significant others, including Brazil, the EU, Kazakhstan, Nigeria, Saudi Arabia, Tajikistan and Uzbekistan (Hall, 2016a, pp. 277–8). The purposes of these deals varied, with some principally security focused and others, especially with East Asian states, more concerned with trade and investment. Some – notably those with hydrocarbon producers – were intended to secure energy supplies to meet India's burgeoning demand.

In parallel, New Delhi also committed India to greater involvement in a series of regional and global institutions, giving the country a seat at the table so that it could – in principle at least – defend its interests and promote its values (Jaffrelot and Singh Sidhu, 2013). Under Vajpayee, in 2003, New Delhi had joined with Brazil and South Africa in the IBSA (India-Brazil-

South Africa) initiative, intended to promote dialogue between the three large developing states with an annual intergovernmental summit and a series of parallel working groups.[27] Under Singh, India became a member of the ASEAN-centred East Asia Summit and an official observer at the Sino-Russian Shanghai Cooperation Organisation, both in 2005. A year later, it joined with Brazil, China and Russia in the BRIC forum, which became the BRICS when South Africa was added in 2010. At the same time, India had also embraced its membership in the revamped Group of 20 (G20), which became central to the global response to the financial crisis during 2008. These developments recognised India's arrival as a major economy and a player of growing political and military weight. But they also signalled a change in attitudes within a New Delhi foreign policy elite historically suspicious of multilateralism outside the UN, in which it had earlier invested so much.

Taken together, India's growing involvement with regional institutions and so-called minilateral groups and forums, plus construction of new strategic partnerships designed to deliver a range of different benefits, signalled a change of approach by Singh's government to those of its predecessors. For some at the time, it signalled a 'neo-Curzonian foreign policy ... premised on the logic of Indian [geographical] centrality, permitting multidirectional engagement...with all major powers and seeking access and leverage from East Africa to Pacific Asia' (Khanna and Mohan, 2006). This 'forward foreign policy' involved the 'revival of commercial cooperation; building institutional, physical and political links with neighbours to circumvent buffer states, developing energy supplies and assets; and pursuing multistate defence agreements and contracts' (Khanna and Mohan, 2006)). For these and other analysts, it looked like India was now pursuing 'multialignment' rather than nonalignment.[28]

Multialignment arose from the imperatives driving the first four points of Singh doctrine – the harnessing of foreign policy to the domestic development agenda, the need to integrate India into the global economy, the focus on the economic dimension of relations with other major powers, and the emphasis on South Asian integration. To deliver the goods – as it were – it also depended on walking a series of tightropes on contentious issues in order to try to maintain good ties with other significant players. It involved a substantial element of 'normative hedging', in other words, recognising that India's influence in the world depended to a degree on how it was perceived in relation to a series of important issues, especially democracy and democracy promotion; what might be broadly termed neoliberal economics, particularly in the area of trade; and humanitarian intervention and the defence of human rights, more widely.

For most of the latter half of the Cold War and all of the 1990s, India had staunchly opposed a series of efforts to reform key elements of the post-war international order led by the West. These included the moves to bring about liberalisation of trade and investment, from the 1970s onwards; attempts to loosen the rules and norms concerning international intervention in conflicts and humanitarian crises, starting in the early 1990s; and post-Cold War efforts to promote liberal democracy as a form of government. Instead, India had advanced its own proposals for reform, especially in the context of the push for a New International Economic Order, which began in earnest in the mid-1970s (Murphy, 1983), and in terms of UN reform. Throughout, it had also declared a strong preference for a multipolar or polycentric order in which hard interpretations of sovereignty, non-intervention and non-interference prevail. It was highly critical even of the UNSC-sanctioned military action to expel Iraqi troops from Kuwait in 1991, and it was flatly opposed to the series of so-called humanitarian interventions that followed in the Balkans, East Africa and elsewhere (Bommakanti, 2017). India stood firm, moreover, on attempts to extend the scope and reach of international criminal justice, refusing the sign the 1998 Rome Statute that established the International Criminal Court. And its scepticism about US- and European-led efforts at 'democracy promotion', by force or by others means, remained palpable (Hall, 2017a, pp. 83–4, 88–9).

Led by Vajpayee and then by Singh, India maintained some of these stances and modified others. It dabbled with ways of supporting democratic transitions and the quality of democratic governance in vulnerable states, becoming a member of the Community of Democracies group in 2000, for example, and under Singh, after 2004, it became a significant donor to the UN Democracy Fund, which supports a range of civil society projects (Hall, 2017a, pp. 85–6).[29] India became less vocally critical about Western economic agendas, though it did continue to obstruct – in the eyes of Western observers, at least – substantive reform of trade and investment regulation, as one of the states blocking progress in the so-called Doha Round of multilateral talks, which began in 2001 and remain unresolved (Hopewell, 2016, pp. 147–75). Moreover, at the Copenhagen Climate Summit in late 2009, it worked with China to stymie agreement on a US-led deal (Hurrell and Sengupta, 2012).

Moreover, India remained deeply reluctant to countenance any change to the basic norms of sovereignty and non-intervention in circumstances of humanitarian emergency. At the UN World Summit in 2005, its diplomats tried to derail agreement on the concept of 'Responsibility to Protect' (R2P), which attempted to bridge the gap between the push by some Western and African states for clearer and more permissive rules for humanitarian intervention and the desire of others to maintain strict interpretations of the norms of sovereignty and non-intervention. After a period in which some states had decided to intervene militarily without UN authorisation, most notably in Kosovo in 1999, R2P was designed to bring the practice back under UN auspices (Hall, 2013, p. 93).[30] To New Delhi, however, R2P was still too permissive, so at the last minute it sought unsuccessfully to unravel the deal struck. India also showed itself reluctant to condemn or criticise human rights abuses in its neighbourhood, during the civil war in Nepal, in Myanmar in the aftermath of the so-called Saffron Revolution of 2007, and in the political crisis in the Maldives in 2008 (Piccone, 2016, pp. 76–9). During a stint in 2011–12 as a non-permanent member of the UNSC, India's representatives also spoke out strongly against NATO's military action against the Muammar Gaddafi government in Libya and resisted similar measures being carried out under a UNSC mandate in the civil conflict then beginning in Syria (Jaganathan and Kurtz, 2014).

Overall, the Singh doctrine arguably served India well until his second term in office. New Delhi was able to prioritise economic development and to focus its attention on deepening partnerships that assisted that project. As GDP grew strongly during this period, at over 9 per cent in all but one year between 2005 and 2009, the approach seemed to work, and the country stood tall. Thereafter, however, growth began to falter, the government seemed to lose its zeal and became mired in corruption scandals, and, just as importantly, the international environment grew less benign. The global financial crisis hit the US and Western economies in 2008; China became more assertive in its claims and behaviour. Progress in developing New Delhi's security-focused strategic partnership with Washington, which had moved quickly in the mid-2000s, began to falter, as doubts crept in on both sides (Pant and Joshi, 2017, pp. 135–6).[31] Despite the two landmark agreements in 2005 and some major purchases of US military equipment, and indeed Singh being given the honour of the first state visit to the US of Obama's Presidency disappointment set in and disputes arose. India passed legislation that made it hard for US firms to bid to build and run nuclear power plants in India, the two squabbled over the latter's ties to Iran (Fair, 2007), and Washington's continued support for Islamabad in the pursuit of the 'War on Terror' irked New Delhi (Pant, 2012). India's long-standing ties with Russia also came under pressure, as Moscow's relationship with the West soured and its partnership with Beijing deepened (Mankoff, 2015). In this context, Singh's government struggled in foreign policy, and some of the lustre around India's re-emergence as a major power was lost (see especially Baru, 2015).

Conclusion

The foreign policy of the Modi government, I argue in the remainder of this book, presents a paradox. On the one hand, Modi himself devoted extraordinary energy to diplomacy, building relationships with other world leaders, crafting joint 'vision statements', and making a particular point of attending multilateral meetings, from the Group of 20 (G20) in Brisbane in November 2014 to the East Asia Summit in Singapore four years later. His government took a series of dramatic, unexpected actions too, approving, as we will see, long stalled proposed defence agreements with the US, confronting China over its infrastructure projects, and ordering raids on militant camps in Pakistan and Pakistani-administered Kashmir in the wake of terrorist attacks. Modi and his allies also took pains to try to craft a new narrative for Indian foreign policy, one that reflected Hindu nationalist understandings of the world, explored in the next chapter, and that tried to build 'Brand India' and leverage 'soft power'. These actions gave rise to the notion that his government was engaged in a wholesale '*Modi*-fication' of foreign policy (Chaulia, 2016, p. 1).[32]

On the other hand, there is evidence that Modi's government did not deviate far from the basic strategy taken by its two immediate predecessors. Its aims were much the same, despite the new language in which it was couched. Like Singh, Modi pledged to put India's economic development first, and devote a substantial part of the scarce diplomatic resources at his disposal to finding markets, securing energy supplies, and attracting investment. This effort – again, like Singh's – flowed from the recognition that the country needed a benign international environment, stronger strategic partnerships with key states, and a more positive image abroad, especially among investors, to bring about the '*acche din*' (good days) promised to voters. The project of India's 'transformation', Modi argued at the Raisina Dialogue in New Delhi in January 2017, was inseparable 'from its external context' – its 'choices at home and our international priorities form part of a seamless continuum' (MEA, 2017a).

Like Singh too, but indeed also like Gujral and Vajpayee, Modi promised to focus attention on India's immediate neighbourhood – on improving bilateral ties with each South Asian state, on upgrading connectivity between them, and on mutual economic benefit. '*Sabka Saath; Sabka Vikas*' (loosely, 'together we go; together we develop'), Modi declared in 2017, recalling a key campaign slogan from three years earlier, 'is not just a vision for India', but for the world, and especially for South Asia (MEA, 2017a). And again like Singh, Modi concentrated on trying to manage relations with the major powers so as to see off any costly clashes of interests and to bolster both India's economy and its security. To do this, he used means established by his predecessors: regular summitry with strategic partners and strategic rivals, and regular attendance at multilateral forums where India can be seen, at home as well as abroad, as a player on the most important stages. He sought – especially early in his tenure – to 'multi-align', trying to extract deals from each of the major powers, seeking investment from China, for example, at the same time as seeking improved security ties with the US.

In Modi's approach to China and the US, in his crisis management with Pakistan, and in what we might call his normative agenda, there was some deviation from the broad lines established by Vajpayee and especially by Singh. All three were keen to promote, build, and use India's soft power'. But as we shall see in Chapter 5, under Modi this exercise took became more urgent and more ideologically-tinged, as Hindu nationalist conceptions of India and its supposed soft power came to the fore, and the government opened up a series of inter-religious and inter-cultural dialogues. 'Spreading the benefits of India's civilizational legacies', as Modi put it, was advanced as what he called 'a global good' (MEA, 2017a). Turning India into a 'world guru' and restoring global respect for its traditions and ideas became a significant objective, backed enthusiastically by Hindu nationalist ideologues and activists.

Modi also won plaudits from the Hindu Right, and from others, for his handling of two challenges: Chinese pressure and Pakistan's backing of terrorism and insurgency. When the PLA was detected building a road through an area of Bhutan claimed by Beijing, at Doklam (Dong Lang in Mandarin), in mid-June 2017, they were confronted by Indian troops. A standoff ensued that lasted for 74 days. Chinese officials and state-run media made a series of dire threats to punish India if it did not withdraw its forces. New Delhi did not, however, back down – at least publicly – and the standoff was resolved diplomatically, with a mutual drawback of troops (Ganguly and Scobell, 2018).

More dramatic still were the Modi government's responses to terrorist attacks in 2016 and 2019. Two military bases were attacked at Pathankot and Uri, both in Kashmir, in January and September 2016, probably by the Pakistan-based jihadi group Jaish-e-Mohammed. Following the second of these attacks, in late September 2016 the Modi government sent special forces across the Line of Control into Pakistani-administered Kashmir. While not unprecedented, these so-called surgical strikes represented a significantly less restrained and more muscular approach, intended to deter further attacks and adventurism by those elements of the Pakistani state thought responsible for backing terrorist groups, and the groups themselves (see especially Gokhale, 2017a). The air strikes conducted by the Indian Air Force after another attack, which killed more than forty paramilitary police officers at Pulwama in Kashmir in mid-February 2019, reinforced this impression that the Modi government had departed from 'strategic restraint' and embarked on a new approach to India's relations with Pakistan and the militants resident there.

This book does not play down these episodes or their implications. But it does seek to put them into a broader context. Despite Modi's centralisation of control over foreign policy in the Prime Minister's Office, and his government having 'many more opportunities' than earlier governments 'to engineer' what C. Raja Mohan has called 'a structural transformation in India's international relations' (Mohan, 2015, p. 19), I argue in what follows that this transformation did not occur in the five years after his election triumph in 2014. Instead, notwithstanding his government's pursuit of a new set of principles to inform foreign policy and a new language in which to describe it, the Modi government struggled to shift national strategy. In part, this occurred because of long-standing and well-known weaknesses in the institutions charged with managing this area: with the woefully under-staffed and under-funded Ministry of External Affairs, and with the Ministries of Defence and Commerce and Industry.[33] But part of the explanation for this failure, I suggest, concerns inherent weaknesses in the Modi government's preferred view of the world and India's role within it, a view deeply rooted in the Hindu nationalist tradition, and in the way in which it sought to use foreign policy for domestic political advantage.

3

Hindu Nationalism
and Foreign Policy

Hindu nationalists have a rich tradition of thought about politics and international relations running back into the mid-19th century, and of course they and others can make use of a range of ancient and medieval Hindu texts that address problems of statecraft.[1] But in the main, Hindu nationalist thinking on foreign policy has long displayed considerable weaknesses. It is often imprecise and does not clearly align with the ways in which international relations are generally practised in the contemporary world, making it difficult to extrapolate clear lines of policy – especially in foreign affairs – from its assumptions and arguments. At the most fundamental level, it conceives of international relations in quite different terms to those with which most observers – at least in the West – are familiar. It sees the key players as civilisations or cultures, and not sovereign states. It often understands the sources of strength and vitality of cultures in racial and gendered terms. It invokes quite different remedies to the security challenges that we face to the ones most often countenanced, arguing that religious paths are the ones to take us beyond our current predicament. And it lambasts what it perceives as Westernised philosophies and practices – especially Nehru's – for its supposed failure to grasp the elements of an authentically Indian approach, as well as its inability to deliver to Bharat the greatness and recognition it deserves.

Modi's attempted reinvention of Indian foreign policy drew, as we shall see, on elements of this Hindu nationalist way of thinking. This is hardly surprising – as I discuss more in the next chapter, Modi knows this tradition well, as do some of his key lieutenants, like Ram Madhav or Sushma Swaraj, and as do many of their supporters, as they were introduced to it at an early age by the RSS or other organisations affiliated with it. As a result, their speeches are peppered with references to concepts, historical arguments and theories drawn from that tradition. I do not argue that Modi and allies tried to implement a foreign policy wholly consistent with the tradition after 2014 – the evidence does not support that conclusion. In significant places, their approach diverged at times from what we might regard as 'orthodox' Hindu nationalist thinking. As with the earlier BJP-led government that ruled India between 1998 and 2004 and as with a number of BJP administrations that have ruled in India's states, it is clear that what has been termed the 'compulsions of politics' entailed departures from elements of the tradition (see Blom Hanson, 1999, p. 224),[2] generating policies that diverged from its tenets. Moreover, as the next chapter explores in more depth, prior to coming to New Delhi Modi had a long track record of selectively appropriating and modifying elements of Hindu nationalist thinking, often combining them with other ideas from different sources, in order to construct what we might term his personal governing philosophy.

The purpose of this chapter is to lay out the resources available to Modi and his allies that they could use for their avowed attempt to displace the existing paradigm underlying Indian foreign policy. By way of introduction, the following section looks briefly at the spectrum of thinking on international relations that exists in India – at what Modi could have drawn on. The remainder of the chapter explores the Hindu nationalist tradition of thought, which I argue is the best context in which to assess what Modi sought to achieve with his attempted reinvention of foreign policy, where his approach diverged from Hindu nationalist 'orthodoxy', such as it is, and what effect the 'compulsions of politics' had on his and his allies' thinking.

The chapter looks first at the origins of Hindu nationalism, found in the Hindu revivalist movements of the 19th and early 20th centuries. It also examines the thought of Swami Vivekananda, one of the most important revivalists, whom Modi claims as a particular inspiration (Hall, 2017b). It then turns to central tenets of the political thought of the core ideologues of the tradition: V.D. Savarkar, M.S. Golwalkar, and especially Deendayal Upadhyaya, cited as another significant influence on Modi's thinking (Mukhopadhyay, 2017). The concluding part then lays out what might be termed the tenets of the Hindu nationalist theory of international relations, as it can be gleaned from those and other thinkers of the past century.

Nehruvianism and its alternatives

In contemporary India, various ways of thinking about and practising foreign policy contend for primacy, some long-established and some relatively new.[3] Historically, the three dominant traditions were what we might call classical Nehruvianism, 'militant Nehruvianism' (Cohen, 2001, p. 41) and 'Neo-Nationalism' (Ollapally and Rajagopalan, 2012, p. 87), which all trace their origins back to Nehru's thinking and – to a degree – to Gandhi's. Although Nehru's own thought is notoriously difficult to classify – combining as it did power political thinking with forms of internationalism (Ollapally and Rajagopalan, 2012, p. 79)[4] – what we might call classical Nehruvianism is an approach that places economic and social development first, puts strict limits therefore on defence spending, relies on diplomacy and the UN to protect the country from external threat, overtly seeks status and acknowledgement of India's size and significance, pursues normative agendas, and espouses solidarity with other developing societies.

Militant Nehruvianism, which was pursued by Nehru's daughter Indira, was less ambitious and less idealistic. Spurred by the 1962 and 1965 wars, it held that India needed to invest in military power, carve out a sphere of influence in South Asia, and build economic self-sufficiency if it was to stay secure, develop, and advance its values. It was largely anti-Western in orientation, and inflected with the Third World socialism of the era (Cohen, 2001, pp. 41–3). Neo-Nationalism, for its part, emerged later, in the 1990s, but again emphasised development and the risks of opening India out to the vicissitudes of the global market, showed a strong preference for UN-based multilateralism and developing world solidarity, as well as for status-seeking, and betrayed a residual suspicion of the West (Ollapally and Rajagopalan, 2012, pp. 87–9).

Running alongside all three of these traditions is a 'Leftist' one that has never been a sustained influence on policy making, but which has provided a means of critiquing the other approaches, and which has long been espoused by India's remarkably tenacious socialist and communist parties, including the Communist Party of India and Communist Party of India-Marxist, and a proportion of its intelligentsia. It is anti-Western and particularly anti-American in orientation, fiercely opposed to liberalisation and globalisation, and convinced of the need for developing world solidarity (Ollapally and Rajagopalan, 2012, p. 100). Opposed to this worldview are the Liberals and a variety of Realists. The Liberals argue that India needs market reforms and deeper integration into the global economy, and that it should become a more 'normal' state, seeking a modicum of military power to provide security, but also relying on multilateral institutions and economic interdependence. The Realists also want India to set aside its inherited ideological prejudices and become more 'normal', but its norm differs from the Liberal version. They argue India needs to spend more on defence, harness its economic heft and pursue its interests more assertively, and behave like an emerging great power (see especially Mohan, 2003).

Finally, there are what some call the 'Hyper-Realists', and of course the Hindu nationalists.[5] The former place great weight on military might, demanding that India build a significant nuclear deterrent and powerful conventional force to manage threats from China and Pakistan, but also to maintain its autonomy. They are suspicious of the West and especially the US, arguing that Washington wants to limit India's ambitions and divert it according to its preferred agenda in the region and the world (see especially Karnad, 2015). They also believe that India's development must be advanced as quickly as possible, to provide the necessary base for the acquisition of military power and the use of economic statecraft in pursuit of the country's interests, but that economy ought to be protected from external pressures insofar as that it possible.

Some Hindu nationalists and a number of significant backers of both Modi and the BJP share some or all of these Realist or Hyper-Realist views. The BJP, after all, represents a broader constituency than just the *Sangh* or Hindu nationalist opinion, attracting votes from the urban middle class and those who aspire to join them, as well as significant support from former military officers.[6] These groups tend to favour more Realist or Hyper-Realist perspectives, as they did during the last BJP-led government between 1998 and 2004, which followed an essentially pragmatic approach to foreign and security policy, and did not generally seek to frame it in overtly Hindu nationalist terms (see especially Ogden, 2014). Modi's attempted reinvention of Indian policy, I argue in the remainder of this book, departed from that precedent, despite his praise for Vajpayee's conduct of international relations and pledge to stay faithful to it that Modi made during the 2014 election campaign (Jaishankar, 2014). Instead, he and his allies couched foreign policy in the language of Hindu nationalism, drawing on the thinking of a series of ideologues from that tradition to justify their approach and provide alternative intellectual foundations to those inherited from previous governments.

Hindu revivalism and communal identity

Hindu nationalist ideology began to emerge between about 1870 and 1920, as a series of intellectuals and political activists reinterpreted India's history and its religious traditions (Jaffrelot, 1996, pp. 11–79). In various ways, they tried to respond to four challenges: first, to the problem of explaining why India had suffered a series of invasions and become subject to 'foreign' rulers; second, to European Christian critiques that questioned or indeed straightforwardly denigrated Hindu beliefs and practices; third, to the perceived need among some Hindus for some reform of elements of ritual and practice, including the caste system, to reground and revive Hinduism; and fourth, to the mobilisation of the Muslims of British India, which led to the so-called *Khalifat* movement in the 1920s and the demand for an independent Muslim-majority state in the 1930s. They also drew on new knowledge and ideas derived from outside India, including European Indology, which was engaged in a search for ancient and medieval texts and their interpretation, as well as studies of contemporary Indian beliefs and practices,[7] and the philosophical movements of the period, including Romanticism, Hegelianism and Darwinism. In some cases, these efforts led to the creation of what were effectively or self-consciously syncretic religions, such as theosophy (see Bevir, 1994). In others, while the object was to recover older, supposedly more authentic Hindu beliefs or practices, the resulting product relied heavily not just on European historiography, but also on borrowed philosophical concepts and theories (see Bhatt, 2001).

Many of these thinkers embraced the idea, advanced by some of the European scholarship and by the Hindu revivalist groups, that Hinduism had once had a 'Golden Age' – the so-called 'Vedic' period, after the ancient texts, the *Vedas* – in which true religious ideas and practices prevailed. They accepted, moreover, the theory that Hinduism had originated among a particular racial group, the Aryans, who had either always been present in the subcontinent or had migrated there in ancient times. Finally, they also borrowed ideas from contemporary European philosophy and national science, especially Social Darwinism and 'vitalism', to build their account of the past successes and travails of Hindus and explain both why they succumbed to foreign conquerors, both Mughal and British, and what they ought to do to reassert themselves in the world (Bhatt, 2001, pp. 7–40). Putting all of this together, they sought to forge a communal identity for Hindus, together with new accounts of what beliefs and practices Hindus ought to affirm (Jaffrelot, 1996, p. 5).

The thought of Swami Vivekananda, born Narendranath Datta in Calcutta (now Kolkata) in Bengal in 1863, illustrates these various processes, and what emerged from them in terms of a recast Hinduism and a new sense of the role that Hindus might play in the world.[8] Having received a British education, including an Arts degree at what is now the Scottish Church College in Kolkata, Vivekananda was well versed in modern European thought. Fascinated in particular by the sociologist and Social Darwinist Herbert Spencer, he translated the latter's *Education* (1961) into Bengali. At the same time, he was an avid student of Indian texts and traditions. When the sudden death of his father impoverished his family, around the time that he took his degree, Vivekananda chose to become a monk. As a student, he had become interested in esotericism and transcendentalism, dabbling with various revivalist groups that drew on Western interpretations of Hindu spiritualism. In this phase, he also met the mystic Ramakrishna Paramahamsa (1836–1886), to whom Vivekananda became devoted after his father's death in 1884.

Ramakrishna's teachings are hotly contested.[9] Early in his life, he apparently had spiritual visions, entering into trances. He became a priest in his late teens, at a temple devoted to Kali, but was drawn to various different traditions in the years that followed: to tantric practices, to the *Advaita Vedanta* Hindu philosophical tradition, and even to Sufi Islam and Christianity, exploring each in turn. Aside from being convinced of Ramakrishna's holiness, Vivekananda admired his openness to ideas and his breadth of interests, though he did not share all of his guru's concerns. He had little sympathy, in particular, for his Kali worship, arguing it was a 'fad' (Sharma, 2013, p. 10). Instead, what Vivekananda took from Ramakrishna was his intuition that all religious traditions had similar underpinnings and objectives, and could somehow be reconciled, albeit under the direction of Hindus. After the guru's death in 1886, Vivekananda founded a *math* (monastery), first at Baranagar and then at Belur, both on the banks of the Hooghly river near Kolkata (then Calcutta), as a foundation for a religious order that would work for the betterment of Hindus and that would preach what he took to be this core message of his guru's teachings. In 1897, this establishment became the Ramakrishna Math and Mission.

Vivekananda integrated Ramakrishna's supposed insights into a much wider account of the history of Hindus and their place in the world. He argued that the essence of Hinduism consisted not in the inherited beliefs and rituals he saw around him, but in the philosophy presented by the *Vedas*, especially the *Upanishads*, and in that part of the *Mahabharata* known as the *Bhagavad Gita*. He criticised fellow Hindus for adhering to 'don't touchism, caste obsession and kitchen religion', arguing that '[s]ocial rules and practices have changed from time to time' (Tapasyananda, 1990, p. xi). He argued that what the *Vedas* taught and what Hindus understand, above all, is that there are many paths to truth and to God. As a consequence, we must accept all religious traditions, not merely tolerate some, as many Westerners advocate (Vivekananda, 1990, pp. 15–17). Hindus should also learn from the Westerners that there is a spiritual value to work and especially to social work in the service of others, and that *sannyasa*, or withdrawal, renunciation and asceticism, commonly valued in Hinduism, should not be the only or the most worthy objective. The spiritual truths that God is One and that all paths should be accepted are Hinduism's gift to the world, and will help remake it, he argued. In order for it to reach its audience, however, Hindus needed to rebuild their nation through what Vivekananda called *karma-yoga* – the *yoga* or practice of work (Vivekananda, 2015). Once that work is done, India can be the *vishwa guru* ('world guru') it is destined to be.

Vivekananda embedded these arguments in a wider account of world history. In quasi-Hegelian style, he suggested that all nations have purposes to realise. The purpose of the English was to maximise 'social independence' through trade; the purpose of the French was to show the way to 'political independence' through revolution. Hindus had a different destiny. Their 'national purpose' was to show the way to 'spiritual independence'. For this reason, despite coming under the political and economic domination of the Mughals and the British, Hinduism had survived (Vivekananda, 2010, pp. 23–5). Now it had the chance to realise its purpose and fulfil its *dharma* by delivering its spiritual message to the world, if Hindus would embrace practical *karma-yoga* and make their nation sufficiently strong to command the respect from the rest of the world necessary for a *vishwa guru*, and for its message to be received as it should. For upon India, Vivekananda declared, 'depends the welfare of the whole world' (1990, p. 88).

These ideas were and remain highly influential, both within India and outside it. In 1893 Vivekananda travelled to the US to carry his message, as well as his broader interpretation of Hinduism, to the first meeting of the so-called Parliament of the World's Religions held in Chicago. He gave talks as he travelled through the US, gathering followers and supporters, delivering powerful and charismatic addresses. In so doing, he became one of the first Hindu religious leaders to speak in the West. The fact that he did so at a relatively young age (he was 30 at the time, and died just nine years later, in 1902), and with such dramatic effect, made him a focus of national pride. This episode, coupled with the message that India had a unique and important mission in the world, also endears Vivekananda to later Hindu nationalists, including Modi, who has cited him repeatedly as a model, inspiration and guide for the country.[10]

The invention of *Hindutva*

Hindu nationalism emerged as a fully fledged political ideology in the 1920s, drawing on ideas established during the earlier period of introspection in which Vivekananda and others like Aurobindo Ghose (1871–1950) played prominent roles, but adding important novel elements.

The appearance of Vinayak Damodar (conventionally, V.D.) Savarkar's book *Hindutva: Who is a Hindu?* (1923) opened this new phase. Born in 1883, as a young man Savarkar became involved in anticolonial groups and anti-Muslim riots. He also studied law, spending a period in London at the Inns of Court, until the publication of his history of the 1857 'Mutiny', *The Indian War of Independence* (1909) and his involvement in anti-British plots led to his arrest. In 1911, he was sentenced to 50 years' imprisonment in the Cellular Jail at Port Blair in the Andaman Islands, in the Indian Ocean. In the event he spent only 13 years there, managing to have himself moved to another prison in India in 1924 after a long campaign of letter-writing.

At Port Blair, Savarkar had composed *Hindutva*, which he succeeded in having smuggled from prison and published under a pseudonym ('A Maratha'). The word *Hindutva* was his invention. For Savarkar it meant 'Hindu-ness', which he contrasted with the narrower concept of Hinduism. One could be a 'Hindu' and not adhere to the beliefs or practices of Hinduism, he argued, since Hinduism was 'only a derivative, a fraction, a part of Hindutva' or Hindu-ness (quoted in Sharma, 2003, p. 124). In principal, this meant that everyone residing in British India – apart from the British themselves – was a 'Hindu', regardless of whether they professed to be Christians or Muslims. What made one a 'Hindu', in Savarkar's idiosyncratic inclusive view, was not following religious beliefs or practices, but rather living within the Indian subcontinent, sharing a set of racial characteristics, and sharing the region's culture, which he termed – borrowing a Sanskrit term – *sanskriti*. This definition allowed Savarkar to assert that local Christians, Muslims, and others who met his three criteria were actually Hindus, even if they or their ancestors had migrated into the subcontinent sometime in the past or had converted to their present faiths (Jaffrelot, 1996, pp. 28–9).[11] They were all members of the same 'race-jati', to use Savarkar's term, or 'race-caste', sharing the *sanskriti* of the region, and sharing, as a consequence, a common 'Hindu-ness' (Sharma, 2003, p. 163).

Despite his differences with the British authorities, Savarkar's political programme was principally concerned with the Muslim presence in India and with ensuring that Hindus defend themselves effectively against the threat he thought they posed and dominate any post-independence polity. As Jyotirmaya Sharma summarises his view: 'The goal of the Hindus was the same as that of the [legendary 17th century Marathi warrior] Shivaji: Re-acquire territory, rehabilitate religion, preserve the *Vedas* and shastras, protect cows and Brahmins, establish suzerainty and diffusion of Hindu fame and glory' (Sharma, 2003, p. 127). Savarkar feared and admired Muslims as strong, single-minded and successful. By contrast, he deplored what he perceived as the weakness of his fellow Hindus, who had 'fallen a prey [sic] to the most decentralising and disabling institutions and superstitions' and displayed 'a general lack of community of feeling and pride and national sympathy' (quoted in Sharma, 2003, pp. 129–30). He admired the passionate and militant nationalism of Guiseppe Mazzini, the racially tinged Social Darwinism of Spencer – one of Vivekananda's inspirations – and turn-of-the-century German nationalism (Jaffrelot, 1996, p. 32). He was convinced that Hindus needed both to be infused with a sense of national spirit and, in order to defend and promote themselves in the perennial struggle for survival between peoples, with a newfound manliness (Sharma, 2003, p. 148). He therefore rejected both Gandhi's embrace of non-violence (*ahimsa*) and the broader appeal of Buddhism, arguing as Vivekananda and others had, that it weakened and distracted Hindus from what needed to be done, which was the establishment of a Hindu *Rashtra* or – very roughly – 'polity'.

RSS and the Hindu *Rashtra*

Savarkar continue to write and agitate until his death in 1966, leading the nationalist *Hindu Mahasabha* group from 1937 to 1943. He was not, however, the only advocate for *Hindutva* during this period. Influenced by Savarkar's ideas, K.B. Hedgewar (1889–1940) emerged as a new force in the 1920s. A former member of the Indian National Congress, he had grown disillusioned of its approach and increasingly concerned about the Muslim presence in a future independent India. In 1925, Hedgewar founded a radical alternative, the Rashtriya Swayamsevak Sangh (RSS).[12] The RSS was designed from the outset as a paramilitary organisation, with uniforms, physical training for its recruits, weapons drills (particularly using *lathis* – the bamboo poles still employed by India's security forces for crowd control) and an unabashedly quasi-fascist salute (the right hand held horizontally across the chest, facing downwards). It was designed to produce a generation of what we might call hardened Hindus, more capable of defending – as they saw it – their communities from others, especially Muslims (Jaffrelot, 1996, pp. 35–8). Alongside this primary function, Hedgewar also gave the RSS the mission of promoting Hindu nationalist ideology. This task was assigned to a specially chosen group – the *pracharaks* (literally 'preachers', but often translated as 'organisers') – who were required to devote their lives to the cause, remain celibate, and practise *karma-yoga* for the betterment of the nation.

Hedgewar did not contribute much in the way of original thinking to Hindu nationalism. That was left to his successor as *Sarsanghchalak*, as the head of the RSS is known, M.S. Golwalkar, known to his followers as 'Guruji'. His *Bunch of Thoughts* (1966) developed and adapted what Savarkar had laid out, alongside other works inspired by the RSS and its ideals and theories, like *We, or Our Nationhood Defined* (1939), once attributed to Golwalkar.[13] He drew not just on Savarkar's thought, but also that of Hindu revivalists and nationalists from late 19th and early 20th centuries, including Vivekananda, Aurobindo, and Bal Gangadhar Tilak. In *Bunch of Thoughts*, he developed a powerful account of what he took to be the 'world mission' of the Hindus, the challenge of building a Hindu *Rashtra*, and the 'Path to [Hindu] Glory' (Golwalkar, 1996).

Like Hedgewar, Golwalkar (1906–1973) was born into a Brahmin family in Nagpur, in Maharashtra, where the RSS still has its headquarters. He studied in both his home town and at Benaras Hindu University in Varanasi, on the banks of the Ganges in what is now Uttar Pradesh, where he met the veteran nationalist activist Madan Mohan Malaviya, the founder of that institution. In the mid-1930s, he joined a Ramakrishna Mission ashram at Sargachi, north of Kolkata, but remained there for only a year, returning to work for Hedgewar's RSS. Shortly before the latter died in 1940, Golwalkar was designated as his successor. Golwalkar remained *Sarsanghchalak* until his death in 1973, becoming the RSS's 'most influential ideologue' (Sharma, 2007, p. xviii).

Golwalkar took the RSS in a distinctive direction. Ostensibly, he assumed the role of what Jaffrelot calls the 'world-renouncer' as 'activist' (1996, p. 40).[14] He eschewed family life and remained a bachelor, setting an example to his *pracharaks*. He renounced 'self' to the cause, leading an apparently highly ascetic life that was greatly admired by his followers, including Modi, who singled out and praised this attribute in his profile of Golwalkar in his book *Jyotipunj* (Modi, 2015a, pp. 39–86), a set of highly personal biographical sketches of leading RSS members. Importantly, he argued that the RSS should be apolitical, remaining (supposedly) aloof from the political fray. He justified this stance by arguing that everyday electoral politics were ephemeral and grubby compared to the depth and purity of *sanskriti* or Hindu culture, which would one day produce a saviour-leader who would transcend the petty squabbles of conventional political life (Sharma, 2007, pp. 18–19). 'Neither political power nor holding political office', he believed, 'could help the Sangh's work, or even protect it from any future threat' (Sharma, 2007, p. 19; see also Golwalkar, 2000, pp. 72–4, 172–5). He refused to campaign against British rule before 1947, thereby also avoiding the imposition of official restrictions on its activities by the colonial authorities. He insisted that the RSS should focus instead on protecting and promoting *sanskriti* – and stuck to this position after independence. In time, this stance paid dividends. When a former RSS activist, Nathuram Godse, assassinated Gandhi in January 1948, leading to a temporary ban on the organisation, Golwalkar and the *Sangh* successfully escaped lasting curbs on their work, partly because they could argue that they would stay out of political life.

Golwalkar's thought, however, did have political and international implications. He was a fervent if eccentric nationalist. Combining his ascetic beliefs about the self and society with ideas drawn from European nationalism, he argued that the dutiful Indian 'had to become a *rashtrabhakta* or worshipper of the nation' and that 'the entire strength and intellect of Hindu society has to be placed at the feet of the nation', Bharat, which was itself divine (Sharma, 2007, p. 13). 'Devotion to the motherland', Golwalkar wrote in *Bunch of Thoughts*, 'of the intense, dynamic, uncompromising and fiery type is the life-breath of a free, prosperous and glorious national existence on the face of the earth'. What Hindus needed to do, he argued, was to fan 'the ancient embers of devotion lying dormant' to generate a 'sacred conflagration which shall consume all the past aggressions on our motherland and bring to life the dream of Bharat Mata [Mother India] reinstated in her pristine undivided form' (Golwalkar, 1996, p. 96).

This 'mission' required Hindus to resist Western ideas and practices, including 'permissiveness', social contract theory, competition, democracy, and capitalism, as well as communism, which Golwalkar particularly disliked (1996, pp. 10–19). It also meant resisting the corrupting effects of the 'narrow' 'Semitic religions – Judaism, Christianity and Islam', with their insistence on a 'single way of worship' (Golwalkar, 1996, p. 103). But above all it meant confronting Muslims, who were 'invaders' and 'tooth and nail opposed to our way of life in all aspects' (Golwalkar, 1996, p. 142). Muslims represented what Golwalkar called, without qualification, 'internal threats' – a category that also included Christians and Communists (1996, pp. 177–201). All needed to be confronted with material power, for the 'world worships only the strong' and '[n]obody cares a whit for the voice of the weak' (Golwalkar, 1996, pp. 270–1). Gandhi's preferred path of *ahimsa* (non-violence) thus had to be rejected as 'perverse' – such an approach would only be adopted by an 'imbecile' (Golwalkar, 1996, p. 272). The *Mahabharata* teaches, he argued, that Hindus should be manly and do what should be done, like the warrior Arjuna, as 'righteousness' cannot be established without 'fearlessness and heroism' (Golwalkar, 1996, p. 274). An 'invincible national will' was needed, since '[m]ilitary power' is more than just the size of an army or the quality of its equipment – it demands a 'well disciplined, intensely patriotic and heroic attitude of the people' (Golwalkar, 1996, p. 277; pp. 278–88).

These ideas – the insistence on the worship of the nation and sublimation of the self into society, the demonisation of out-groups, and the glorification of strength – have given rise to the assertion that Golwalkar was a fascist (Jaffrelot, 1996, pp. 50–8). But as Rahul Sagar (2014, pp. 242–5) observes, this characterisation of Golwalkar might lead the reader astray in terms of understanding his philosophy of international relations, such as it was. Unlike mid-20th century European fascists, who embraced a hybrid Social Darwinist-Nietzschean view that nations were locked in a perpetual struggle for survival and dominance over others, Golwalkar did not think conflict between nations was inevitable or perennial. Early in *Bunch of Thoughts*, he argued that nationalism could never be 'rooted out', as some liberals and communists thought, and for that reason, Golwalkar maintained, the League of Nations had failed and the UN would too (1996, pp. 2–3). But this did not mean that 'world unity' was impossible. Instead, he avowed the Vivekanandan view that it could and would come about when the world, led by Hindus, embraced the truth of the *sanatana dharma* (loosely, 'true religion').

Teaching the world about these truths was the 'sacred trust' and 'world mission' (Golwalkar, 1996, pp. 6–7) of the Hindu people, who would thereby lead the world, as a *vishwa guru*, beyond conflict and toward peace. It is 'evident', Golwalkar (1996, p. 5) wrote,

> that world unity and human welfare can be made real only to the extent that mankind realises the common Inner Bond which along can subdue the passions and discords stemming from materialism, broaden the horizon of the human mind and harmonize the individual and national aspirations with the welfare of mankind.

The ills of the world can only be addressed, he argued, through Hindu transcendentalism – by giving up worldly desires and quelling the 'restless mind' (1996, p. 14) in favour of mental peace, brought about by following the teachings of the *Vedas* (Sagar, 2014, p. 243).

Integral Humanism and *dharma rajya*

Golwalkar might have been the biggest influence on RSS thinking in the 20th century, but others also played significant roles in developing Hindu nationalist political thought and practice, including Deendayal (or Deen Dayal) Upadhyaya (1916–1968).[15] Born in what was then the United Provinces, now Uttar Pradesh, Upadhyaya earned a First Class degree in English, but spurned a possible civil service career in favour of the RSS, which he joined in 1937, becoming a *pracharak* in 1942. During the 1940s, he established himself as a journalist and commentator, creating a periodic called *Rashtra Dharma*, and then, after its establishment in 1941, writing for the RSS paper, *The Organiser*. In 1951, he was deputed from the RSS, with Golwalkar's apparent blessing and despite the latter's personal antipathy to politics (Sharma, 2009, p. 21), to work with Syama Prasad Mookerjee to found a political party, the Bharatiya Jana Sangh (loosely, Indian People's Association, or BJS), a forerunner of the BJP.[16] Upadhyaya became BJS General Secretary the following year and remained in that position until shortly before he died. During the 1950s and 60s, he also continued to write for periodicals, and produced a number of books, including a novel for children about the ancient Indian king Chandragupta (Mukhopadhyay, 2017). At the same time, he developed his distinctive political philosophy, which he called 'Integral Humanism', and which was adopted by the BJS in 1965 and has been the avowed creed of the BJP since 1985 (Andersen and Damle, 2018, p. 8).

Like other Hindu nationalists before him, Upadhyaya situated his philosophy in a sweeping interpretation of India's past.[17] For much of the modern period, he lamented, Hindus had not been able to 'contribute to world progress' because they had been 'engaged in fighting for independence or staving off new hordes of invaders' (Upadhyaya, 1992, p. 14). But like Golwalkar, Upadhyaya believed that India's moment had arrived, as the West was riven by the tensions generated by the contradictions inherent in nationalism, democracy and socialism, and as it became increasingly evident that Western-created international institutions like the League of Nations and the UN were unable to manage them (Upadhyaya, 1992, pp. 15–19). The time was ripe, he thought, for 'Bharatiya culture' to pass on the 'truth' of the *Vedas*: that 'unity in diversity', grounded in the interconnectedness of all things, was possible and necessary. The Western dominated period was coming to an end, and the time was nigh when a *dharma rajya* – a polity guided by *dharma* – could lead the world in a different direction. In order to do fulfil this task, Upadhyaya argued that India – or Bharat, as he termed it in his lectures on *Integral Humanism* – needed to tend its 'neglected self', set aside those Western ideologies that were patently flawed, and recover its distinctive identity (Upadhyaya, 1992, pp. 18–19). Indeed, he argued that 'Independence can be meaningful only if it becomes an instrument for the expression of our culture' (Upadhyaya, 1992, p. 24).

That culture taught something quite different from the West. It maintained that 'life' is an 'integrated whole', Upadhyaya argued, echoing the *Advaita Vedanta* tradition to which Vivekananda and Aurobindo belonged. It rejected what he took to be the Western view that the best way to comprehend 'life' – that is, the natural and social worlds – was to divide it into parts, classifying it and splitting it into taxonomies. That approach failed to appreciate that '[t]he diversity in life is merely the expression of the internal unity' of all things (Upadhyaya, 1992, p. 25). This truth also had implication, Upadhyaya maintained, for social and political thought. Whereas Western theories held that diversity leads to conflict, Integral Humanism recognises that this is not the natural state of things, but rather a 'perversion'. Cooperation is the norm, demonstrated by the sustenance given by living things to other living things, and it ought therefore to be recognised as such, and nurtured (Upadhyaya, 1992, pp. 26–7).

Our aim as human beings, Upadhyaya argued, should be to lead an 'integrated life' (1992, p. 29). This can be achieved if we ensure that *dharma* (which he observed should be translated as 'law' not 'religion') regulates nature. Hindus, he asserted, knew this. They recognise the importance of an integral approach to the 'longings in man', which are *Dharma*, *Artha*, *Kāma*, and *Moksha*, and the importance of not merely trying to satisfy the body, as Westerners would apparently have it (Upadhyaya, 1992, p. 32). *Dharma* must be upheld to allow *Artha* (business and politics) to flourish and *Kāma* (bodily desires) to be satisfied. If this is done, *Moksha* (enlightenment) will follow. But at all times, a balance has to be struck between them. If one of these is pursued at the expense of the others – if money or power is sought too avidly or ruthlessly or if greed prevails – individual life will fail, and so too do societies.

For these reasons, Upadhyaya rejected Western social contract theory, arguing, as Golwalkar has implied, that it misconceived 'life' and the true relationship between individuals and societies. Societies are 'self-born' and 'organic'.[18] Like individuals, they have their own 'body, mind, intellect and soul' (Upadhyaya, 1992, p. 37). Social contracts could, he acknowledged, create states, but they were just temporary institutions sometimes necessary when *dharma* was in decline (Upadhyaya, 1992, pp. 43–4). They were contrivances compared to societies and, above all, nations – the ultimate form of societies – which were living things, complete with souls. 'When a group of persons lives with a goal, an ideal, a mission, and looks upon a particular piece of land as motherland', he argued, 'this group constitutes a nation' (Upadhyaya, 1992, p. 40). Such entities have souls that persist even when individual members die, just as souls pass from one body to another according to Hindu philosophy. And the national soul – he termed the concept *Chiti*, translated as 'consciousness' by some of his interpreters (Sharma, 2009, p. 24) – gives nations their direction.

Swadeshi and *Sarvodaya*

The specifics of Upadhyaya's political agenda, including for international relations, were more mundane, overlapping with positions held by Congress leaders, especially Gandhi, and sometimes unclear. For these reasons, he and other Hindu nationalist activists have been criticised for according economic policy, in particular, 'low priority', and displaying little interest in its development (Blom Hansen, 2001, p. 296). This is only partly fair. From Savarkar onwards, the Hindu nationalists did pay attention to economic and other areas of policy, including foreign policy, but they were insistent that these topics should not be the sole or most important focus. In the late 1930s, for example, Savarkar urged his Hindu Mahasabha to develop a coherent economic policy that would serve the nation while avoiding the twin pitfalls of conceiving 'man' as merely an 'economical being' and thinking that an 'economical programme alone will ever suffice to solve all cultural, racial, and national dangers that threaten [Hindus]' (Savarkar, n.d., pp. 59–60).[19] 'Taking into consideration the special circumstances obtaining in India and the stage of social progress', he argued in favour of what he called 'Nationalistic' economics – essentially authoritarian corporatism (Savarkar, n.d., p. 60; p. 61). The aim, he thought, should be national self-sufficiency achieved by rapid modernisation. 'This is a Machine age', Savarkar declared, so technology must be embraced, and '[n]ational production' should be on 'the biggest possible machine scale'. He envisaged some nationalisation and even 'State cultivation' in agriculture, though private property ought to be treated as 'inviolate' (n.d., p. 61).

Golwalkar and Upadhyaya were less clear on their preferred agendas. Golwalkar was insistent that India had to be protected from all foreign influences, since *dharma* is what will 'save' the world from 'military aggression', 'excessive consumerism', and 'exploitation of natural resources', so favoured protectionism over openness (Blom Hansen, 1999, p. 229). He argued that the 'right structure' for both politics and economics was one that rested on 'original concepts reflecting the genius of our own soil', albeit with borrowings from elsewhere if 'positive elements' could be found (Golwalkar, 1996, p. 30). Upadhyaya was arguably more definitive, but again more categorical about what he opposed than what he wanted. He rejected Savarkar's preference for machines, arguing that mechanisation was inappropriate to India's economy (Sharma, n.d., p. 8). He was also highly critical of Nehru's attempt to achieve economic development by central planning and large-scale infrastructure and industrial projects, critiquing them most notably in *The Two Plans: Promises, Performance and Prospects* (1958) and his *Political Diary* (1968).

Only in *Integral Humanism* (1992 – first published in 1965), however, did Upadhyaya try to sketch out an alternative economic policy from the kinds of autochthonous materials Golwalkar recommended.[20] There he argued that the strengthening of the nation and achieving 'supreme happiness', as Golwalkar called it (1996, p. 17), should be the aims of economic policy. Upadhaya argued:

> We must have such an economic system which helps in the developments of our humane qualities, or civilization and enables us to attain a still higher level of all round perfection. We should have a system which does not overwhelm our humane quality; which does not make us slaves of its own grinding wheels. According to our concept, man attains God like perfection as a result of development. (Upadhyaya, 1992)

This could not be done by emulating Western capitalism, which does not just aim at satisfying needs, but also at stimulating new desires, and which is wasteful, unnecessarily using up scarce natural resources and 'disturbing' the 'equilibrium of nature'. The notion of 'economic man' must be resisted, for treating people as commodities and consumers will not aid the 'development of an integral human being'. Both the capitalist and communist systems, he argued:

> ... have failed to take account of the Integral Man, his true and complete personality and his aspirations. One considers him a mere selfish being lingering after money, having only one law, the law of fierce competition, in essence the law of the jungle; whereas the other has viewed him as a feeble lifeless cog in the whole scheme of things, regulated by rigid rules, and incapable of any good unless directed. The centralization of power, economic and political, is implied in both. Both, therefore, result in dehumanization of man. ... We must re-establish him in his rightful position, being him the realization of his greatness, reawaken his abilities and encourage him to exert for attaining divine heights of his latest personality. This is possible only through a decentralized economy. (Upadhyaya, 1992)

The 'system' needed was one based not on the 'exploitation of nature' but one that would 'sustain' it. It had to offer all an education and a 'guarantee of work'. It would use technology, as it aids labour and increases productivity, but cautiously, especially when it came to foreign equipment. In time, appropriate 'Bharatiya machines' should be developed for the nation's particular purposes.

In short, Upadhyaya favoured a different approach to Savarkar – one much more like that which Gandhi had envisaged. Self-sufficiency was the aim – *swadeshi* being necessary because if the nation became dependent on 'foreign articles' '[w]e shall forget our individuality and become virtual slaves once again', as India had under the British (Upadhyaya, 1992). Both markets and planning had to be avoided – neither were paths to the realisation of 'Integral Man'. That meant setting aside Nehru's attempt to achieve modernisation through centralisation and state control. Instead, a protected, decentralised economy was preferable, with cottage industries and small traders as its mainstays. In this way, *sarvodaya* or the 'uplift' of all and *antyodaya* or the 'rise of the last person' (that is, the poorest or most disadvantaged) – more of Gandhi's concepts appropriated by Upadhyaya – could be achieved without Bharat succumbing to consumerism or communism. Moreover, development could be achieved in ways that were not so destructive of the environment, in line with his understanding of the integrated nature of all living things (Andersen and Damle, 2018, p. 132).

These commitments to *swadeshi* and to a version of *sarvodaya* remain powerful within elements of the Hindu nationalist movement. There are those who would like the BJP to return to its original commitment to 'Gandhian socialism' or something like it. The *Swadeshi Jagaran Manch* (loosely, 'Self-Reliance Awareness Platform' – or SJM), another offshoot of the RSS created in 1991 to oppose liberalisation, still campaigns against the opening of India's markets to foreign trade and capital. During the 1990s, the SJM played a leading role in campaigning against the construction and operation of a power plant in Maharashtra by a firm owned by the now-defunct US company Enron (Blom Hansen, 1999, p. 222). Another organisation, the Bharatiya Mazdoor Sangh ('Indian Workers' Association' – BMS), created by the RSS in 1955 and led first by another key economic thinker within the Sangh, Dattopant Thengali, still organises regular protests against the liberalisation of India's markets for goods and capital.[21] Both the SJM and BMS, indeed, have publicly criticised BJP-led governments for their economic policies, including Modi's NDA coalition (Andersen and Damle, 2018, pp. 125–9).

Power and nonalignment

In contrast to Upadhyaya's thinking on economic policy, his views on power and conflict in international relations were significantly more 'mundane', to use a word he himself employed (Upadhyaya, 1968, p. 51).

In a number of the essays collected in his *Political Diary*, and even in his *Integral Humanism* lectures, these issues are addressed in acute and nuanced ways, but not in a fashion that makes clear the link with his underlying philosophy. Nor does it clearly evince Golwalkar's apparent belief that transcendentalism will eventually free the world from war. Upadhyaya's tone is frank bordering on blunt. Its content is robustly anti-communist and his core concern is frequently the threat posed to India by China. That threat is treated as real and pressing, but not entirely damaging, as the 1962 war, he notes, did help Indians to 'recognise ourselves' so that they 'stood united' and recovered, to some extent, the 'sense of self' the country needs to drive it forward in the right direction (Upadhyaya, 1992).

On the whole, Upadhyaya's thinking was broadly 'realist' in form. The BJS, he observed in one key essay in February 1963, held that foreign policy 'should be framed with the sole objective of securing the enlightened self-interest of the nation' and must be 'realistic' (Upadhyaya, 1968, p. 51). In that spirit, Upadhyaya pointed to China as a 'new aggressive force threatening the peace of Asia and the world' and called for India to align itself with other states willing to resist Beijing's designs. New Delhi, he argued, should build an 'A-Bomb', invest in India's military to secure the country, withdraw its recognition of the People's Republic and its 'suzerainty' over Tibet, and assist in that country's liberation (Upadhyaya, 1968, pp. 50–3). In parallel, India should patch up its relations with the US, damaged by the leftist activism of Nehru's representatives, including Krishna Menon, and persuade Washington to cease or slow its assistance to Pakistan, which distracts India from 'her fight against the [Chinese] Reds' (Upadhyaya, 1968, p. 46).

The wider problem, Upadhyaya argued, was that the policy of nonalignment had not benefited India in the way that Nehru and his acolytes had envisaged. It had alienated Western – and especially US – opinion, and made it harder, not easier, to secure support from the West when it was needed, as the 1962 war had shown (Upadhyaya, 1968, p. 32). There might have been a time when nonalignment was appropriate, but things change, and the time had passed – and 'a foreign policy like any policy cannot become a creed', still less a 'fetish' (Upadhyaya, 1968, pp. 51–2). The Chinese threat, in particular, meant that it needed to be set aside, as India needed friends or even allies to manage it.

Conclusion

Constructing something that approximates to what we might call a 'Hindu theory of international relations' from all of the various parts discussed in this chapter is not a straightforward or uncontroversial exercise. But it is necessary to do so, to get a stronger sense of how those who see themselves as the heirs of this tradition of thought conceive of foreign affairs. This chapter should have made clear that the Sangh and those parts of the BJP most closely affiliated to it have a worldview that includes within it an account of India's place in the world and how it ought to interact with others. The building blocks of the world are societies defined racially, at times, and certainly culturally, rather than – as conventional international relations theory would have it, sovereign states. These societies are not immortal, but they are long-lived, and endowed with something akin to a soul. They also have missions – distinct purposes to fulfil in the world. Their paths for development are conditioned by both their cultures and missions – and to realise the latter they need to find ways to advance, socially and economically, in keeping with the former.

In the case of India – or Bharat, to use the Hindu nationalists preferred term – this theory implies that the country must safeguard its cultural essence against all challengers, inside and outside the country, in order for the country to fulfil its purpose. Indeed, it conceives of a kind of continuum between these internal and external threats, with Indian Muslims connected to Pakistan, in particular, and the wider Islamic world, Indian Christians to the West, and Indian 'secularists' – Nehru especially – also to the Western world. These groups need therefore to be held in check within India if it is to develop as it should and regain the wealth and power it once had. The best path for that development is, moreover, one in which policies arise from authentically Indian philosophies and technologies, ones that will not undermine or displace *sanskriti*. Through *swadeshi* India can achieve *sarvodaya* and *antyodaya*, and then fulfil its mission, which is to serve as a 'spiritual corrective' to the rest of the world, to wean it away from war and materialism (Blom Hansen, 1999, p. 229). In the meantime, of course, it may have to acquire military power and use it, and as Upadhyaya in particular makes clear, it may also have to align itself with other states with different missions, including Western states. In time, however, 'Bharatiya culture' will lead others to the recognition of the truths of the *sanatana dharma* and its message, taken from the *Upanishads*, that *vasudhaiva kutumbakam* ('the world is one family').

4

Modi and *Moditva*

Modi's rise to become India's fourteenth Prime Minister is a tale of persistence, luck, ruthlessness, and indeed, talent. At some points, the facts of the story are also unclear and the evidence subject to competing interpretations. There are good reasons for this murkiness. Modi's biography – as for any politician – furnishes key elements in the wider narratives he and his allies would like to advance about his character and capacities. As a result, stories about him are carefully policed – as some of his biographers have found, when they have got too close to certain topics – by Modi and his supporters.[1] For these reasons, and despite the publication of multiple studies of his life, what we know about his background, his rise to prominence, his political thinking, and his style of governing is patchy and overlain with at least two decades of mythmaking. But given the manner in which Modi personalised Indian foreign policy after 2014, and centralised decision making in his hands, the story of his life and of political career cannot be avoided.

Three particular things, I argue, are crucial to understanding Modi's reinvention of Indian foreign policy. The first is his character – his oft-noted ego and ambition, but also about his intellectual self-confidence, manifest in his apparent conviction that he is capable of learning and grasping the essentials of international relations and diplomacy, as he has with other areas of government. The second is Modi's political thought, including his beliefs about foreign policy, and how they converge with – and just as importantly, diverge from – the thinking of the broader Hindu nationalist movement, and especially to the *Rashtriya Swayamsevak Sangh* (RSS), which he joined as a boy. The last is his style of leadership and preferred mode of governing. In that area – and indeed in his thought – it shows how Modi's distinctive approach both adheres to and departs from the Hindu nationalist norm, such as it is.

To explore each of these issues, this chapter is divided into five sections. The first looks at Modi's upbringing, the break that he made with his family in the late 1960s, and his early days in the RSS. The second explores Modi's time as an RSS *pracharak* during the 1970s and his transition into the BJP in the 1980s. The third and fourth examine Modi's time as Gujarat Chief Minister, focusing particularly on the Godhra incident and its aftermath, and then on the making of his style of governance, labelled *Moditva* (or Modi-ness) by some of his supporters. The last looks at Modi's political style and charts the principal ways in which that shaped his approach to government and foreign policy after May 2014.

Family and *Sangh*

Modi was born to Damodardas Mulchand and Hiraben (or Hiraba) Modi on 17 September 1950 in the town of Vadnagar, in what was then still part of Bombay State, but which is now in Gujarat. Modi was the third of their six children. His parents belonged to the *Ghanchi* caste, traditionally oil pressers – a group now classified as an 'Other Backward Class' (OBC) – and the family lived in humble circumstances. His father sold tea at the local railway station, and when Modi was old enough and the trains stopped on their way through the town, he joined him in that trade (Verma, 2014, pp. 2–3).

In academic terms, Modi was apparently not particularly successful at school, but some biographers suggest he had a special interest for debating and drama (Nag, 2013, p. 37). He was apparently devout, regularly attending local temples and fasting (Mukhopadhyay, 2013, p. 28). There are suggestions from more sympathetic biographies that he developed an ascetic streak early in life, forgoing certain foods, and showing an interest in *sadhus* (holy-men) and *sannyasis* – those who renounce worldly things and family ties to pray and wander (Kamath and Randeri, 2013, pp. 6–8; Marino, 2014, pp. 8–9). He was also apparently a physically active boy – whether or not we believe the stories about his swimming in crocodile infested local lakes and the other tall tales told about him in some of the biographies.[2]

Modi's restlessness was probably what led him, at eight years old, to join the RSS, an organisation that was controversial then and remains so today (Marino, 2014, p. 16). Founded in 1925 by K.B. Hedgewar, who became its first leader or *Sarsanghchalak*, the RSS was designed to train young men in the means by which to defend Hindu communities.[3] From the start, as I observed in the previous chapter, this training had two components, one designed to harden bodies and the other to build character. At their *shakhas* (local branches, modelled on traditional Indian gymnasia) recruits gather for games, exercise, and drill – the latter involving training in the use of the *lathi* – and parading in the quasi-paramilitary uniforms of khaki shorts and white shirts (Jaffrelot, 1996, pp. 35–40).[4] The intention is to hone fit and strong men capable of resisting attacks on Hindu homes or communities and able, some allege, to perpetrate attacks on those of others, should the circumstances arise.

In parallel, RSS recruits are also inducted into a programme of ideological education known as 'character building' (*chaaritya nirman*) that is intended, according to a recent, relatively sympathetic study, to 'create a cadre of men who would unify a highly pluralistic country, using their own perfected behaviour as a model for other Indians' (Anderson and Damle, 2018, p. xii). At the *shakhas*, members sing patriotic songs or hear talks about history or social issues. They learn about Hindu philosophy and are taught to memorise supposedly pertinent aphorisms or quotations – *subhaashits* – derived from '*shlokas* [epic verse]... ancient scriptures, or speeches of great leaders' (Sharda, 2018, p. 105). As boys get older, they are also given practical tasks to complete, and if they show promise, they are appointed to lead small groups in activities (Sharda, 2018, pp. 108–9). This training is especially intense for a chosen few who decide to commit themselves fully to the RSS, foreswearing the right to marry and have a family, and becoming full time *pracharaks* ('preachers' or 'organisers') at the disposal of the organisation.[5] Today numbering about six thousand in total (Andersen and Damle, 2018, p. xi), these *pracharaks* form the backbone of the RSS, supporting it and its various affiliates, including the BJP, which together form the *Sangh Parivar* ('Family of Organisations').

Initially, the RSS likely appealed to Modi, as it did and continues to do for other boys, because it provided a place to escape from home and schoolwork, and spend time with friends (Marino, 2014, p. 16; Verma, 2014, pp. 16–17). For boys like him and of a similar age, the organisation offered somewhere to play games, and learn different skills. As 'a child', he later told one biographer, 'it was just a playground' (quoted in Mukhopadhyay, 2013, p. 56). But over time it is clear that he was deeply influenced by its way of thinking – by its account of good character and social responsibility, its understanding of India's culture, history and politics, and its thinking about the relationships between Hindus and other communities, especially Muslims and Christians. The RSS provided Modi with an ideology that gave him a set of rules and values by which to live, as well as a framework for interpreting the world around him and the role that might be played by people who shared its beliefs (Verma, 2014, p., 19). It inculcated a 'sense of responsibility' and 'what it means to be responsible', as well as a sense of how organisations worked and 'how to work within it' (quoted in Mukhopadhyay, 2013, p. 52). It gave him role models outside his family who in time would become more important to his personal and political development than his relatives. And combined with Modi's asceticism and curiosity about *sadhus* and *sannyasis*, the RSS seems to have nurtured in him a desire to live a different life from that conventionally pursued (Nag, 2013, p. 36).

Modi's involvement with the RSS also helped to open, or perhaps just widen, a rift with his family. Some of his sympathetic biographers suggest that the first signs of disagreement emerged in 1962, amidst the national trauma inflicted by China's punitive border war, which ended in a humiliating defeat for India's forces. Modi was then 12, and when not in school, he was helping his father serve tea at the railway station in Vadnagar. There he apparently saw troops heading to the front to fight the Chinese forces and would have heard news and rumours about the conflict (Marino, 2014, p. 18). At the same time, at the RSS *shakha*, he would also have been exposed to a Hindu nationalist critique of the Nehru government's alleged failure to prevent the Chinese attack or make adequate preparations for the country's defence (Marino, 2014, p. 17; Mukhopadhyay, 2013, pp. 72–3).

Thus fired by an apparent desire to do his duty for his country, Modi supposedly responded to these events by telling his father that he wished to enrol in a nearby *Sainak* or military academy and afterwards join the army. To his annoyance, however, this request was denied, probably because the family could not afford the costs of sending him away to the academy (Marino, 2014, p. 19).[6] Soon after, other points of contention emerged. When Modi was about six, his father had made a preliminary arrangement for his marriage, as was customary at that time and in that community (Verma, 2014, pp. 9–10). By the time he was 13, however, he seems to have begun to protest against the idea of marrying (Mukhopadhyay, 2013, pp. 65–6; Marino, 2014, p. 21). Nevertheless, a ceremony was conducted at some point with Jashodaben, his intended spouse, either when Modi was 13 or 16 (his biographers disagree on the details) (Verma, 2014, p. 10). Another was performed to seal the marriage when Modi was about 17, at which point the couple were meant to live together, with his wife joining his parents' household. This situation did not last long. Within weeks, he broke with both his spouse and his family. He left home and thereafter did not return, except very briefly, to either his wife or his parents.

Instead, Modi apparently roamed across India for about two years. According to some, he first travelled to the Ramakrishna Mission at Belur in West Bengal, and then to the Mission's branch in Rajkot, in Gujarat, about 300 km away from Vadnagar. At one or both Missions, he apparently expressed the desire to become a monk, citing his devotion to the order's founder, the important late 19th century Hindu nationalist intellectual and activist, Swami Vivekananda (Mukhopadhyay, 2013, pp. 59–60; Verma, 2014, pp. 14–15). The Missions sent Modi away, however, supposedly telling him to devote his life to social work and to help regenerate his community and the nation, as Vivekananda himself had advised Indians to do (Marino, 2014, pp. 24–7). Disappointed, Modi then travelled north to the Himalayas, and at least one biography includes a picture of him dressed in the saffron robes of a *sannyasin*, sitting next to a river swollen with snow-melt (see Mukhopadhyay, 2013).

Becoming a *pracharak*

By now 19 or 20 years old, Modi returned to Gujarat sometime in 1970, but not to Vadnagar, his parents, nor his spouse. After a brief visit to see his mother, he went to live and work with his uncle in the state's largest city, Ahmedabad, about hundred kilometres to the south (Kamath and Randeri, 2013, pp. 9–10). There he renewed his contacts with the RSS, and at some point around this time determined that he wanted to work for that organisation as a full-time volunteer. In 1972, he left his uncle's house and joined a number of other RSS members living at its headquarters in Ahmedabad, the *Hedgewar Bhavan* (Hedgewar House), which was overseen by an influential *Sangh* leader, Lakshmanrao Inamdar. Better known as Vakil Saheb, he became Modi's first personal and political mentor, someone whom he greatly admired (Kamath and Randeri, 2013, p. 11).[7] In the idiosyncratic collective biography of a series of RSS leaders, *Jyotipunj*, which Modi published some time later, in 2001, he called Vakil Saheb a 'fascinating personality' and 'inspiration to a great number of youths', and praised both his perseverance with and devotion to the *swayamsevaks* in his care (Modi, 2015a, p. 135).[8]

After moving into the *Hedgewar Bhavan*, Modi became, in effect, one of Vakil Saheb's servants – at least when the latter was in Ahmedabad – and then, as he supposedly proved his worth to the organisation, one of his trusted lieutenants (Nag, 2013, p. 39; cf. Verma, 2014, p. 27). He also began to involve himself in political activities, participating in the protests that were held in response to the Pakistani army's crackdown on dissent in what was then East Pakistan in 1971, and then in anti-government demonstrations in Gujarat (Mukhopadhyay, 2013, p. 111). One biography says that Modi was arrested and held for a short time in Delhi's Tihar prison after one of the anti-Pakistan rallies (Kamath and Randeri, 2013, p. 12). In return, Vakil Saheb repaid his labour and commitment to the cause with advice and advancement. Sometime in 1972, a little earlier than perhaps normal, Modi became an RSS *pracharak*, a full-time worker for the cause. Over the next few years, despite some inadvertent disruptions, he completed the organisation's required so-called officer training course given for *pracharaks* in Nagpur, where the RSS was founded, and assumed greater responsibility within its ranks (Verma, 2014, p. 29).

At the same time, Vakil Saheb also seems to have also persuaded Modi to complete his formal education (Kamath and Randeri, 2013, p. 12). Sometime in the early 1970s, he apparently enrolled – or pretended to enrol – in a political science degree by correspondence at Delhi University (Verma, 2014, p. 27).[9] This arrangement may have been helpful to the RSS. An opportunity for Modi to play a bigger role within the organisation – and to use his enrolment in university to its advantage – came with Indira Gandhi's suspension of democratic politics and a draconian clampdown on such opposition groups known as the Emergency, from late June 1975 until March 1977 (Marino, 2014, p. 41). Like most of the RSS leadership, he went underground for a period. In hiding, Modi apparently worked at publishing and distributing a series of anti-government pamphlets (Verma, 2014, p. 36). One now-famous contemporary photograph shows Modi involved in these activities disguised as a Sikh, with beard and turban (Kamath and Randeri, 2013).[10]

His university studies, however, also gave him a legitimate reason to travel from Gujarat to Delhi. It seems that with that 'cover', the RSS also used Modi to act as a courier, taking messages backward and forward to senior Hindu nationalists and Opposition politicians (Mukhopadhyay, 2013, p. 122).[11] In parallel, his academic work also provided him with the chance to work with other elements of the broader Hindu nationalist movement. He became involved with the powerful RSS affiliate, the *Akhil Bharatiya Vidyarthi Parishad* (ABVP or 'All India Student Council'), during or after his undergraduate degree. By the time some suggest that Modi began work on an MA in political science, this time at the University of Gujarat, he had been promoted to run ABVP's operations in the state (Nag, 2013, p. 42). The knowledge that he gleaned from these various activities was put to use by the RSS, with one of its key leaders, Dattopant Thangali, commissioning him to write an internally circulated history of the organisation's work during the Emergency (Marino, 2014, p. 52).

When the Emergency ended, Modi was given the task of mobilising voters in Gujarat in the 1977 general election, which led to a win by the *Janata Dal* (People's Party) and the first taste of government for important Hindu nationalist leaders like Atal Bihari Vajpayee, later Prime Minister, who became Minister of External Affairs. Soon after, Modi was promoted within the RSS, becoming a *vibhaag pracharak*, responsible for overseeing the *shakhas* in six districts, and then a *sambhaag pracharak*, in charge of a wider area in Gujarat (Kamath and Randeri, 2013, p. 24). His move into politics proper did not come, however, until 1986, when he was assigned by the RSS to assist the BJP, the political party formed six years earlier to represent the Hindu nationalist cause (Mukhopadhyay, 2013, pp. 148–9, 157; Marino, 2014, p. 67). His skills had apparently come to the attention of then-BJP President, L.K. Advani. Soon, Advani became his second mentor, greatly aiding his advancement within the BJP (Advani, 2010, p. 325).

Modi's job – informal at first, but then formalised in 1987 – was to help orchestrate the BJP's ultimately victorious effort to win municipal elections in Gujarat. He laboured in the BJP's backroom for three more years, organising campaigns on several issues, including the sale of alcohol in that state. In that capacity, he played a key role in organising several *yatras* – literally ceremonial processions, but in this case effectively long campaign marches through the country to promote the Hindu nationalist cause. These included the *Nyay Yatra* or 'Journey for Justice', which aimed at highlighting the plight of famine-affected areas of Gujarat, and a number of others (Kamath and Randeri, 2013, pp. 34–5). By far the biggest and most consequential, however, was Advani's famous *Ram Rath Yatra* in 1990, which was meant to travel from Somnath in Gujarat to Ayodhya in Uttar Pradesh, thought by some to be the birthplace of Lord Rama, and the site of an important mosque, the Babri Masjid, supposedly built on top an earlier Hindu temple dedicated to that Hindu god.[12] Modi was responsible for the first stage, running through his home state, and helped with the parallel national campaign (the *Ram Shila Pujan*) to gather bricks for the new temple (Nag, 2013, p. 54).[13]

The *Ram Rath Yatra* was a highly significant event in contemporary Indian political history. It constituted a major escalation in the longer-running campaign to demolish the mosque, which culminated in the Babri Masjid's destruction in December 1992, followed by riots that resulted in the deaths of over two thousand people.[14] It also marked the emergence of the Hindu nationalists as a mainstream political force, playing as it did on themes and symbols familiar to most Indians. Advani rode in a Toyota truck decorated as an ancient chariot; loudspeakers played music from the recently aired – and wildly popular – TV adaptations of the ancient epics, the *Ramayana* and *Mahabharata*. The RSS described the parade as nothing less than the start of a *dharma yuddha* ('holy war') against the enemies of India (Blom Hansen, 1999, p. 164). In any event, even among voters without sympathy for the RSS, the *Ram Yatra* delivered the BJP a significant boost to its political fortunes. The so-called *Ramjanmabhoomi* agitation of which the *Yatra* was part helped popularise *Hindutva* and aided the BJP at the polls, despite the communal tensions and violence that went with it. Partly as a result, the BJP won almost 20 per cent of the vote in the 1991 general election and an unprecedented 119 Lok

Sabha seats, despite a significant sympathy vote to Congress caused by Rajiv Gandhi's assassination during an early phase of campaigning (Blom Hansen, 1999, p. 166).

Modi had been integral to this effort, and might have expected a reward, but during the early 1990s his career stalled, as he fell out of favour with the leadership of the BJP in Gujarat. After the *Ram Rath Yatra* he remained in his home state, but kept a relatively low profile. He played no part in the destruction of the Ayodhya mosque in early December 1992, remaining in Gujarat during that episode (Mukhopadhyay, 2013, p. 190). Instead, he went back to work with the RSS, though according to one biographer he also helped organise the underground activities of the local branches of *Vishva Hindu Parishad* (VHP), the Hindu nationalist umbrella group, after the VHP was temporarily banned from operating following the demolition of the Babri Masjid (Verma, 2014, pp. 54–5). Modi also took the opportunity to travel abroad for the first time. In 1993 and apparently again in 1994, he left India for the US together with some other RSS workers, including G. Kishan Reddy, later a key BJP leader in Telangana state. He travelled widely through the country, from New York to Los Angeles, and to Washington, DC, reputedly with few clothes or other possessions, using cheap air tickets and staying with the families sympathetic to the Sangh (*Deccan Chronicle*, 2014).

The following year, Modi returned to frontline politics. Advani, his principal patron in the national capital, had regained the presidency of the BJP, aiding his cause. Modi helped the BJP seize power in the 1995 election for the Gujarat Legislative Assembly, helping to design a strategy that promised to keep the state free from fear, hunger and corruption, but which also played on concerns about communal violence and terrorism, as well as poor governance (Shah, 2001, p. 259). Soon, however, Modi was once again sidelined due to factional conflict within the BJP and the *Sangh*. Having helped the new Chief Minister, Keshubhai Patel, into power, Modi was then given the job of limiting the influence of his rivals within the party and the wider movement, led by Shankarsinh Vaghela and Kashiram Rana. As a result, he became the object of considerable resentment among those who came to believe that he was too influential over Patel's government (Shah, 2001, p. 262). Increasingly, Modi was perceived by some as overbearing and arrogant – and as the power behind the throne. When a showdown came between the factions, Patel was forced to step down in favour of Suresh Mehta and Modi was 'banished' from the state (Verma, 2014, pp. 56–9).[15]

At this point, his mentor Advani stepped in once more, helping Modi find work elsewhere. He was sent on party business to Haryana, Himachal Pradesh, Punjab, and – sometime later – Jammu and Kashmir. During the 1996 general election that briefly brought the BJP to power in New Delhi, Modi was based in Chandigarh, the shared state capital of Haryana and Punjab. During the 1998 election, which again put the BJP into government, with its National Democratic Alliance (NDA) partners, he played a bigger national role as a strategist. For these labours, Modi was rewarded after the election with the national posts of BJP General Secretary (one of a total of five) and party spokesperson (Verma, 2014, pp. 77–9). He stayed in these roles, building his public profile, for almost three years. He made regular appearances on Indian television, honing his skills, and in 1999 went again to the US, this time for a three-week or three-month – the details are unclear – media management course (Jeffrey, 2015).

Gujarat and Godhra

In early October 2001, having just turned 51, Modi finally made the move from being a 'humble party worker' – his self-description (quoted in Mukhopadhyay, 2013, p. 225) – into a significant position of leadership. The sitting Gujarat Chief Minister, Keshubhai Patel, was ailing physically and politically. His BJP government faced accusations of corruption and incompetence, compounded by the mismanagement of the recovery effort following an earthquake in late January 2001 that had killed up to twenty thousand people and displaced hundreds of thousands. The national party leadership, including then Prime Minister Atal Bihari Vajpayee and Advani, decided Patel needed to be replaced if the BJP was to hold its position in Gujarat. Whether Modi was reluctantly drafted as Patel's replacement, as his sympathetic biographers suggest, or actively lobbied for the job, as more critical observers hint, is disputed.[16] In any event, by the second half of 2001 Modi had been identified as the next Chief Minister by the national leadership, and after a brief interregnum, in which he had to be found a seat in the Gujarat Assembly, he formally took up the post on 24 February 2002.

Three days later, the Godhra incident occurred. A train carrying Hindu nationalist pilgrims and activists was attacked by a group of local Muslims, and in the midst of the chaos that ensued, some of the carriages ended up ablaze, either as a result of deliberate action by the mob, or, as some argue, by accident (Nussbaum, 2007, p. 19). A total of 59 passengers died, with many others injured. The response to this tragedy was furious. Allegedly incited by politicians, among others, communal violence erupted across the state, in major cities like Ahmedabad and Vadodara, as well as in rural areas. The official figures put the death toll from these riots at just over one thousand. Other estimates suggest perhaps two thousand or more were killed, with tens of thousands injured, expropriated, or displaced. Rape was a particularly prominent feature of the incident; women and children were specifically targeted for abuse, humiliation, sexual violence or murder. Dozens of mosques were also attacked.[17]

Modi's response to the post-Godhra riots soon became -- and still remains – a matter of considerable controversy. It has been suggested that he or his government ordered security forces to stand aside during attacks on Muslim communities or otherwise discouraged them to act positively to stop them. Modi has also been accused of more serious charges, notably of being complicit in an organised anti-Muslim pogrom, which some have cast as 'state terrorism'. Members of the RSS, VHP, and another Hindu nationalist group affiliated with both, the Bajrang Dal, have been accused of orchestrating violence, distributing addresses for targeting, and supplying weapons, petrol, and money to rioters. Modi's statements immediately following the Godhra incident, in which he referred to the burning of the train a deliberate act of terrorism have also been interpreted as incitement (Nussbaum, 2007).[18]

In the short term, at least, Modi's political position in Gujarat was severely shaken. Within the BJP there were serious doubts – shared by Vajpayee, the Prime Minister – about whether he could continue as Chief Minister. At a BJP National Executive meeting in Goa in April, Advani made it clear that Modi should show contrition and at least offer to resign. Modi did so, but the leadership decided that it should refuse to accept that offer, allowing him to remain as Chief Minister (Advani, 2010, pp. 842–4). Crucially, Advani sustained his support throughout this episode, defending his protégé and maintaining that on the more serious charges of orchestrating the violence or ordering the security forces to turn a blind eye, he was a blameless 'victim of [a] vilification campaign' (Advani, 2010, pp. 758–60). Modi thus survived, but critics argued long afterwards that Modi and his allies went on to use the Godhra incident and the anti-Muslim violence that followed for electoral advantage.[19] Certainly, he refused to delay the election due at the end of that year, as he might have done, going to the polls in December 2002 while many Muslims remained in displacement camps. During the campaign, he also continued to employ fiery rhetoric nominally targeted at Pakistan-sponsored terrorists, but interpretable as more broadly anti-Muslim. In the end, having survived the crisis, Modi won the election by a landslide, taking 127 seats out of a total of 182 (Kumar, 2002).

Despite the victory, the Godhra episode left a lasting mark on Modi. In its wake, he was denounced not just as a communalist, but also as a 'fascist'. In a famous article for *Seminar*, the veteran political psychologist and critic

Ashis Nandy (2002) called Modi's public statements on Godhra and the riots as 'a slur on civilised public life', compared him to Serbian leader Slobodan Milošević and suggested that he should face an international tribunal for what looked like 'crimes against humanity'. Nandy recalled interviewing him when he was 'a nobody, a small-time RSS *pracharak* trying to make it as a small-time BJP functionary' (2002), long before he became Chief Minister. To Nandy, Modi had come across as 'a classic, clinical case of a fascist' – a term he emphasised he was not using as one of abuse, but rather as 'a diagnostic category comprising not only one's ideological posture but also the personality traits and motivational patterns contextualising the ideology' (2002). He went on:

> Modi … met virtually all the criteria that psychiatrists, psycho-analysts and psychologists had set up after years of empirical work on the authoritarian personality. He had the same mix of puritanical rigidity, narrowing of emotional life, massive use of the ego defence of projection, denial and fear of his own passions combined with fantasies of violence – all set within the matrix of clear paranoid and obsessive personality traits. I still remember the cool, measured tone in which he elaborated a theory of cosmic conspiracy against India that painted every Muslim as a suspected traitor and a potential terrorist. I came out of the interview shaken and told Yagnik [Achyut Yagnik, the journalist with whom Nandy interviewed Modi] that, for the first time, I had met a textbook case of a fascist and a prospective killer, perhaps even a future mass murderer. (Nandy, 2002)

After Godhra, Modi had initiated what might well evolve into a second Partition of India, Nandy concluded, complete with the vicious communal violence that had accompanied the first (Nandy, 2002).

Not all agreed with Nandy's assessment, but enough shared similar views of his conduct after Godhra to make Modi a reviled figure for the BJP's political opponents. Moreover, he was denied a visa to visit the US in 2005 on the grounds that he had allegedly engaged in 'severe violations of religious freedom', becoming the only individual ever banned from entering the country for that reason (Mann, 2014). Throughout the 2000s, senior Western diplomats were ordered to steer clear of Modi and his government, although he did visit the UK in 2003 (Price, 2015, p. 40). At the same time, he was pursued through the courts by victims and their advocates, and multiple inquiries were instituted by the national government, by the Gujarat government, by

Indian and foreign organisations, and by a series of local and international researchers. None of these bodies succeeded, however, in bringing Modi to trial, still less securing a conviction for the Chief Minister, although one of his ministers, Maya Kodnani, was found guilty of involvement in murder, along with the leader of the *Bajrang Dal*, Babubhai Patel, also known as Babu Bajrangi.[20] In 2012, the Special Investigative Team charged with looking into whether the Chief Minister had been involved in one notorious episodes of violence, the so-called Gulberg massacre, concluded four years of work by clearing Modi of any involvement (Jaffrelot, 2012).

Making *Moditva*

After 2002, the embattled Chief Minister set about building a formidable political machine in Gujarat, sidelining his rivals, crafting a distinctive style of governing, and transforming his own image, morphing from communal firebrand into a business-friendly, tech-savvy *vikas purush* ('development man') – a different kind of politician to the kind with which Indians are familiar (Jaffrelot, 2016, pp. 196–7). One of Modi's most sympathetic biographers – the British journalist Andy Marino – suggests that he did this in part because he realised at least some of the errors of his ways, especially his hard-line anti-Muslim rhetoric and his erstwhile commitment to what he now realised were outmoded elements of the Hindu nationalist creed. Marino argues that in this period, in the year immediately after 2002, Modi 'slowly detach[ed] himself from … Sangh Parivar orthodoxy', showing that he was 'nobody's man', and carrying out a 'demolition exercise' on the nastier elements of the movement in Gujarat (Marino, 2014, pp. 163–4). This reading of history, which closely aligns with Modi's own, should be treated with scepticism. It is clear, however, that he did seek to both distance himself from some of the more extreme parts of the *Sangh* and deal with some long-standing political enemies within its ranks.[21]

In their place, Modi drew in technocrats and businesspeople. When appointed Chief Minister, he called the state's top civil servants to a quasi-corporate leadership retreat to assess their skills and capacity. Modi assessed them personally to determine which to keep in their positions and which to move on and replace (Fernandes, 2014, pp. 35–6). He demanded his bureaucrats deliver innovative solutions to policy challenges – and learn how to make PowerPoint presentations in order to pitch their ideas to him and his cabinet (Menon, 2014, p. 67). He drew in private consultants and experts to provide additional strategies and techniques, as well as public relations specialists to improve his own image and Gujarat's. He evinced a 'philosophy of governance' and talked – using the language of New Public Management that has seeped through governments elsewhere – of 'whole of government' approaches and 'silo-breaking' (Fernandes, 2014, p. 14, pp. 36–8).[22] And partly as a result, Modi was increasingly perceived by many as an efficient 'can do' politician, capable of driving the stubborn bureaucracies notorious in India and delivering the goods. To his supporters, especially in the growing, aspiring middle class, he became a different kind of Chief Minister from the usual type – a 'super-CEO', not a normal *neta* ('politician').

In parallel, Modi wooed the business community in Gujarat and further afield. In 2003, he launched the first of a series of biennial 'Vibrant Gujarat' summits to showcase opportunities in the state to Indian and foreign businesses – and to try to address the damage done to the state's image after the communal violence (Bobbio, 2012). Formally, these events were a forum at which local officials and entrepreneurs could meet banks and financiers, as well as senior politicians from the state capital, Gandhinagar, and from New Delhi (Maini, 2015). But the summits also allowed Modi to share a stage and to build relationships with key figures in the Gujarati and national business community, including Gautam Adani, who runs a major multinational conglomerate, Mukesh Ambani, head of the industrial giant, Reliance, and C.K. Birla, chair of his eponymous Group. Initiating and sustaining these ties with the promises that he would fast-track approvals, cut red tape, and remove bureaucratic obstacles, he determined, was crucial to developing the state. Modi's reputation as a business-friendly politician grew as a result, allowing him to bring major projects to Gujarat. Perhaps the best known of these – partly because he made much of the story during the 2014 campaign – was the investment by the Tata Group in a manufacturing plant to build the budget Nano car. After the company's application to build the plant in West Bengal was rejected, Modi supposedly convinced its boss, Ratan Tata, to bring his business across the country to Gujarat with a one-word text message that read 'welcome' (Gupta, 2008; cf. Price, 2015, p. 60).

Exactly how far these initiatives stimulated economic activity and brought about sustained social development is, however, a matter of much debate. Gujarat did experience impressively high and sustained rates of economic growth through Modi's period in office, up to 10 per cent in some years. But Gujarat – historically one of the wealthier and more entrepreneurial parts of India – had performed well for some years prior to 2001. Indeed, throughout the 1990s, the state's GDP had risen at a similar annual rate (Ghatak and Roy, 2014). Economists are divided as to whether his government succeeded in significantly accelerating growth beyond what was already the norm for the state, though they concede that Gujarat did markedly better than the rest of India during the 2000s and early 2010s (see especially Ghatak and Roy, 2014). And analysts also disagree about whether key social indicators improved during his time as Chief Minister. They observe that high economic growth rates did not translate into improved literacy or better health care provision (Chandhoke, 2012). Moreover, some argue that economic development under Modi was not as inclusive as it was billed, with Muslims, in particular, remaining disproportionately disadvantaged (Jaffrelot, 2015b).

In any event, Modi's appeal in Gujarat did not wholly rest on his government's economic record. Commerce was only one element in the 'heady mix', as Mukhopadhyay (2013, pp. 343–4) observes – culture was the other. Although he mostly moderated his anti-Muslim rhetoric, no longer overtly seeking to be, as Jaffrelot (2016) puts it, a *Hindu Hriday Samrat* ('King of Hindu Hearts'), Modi continued to use identity politics to polarise and galvanise key segments of the electorate and consolidate support for his administration. Rather than a Hindu-wide appeal, however, Modi focused instead on a sub-nationalist programme focused on the *asmita* (loosely, 'sense of self' or 'identity') of Gujaratis, drawing contrasts between their character traits and history and those of other Indians. Employing a classic populist technique, he portrayed Gujarat as a state unfairly traduced over Godhra and past communal violence. He argued that it was neglected by the national political elite in New Delhi – the 'Delhi Sultanate', as he sometimes referred to it – despite or perhaps because of its success in business and trade, and the economic and social progress it had achieved (Suhrud, 2008). Modi contended that India's elite had blemished the honour of Gujaratis in supposedly casting them as inherently or unusually divided on communal lines and prone to religious conflict, not recognising that in fact, they had long welcomed people of many different faiths and traditions into their plural community.[23] He posed in this context as the defender of Gujarati *asmita* against those who would malign it, casting himself as just another victim of a wider campaign to tarnish the state's image (Jaffrelot, 2016, pp. 198–200).

At the same time, Modi sought to associate himself with the achievements of Gujaratis both great and small. At 'Vibrant Gujarat' and elsewhere, he celebrated the fabled commercial acumen of the state's inhabitants and their past and present success in overseas trade – a business other Indians were historically loath to embrace, because of the loss of caste some Hindus believe comes if they travel overseas (Bobbio, 2012). Modi also went to considerable lengths to burnish the reputations of major figures of Gujarat's past, including Gandhi (the *Mahatma* or 'Great Soul') and the so-called Iron Man of India, Sardar Patel, and to associate himself with the cultivation of their legacies (Jaffrelot, 2013).

In the cases of both Gandhi and Patel, this involved some ideological gymnastics for a Hindu nationalist like Modi, as the first was murdered by a former member of the RSS, and the second, a leading member of the Congress Party, was responsible for briefly banning that organisation after the Mahatma's assassination in January 1948. In both cases, however, appropriating these figures allowed Modi to develop a new image as an inclusive leader governing for all Gujaratis (Jaffrelot, 2016, pp. 202–3). His sponsorship of a scheme to construct a giant statute of Patel – at 182 m high, on top of a 58 m high base, one of the largest in the world – overlooking the state's Narmada Dam demonstrated this effort well. On the one hand, it celebrates a great Gujarati and associates his legacy with Modi; on the other, its title – the 'Statute of Unity' – gives the monument additional political significance, acknowledging Patel's key role in bringing consolidating the Indian state after 1947, and implying that there is work yet to be done by the contemporary generation (Jaffrelot, 2016, p. 202).

To transmit these various messages, Modi did not just rely on traditional means. He embraced new communications technologies, as well as making extensive use of television, which were by the early 2000s more readily available to relatively prosperous Gujaratis than to other Indians (Jaffrelot, 2015c). Modi's own use of various devices was highlighted to the electorate, to demonstrate his personal technocratic credentials – as Chief Minister, he reportedly used three laptops and carried a mobile phone to manage government and communicate with voters. His 2007 election campaign used SMS messages sent to the personal mobile phones of ordinary Gujaratis, who by this point owned them in large numbers, and posted videos on YouTube, as well as saturation coverage in conventional media, including newspapers, radio and television (Jaffrelot, 2008, p. 14).

Together, Modi's friendliness to business, emphasis on efficient governance, appeal to the Gujarati *asmita* and use of technology helped him not just to forge a new image for himself but also for the BJP in Gujarat. The 'wonder product' of '*Moditva*' – a brand of what Jaffrelot called 'high-tech populism' (2013)[24] – emerged to displace *Hindutva*, which had questionable and limited appeal among Indian voters in Gujarat and further afield in the 2000s, as the BJP's defeat in the 2004 general election appeared to both critics and friends to demonstrate (Kanungo and Farooqui, 2008). *Hindutva* seemed old-fashioned and stale; a poor fit with the economic and social aspirations of ordinary Indians. *Moditva*, on the other hand, spoke directly to those desires, and delivered the BJP success in Gujarat provided that it continued to focus on Modi. This it did in both conventional election materials and increasingly on newer platforms, with the Chief Minister front and centre in productions like the YouTube video 'India Tomorrow: The Gujarat Miracle' (Kanungo and Farooqui, 2008, pp. 229–30).

Modi did not, of course, entirely escape criticism during his time in Gujarat. His handling of Godhra and its aftermath, as well as his hostile language about Muslims, continued to concern many and continued to be focal point for his political opponents. Congress Party President Sonia Gandhi's famous remark, made during the 2007 state election campaign, implying that the Chief Minister was a '*maut ke saudagar*' ('merchant of death') (Times of India, 2007), captures the extent to which he became a *bête noire* to his rivals. Modi continued to rely on communal polarisation as a key strategy in state elections, and on subtle and not-so-subtle anti-Muslim remarks as a means of firing up Hindu nationalist voters, again to the disgust of critics (Jaffrelot, 2016, pp. 205–10).

At the same time, Modi also attracted the ire of disgruntled sections of the *Sangh*. As his tenure as Chief Minister went on, he increasingly appeared to at least some of them as egocentric and heavy-handed, as well as insufficiently committed to *Hindutva* and the social norms of the movement. Figures in the Gujarat RSS complained that they were not consulted by Modi as they expected to be, nor treated with due regard. His 'autocratic style' was said to grate on an organisation that traditionally emphasises a more 'collegial' approach (Fernandes, 2014, pp. 22, 151). Indeed, one anonymous RSS leader is quoted as saying that the RSS's 'behavioural indoctrination' intended to inculcate this approach had failed with Modi (Mukhopadhyay, 2013, p. 209). His business-friendly approach and openness to foreign direct investment also generated concern, diverging as it did from the conventional Hindu nationalist preference for policies that promote *swadeshi* or self-reliance (Fernandes, 2014, p. 47) – something discussed further in later chapters. Modi's visits to China – which some in the RSS consider an enemy – in search of investment funds irritated too (Nag, 2013, p. 170). By 2012, relations with some in the Gujarat RSS had apparently soured to the point that some of leaders expressed the hope that Modi might lose the state election that year (Nag, 2013, p. 11).

Others in the Hindu nationalist movement, however, saw something promising in *Moditva*. They included Modi's long-time patron, Advani. In his memoirs, first published in 2008, he argued that the Chief Minister of Gujarat was showing the way for the BJP elsewhere in India, including at the national level. His success in the 2007 state election, Advani declared, 'dispelled the conventional wisdom that [a] focus on good governance does not make good politics' and that elections could only be won by 'appealing to people's caste and communal sentiments' (Advani, 2010, p. 759). By this point, it was becoming apparent that *Moditva* might make possible for Modi a move from state to national politics that many would have been thought impossible in 2002, after Godhra. When the BJP lost the general election in 2009, ending up with 22 fewer seats than it had won when it lost government in 2004, the odds improved even more. By the time Modi was finally acknowledged as the BJP's choice for Prime Minister, in mid-September 2013, it had been clear for several years that he stood head and shoulders above the other possible candidates. Although by then relations with Advani had soured to the point at which the latter briefly resigned his post as BJP President in protest at Modi's selection, many in the broader Hindu nationalist community perceived him as the leader most likely to delivering the rapid economic growth and development that ordinary Indians desire, despite concerns within the BJP and the wider *Sangh* about his style and his ego (Mehta, 2010, p. 591).[25]

Conclusion

Although the slogan *Moditva* did not survive Modi's move from Gujarat to New Delhi, despite the efforts of some Hindu nationalists to promote it,[26] it is clear the core elements of his political style were translated into national government. In New Delhi as in Gujarat, above all, Modi himself remained the focus of attention and the locus of decision making (Kulkarni, 2016, p. 122). He centralised power in the Prime Minister's Office and attempted to impose strict discipline over his ministers, ensuring key policy decisions were approved by the Prime Minister or by his direct proxies, and that their public presentation was effective (Nag, 2016). He continued to advocate technocratic and technological solutions for public policy problems and 'service delivery'. To aid him in this effort, Modi brought with him from Gandhinagar, the Gujarati capital, a group of bureaucrats that had served him as Chief Minister, including P.K. Misra, his former Principal Secretary, as well as another 30 or so senior administrators (Gahilote, 2015). He also brought with him the evaluation techniques he used for assessing public servants, including so-called 360 degree reviews, and shaken up the promotions system within the Indian Administrative Service (IAS) to try to ensure the best rise to the top (Ghosh, 2016). In June 2018, moreover, he opened up the IAS to competition for senior posts, allowing Indian Police Service officers and those from other services, like the Indian Forest Service, to submit applications, and permitting candidates from outside the bureaucracy to put themselves forward for limited number of positions (Das Gupta, 2018).

In New Delhi, Modi also remained close to business and remained keen to promote not just his friendliness to big business in general, but also to particular business people, though over time he took pains to downplay some of these connections. His attempts to impress and entice international investors in Asia, Europe, the Middle East and the US have already been noted. Equally significant, however, was the support he gave for major Indian industrialists, among them individuals like the Gujarati Gautam Adani, a long-time supporter. During the first year of Modi's government, Adani regularly accompanied the Prime Minister on his foreign trips (Langa, 2015). Following criticism of his closeness to these business interests, however, he moved in the second year of his government to distance himself from them in public, positioning himself as a more independent figure. As more than one analyst has argued, this shift coincided with the emergence of a more economically populist line in policy, with a new focus on poverty alleviation, women's safety and the plight of farmers (Jagannathan, 2016, p. 84).

To sell policies, Modi employed the same calls for popular mobilisation and similar quasi-high-tech, quasi-folksy rhetoric, complete with frequent alliteration, in both domestic and foreign policy. These initiatives included Swachh Bharat, the mission to deliver a clean India through toilets and drainage; 'Make in India', the push for foreign investment in manufacturing; 'Digital India', 'Startup India', and 'Stand Up India'; the Aadhaar national identification programme; and the promised universal healthcare system, Ayushman Bharat, nicknamed 'Modicare' by the Indian media – all designed to build Modi's 'New India'. In foreign policy, a series of similar slogans appeared: 'Neighbourhood First' covered South Asia; 'Look East' was rendered 'Act East'; 'Link West' was unveiled for India's Middle East engagement; and 'Project Mausam' was introduced as a counter to China's increasing influence in the Indian Ocean region. At the Raisina Dialogue in January 2017, Modi pledged an approach oriented around 'realism' (*yathaarthavaad*), 'coexistence' (*sah-astitv*), 'cooperation' (*sahayog*), and 'partnership' (*sahabhagita*). Eighteen months later, at the Shangri-La Dialogue, this philosophy had mutated into five S's: *samman* (which he translated as 'respect'), *samvaad* ('dialogue'), *sahayog* ('cooperation'), *shanti* ('peace'), and *samriddhi* ('prosperity') – a formulation echoing Ram Madhav's earlier *Panchamrit*.

Finally, Modi continued to rely on identity politics, albeit not of the same kind to that he used prior to becoming Gujarat Chief Minister and during his early years in that office. In the 2014 campaign and in government, his language was generally more temperate, but remained pointed, leaving others – such as his enforcer Amit Shah – to use more divisive language. Modi instead confined himself to hints and suggestions: for example, using an Urdu word derived from Persian, *shehzada* (prince), when deriding his main political opponent Rahul Gandhi, rather than a Hindi alternative (Price, 2015, p. 104). Instead, he sought to portray himself as a leader for all, following on from his earlier effort to be seen in Gujarat as an inclusive *vikas purush*, and as a *pradhan sevak* or 'Prime Servant' of the nation,[27] rather than a Prime Minister, as he put it in his first Independence Day speech in August 2014 (Press Trust of India, 2014a). He worked, he told the crowd from the ramparts of the Red Fort in Delhi, to realise the 'destiny' of India envisaged by the great nationalist leaders of the struggle for independence (Modi, 2014a).

As Modi's government wore on, however, and especially as the 2019 election loomed, identity politics loomed much larger. A year out from the polls, he began to refer to the Congress party as a 'party for Muslims', pouncing on remarks reportedly made by Rahul Gandhi to a gathering of Muslim intellectuals (Kang, 2018). He seized too on the opposition leader's decision to contest the election from Wayanad in Kerala, as well as from the family stronghold of Amethi in Uttar Pradesh. Modi implied that Rahul Gandhi was too cowardly to run in a Hindu-majority constituency, and was fleeing to one in which there was a larger proportion of Muslim voters (Prakash and Ahuja, 2019). For his part, Modi's key ally Amit Shah referred on the campaign trail to Muslim immigrants from Bangladesh as 'termites', floating the idea of a 'Muslim ban' similar to that attempted by the Trump administration (Dhume, 2019). And above all, the Prime Minister capitalised on the Pulwama terrorist attacks in mid–February 2019 and the Indian air strikes that followed, suggesting that the Congress party was weak on terrorism and on dealing with Pakistan.

5

World Guru India

On 11 March 2016, Modi took the stage to address a huge gathering held on the flood plain of the Yamuna River, southeast of Delhi. The event at which he spoke – the World Culture Festival – was apparently attended by as many as three and a half million people and watched by a similar number on television and the internet. It was organised by a group called the Art of Living Foundation, led by the spiritual guru and self-styled humanitarian Sri Ravi Shankar.[1] It was no ordinary gathering of followers or faithful. The Modi government was a prominent sponsor, contributing some 2.25 crore rupees (22.5 million rupees or about $370,000) towards the cost of staging the event (Jain, 2016). Some one thousand religious leaders and 750 'key' politicians also took part, according to the organisers (Art of Living, 2018). Apart from Modi, former French Prime Minister Dominique de Villepin, the Pakistani senator and sometime ambassador to Washington, Sherry Rehman, Syria's Grand Mufti, Ahmad Badreddin Hassoun, the Buddhist leader Hsin Tao, the former President of Nigeria, Olusegun Obasanjo, and the erstwhile Norwegian Prime Minister, Kjell Magne Bondevik, all addressed the participants. And they were joined by a number of senior Indian ministers, including Arun Jaitley (Finance Minister), Sushma Swaraj (External Affairs Minister), Rajnath Singh (Home Minister) and Ravi Shankar Prasad (Law and Justice Minister), as well as Modi's key lieutenant, BJP President Amit Shah.

From the most part, these dignitaries delivered innocuous messages, intended to be inspiring and uplifting. Modi's short speech, however, was more pointed. He lavished praise on Ravi Shankar and his Art of Living Foundation for the work that they had done not just in promoting interreligious dialogue, but in restoring confidence to India, making its art and music known to the world, and boosting what he called – lapsing into English – India's 'soft power'.[2] They and similar organisations were helping to spread knowledge of the truth of *vasudhaiva kutumbakam* beyond India, he observed, extending its cultural influence (Modi, 2016a).

This speech – quite apart from the government's substantial investment in the festival – was significant for three reasons. First, it highlighted the extent to which many Hindu nationalists believe that culture – or, to use the word Modi himself employed in the World Culture Festival speech, *sanskriti* – is one of India's greatest assets in foreign affairs. Second, it alluded to the connection they see between India's standing in the world and the sense of pride, dignity, and honour felt by Indians – the link between international relations and *samman*, as Hindu nationalists like Ram Madhav would have it. And third, it hinted at the role Modi and his allies saw for dialogue between societies that runs parallel to official diplomacy between states – for *samvad*, to use another term preferred by Madhav, which has also appeared in prime ministerial discourse.

Modi's brief address to the World Culture Festival, together with his presence and that of so many senior ministers, points, in other words, to a distinctive way of thinking about international relations and practicing foreign policy. It is one that arises from the Hindu nationalist worldview outlined in Chapter 3 – and one that helps explain some of the unorthodox or even paradoxical aspects of the Modi government's conduct of Indian foreign policy. In particular, it accounts for Modi's devotion to religious diplomacy, to visits to religious sites, to gifts with religious or cultural significance, and to dialogue with religious leaders, which was so intense that it reportedly caused 'consternation and confusion' among India's diplomats (Ramachandaran, 2015).[3] It accounts too for the Modi government's at first glance paradoxical neglect of the instruments of public diplomacy, notably within the Ministry of External Affairs (MEA), that seem to run counter to its overt commitment to the notion of 'soft power'. And it accounts – at least in part – for the Modi government's extensive employment of non-governmental quasi-diplomatic instruments and forums, using private foundations run by spiritual or religious leaders, as well as other non-governmental tools, especially the BJP's in-house foreign affairs department and think tanks aligned with elements of the *Sangh*, and, of course, India's far-flung and diverse diaspora. These efforts are, I argue, infused with that 'sense of destiny' in contemporary India recently and vividly described by Alyssa Ayres (2018, p. 7). This is a notion central to Modi's attempt to reinvent Indian foreign policy, which aims – at least nominally – at rendering the country into the 'world guru' (*vishwa guru*) Hindu nationalists have long promised it will become.

Guru to the world

The notion that India has a unique mission in the world and unique wisdom to convey ran throughout Modi's rhetoric on foreign policy and that of his government before and after the 2014 election. It was central to the BJP's manifesto; a consistent theme in the most important of Modi's speeches, including his Republic Day addresses, delivered from the ramparts of Delhi's Mughal-era Red Fort; and a favourite of his allies in the RSS, especially its *Sarsanghchalak*, Mohan Bhagwat. It was a key element in the BJP's appeal to the Indian electorate under Modi, illustrating, as we shall see, his use of foreign policy for domestic political purposes.

The BJP manifesto for 2014 opened with an expansive preface penned by the veteran Hindu nationalist Murli Manohar Joshi, then eighty years old, and still a keen devotee of Upadhyaya's thinking (see Flåten, 2017). It opened: 'India is the most ancient civilization of the world and has always been looked upon by the world as a land of wealth and wisdom', and continued in that vein. Before the British, Joshi went on, 'Indian prosperity held the world in thrall'. 'India was a land of abundance, prosperity, affluence' and 'a land of sharing and caring living in perfect harmony and peace with the nature'. It was necessary to reassert these verities, he argued, because 'no nation could chart out its domestic or foreign policies unless it has a clear understanding about itself, its history, its roots, its strengths and failings'. A 'clear vision of the civilizational consciousness of India' had to be their foundation.

Sadly, Joshi argued, this vision had been lost under Nehru and his successors, as they 'adopted the institutional framework of administration created by the Britishers [*sic*] which was quite alien to India's world-view' (BJP, 2014a, p. 1). What was needed, he insisted, in the manner of Golwalkar and Upadhyaya, was a 'socio-economic and political paradigm of governance' which would allow it to 'play its destined role in the comity of Nations' and 'make its voice heard for creating a peaceful and egalitarian world order' (BJP, 2014a, p. 2).

These ideas were echoed throughout the manifesto, which made the case that the past ten years of Congress-led United Progressive Alliance (UPA) rule had been a 'Decade of Decay' in which the opportunity to make India an 'Emerging Superpower' had been lost (BJP, 2014a, p. 4). 'India is seen to be floundering', it asserted, 'whereas it should have been engaging with the world with confidence' (BJP, 2014a, p. 40). The BJP's aim, by contrast, was clear: 'a resurgent India must get its rightful place in the comity of nations and international institutions' (BJP, 2014a, p. 39). It was less forthcoming, however, about the approach to achieving these goals. There were references to being pragmatic, recognising the truth of the well-worn maxim that the 'world is one family' (*vasudhaiva kutumbakam*), but grounding policy in a firm appreciation of 'best National Interests'; creating a 'web of allies' but not being 'led by big power interests'; engaging the neighbourhood; and playing a 'greater role on [*sic*] the international high table'.

None of this was spelt out, however, in detail. Instead, most attention was focused on what the manifesto called 'the full extent and gamut' of India's 'soft power potential'. 'There is a need', it argued in a multi-layered paragraph:

> ... to integrate our soft power avenues into our external interchange, particularly, harnessing and focusing on the spiritual, cultural and philosophical dimensions of it. India has always played a major role in world affairs, offering a lot to the World. This has been its tradition since time immemorial. The magnetic power of India has always been in its ancient wisdom and heritage, elucidating principles like harmony and equity. This continues to be equally relevant to the world today in today's times of Soft power. We will adopt Proactive Diplomacy to spread the same. India was reckoned not only as Vishwaguru but also a vibrant trading society.

'We will', the manifesto concluded, with Modi-esque alliteration, 'revive Brand India with the help of our strengths of 5 T's: Tradition, Talent, Tourism, Trade and Technology' (BJP, 2014a, p. 40).

These various arguments recurred in Modi's speeches before and long after the BJP won power.[4] On 15 August 2014, for instance, he appeared at the Red Fort – the Lal Qila, once the seat of Mughal Emperors – to deliver his first Independence Day speech. He spoke for 65 minutes in total, nearly twice as long as had become commonplace under his most recent two predecessors. He ranged widely outlining various hopes and desires, as well as Modi's apparent disappointment at the condition of the bureaucracy he had inherited. The core theme, however, was the need for national unity and the united effort that would be needed to 'take the country forward' both to advance economic and social development and to realize the 'destiny of India' (Modi, 2014a). That destiny, Modi argued, was the recognition of India as a guide to the world. 'I am reminded', he observed, 'of the words of Swami Vivekananda':

> He had said – 'I can see before my eyes Mother India awakening once again. My Mother India would be seated

as the World Guru. Every Indian would render service towards welfare of humanity...' [...] Friends, the words of Vivekananda ji can never be untrue. The words of Vivekananda ji, his dream of seeing India ensconced as World Guru, his vision, it is incumbent upon us to realize that dream. This capable country, blessed with natural bounty, this country of youth can do much for the world in the coming days. (Modi, 2014a)

'Brothers and sisters', he went on, 'I assure that this country has a destiny. It is destined to work for the welfare of the world, it was said by Vivekananda ji' (Modi, 2014a).

Modi returned to this theme repeatedly in later speeches to both overseas and domestic audiences, including those delivered at a rally for the diaspora in Sydney in November 2014 (Modi, 2014d), at a meeting of Indian Administrative Service probationers in February 2015 (Modi, 2015b), at another diaspora event in Toronto in April 2015 (Modi, 2015c), and so on. In parallel, it was taken up by key allies, including Mohan Bhagwat, the head of the RSS, becoming a central theme of BJP and *Sangh* discussions of India's foreign policy.

In an address marking the 90th anniversary of the founding of the organisation delivered in Nagpur in October 2014, for example, the *Sarsanghchalak* spoke at length on what needs to be done to achieve what he described as 'our goal of making Bharat the "Vishwa-guru" of the world, a model nation that runs on the principles of happiness, peace and harmony' (Bhagwat, 2014). Echoing Golwalkar and Upadhyaya, Bhagwat argued:

> Humanity can live a happy, peaceful and beautiful life only when we understand and follow the principles of loving and respectfully accepting the plurality inherent in nature; move with a sense of coordination, cooperation, empathy and dialogue and; adopt the path of non-violence and constitutional middle path instead of practicing unilateral fanaticism and violence in our practices in matters related to ideological and religious conduct. This truth has been intellectually preached...since the beginning of known world history. (Bhagwat, 2014)

The difficulty, he went on, is that Western 'nations and large multinational companies' are wedded to a 'single minded materialistic, consumerist and a self centred ideology', which has not only wrought terrible damage to society and the environment, but also provoked terrorism through its 'self-centred greed'. To establish social harmony, protect the environment, and end political violence, we must 'first completely eradicate the selfishness, fear and absolute materialistic fundamentalism from their own hearts and adopt an integrated and holistic view that looks for happiness of one and all' (Bhagwat, 2014).

For Bhagwat, only one country could lead this fight. 'In the history of past one thousand years', he observed, 'Bharat has been the only example which has made genuine efforts in this direction through the path of truth and non-violence' (Bhagwat, 2014). Taking what many would consider liberties with history, he argued:

> With Bharat's deep faith in the mantra of 'Vasudhaiv Kutumbakam' (i.e. entire world is one family), a wide range of her Rishis, Munis, Bhikshus, Shramanas, Saints, scholars and experts travelled across the world from Mexico to Siberia in olden eras. Without attempting to conquer any empire or without destroying way of life of any society, prayer systems or national and cultural identity, they shared with them the Bharatiya ethos of love, affection and universal welfare. (Bhagwat, 2014)

To enable such individuals to once again achieve such ends, Bhagwat continued, and make 'Bharat into the guide and torch bearer of the whole world', work needed to be done at home:

> We have to develop India consistent with the present times and conditions, which can stand on its own as an all capable, beautiful and prosperous nation in every manner; a nation that looks at the entire world with a holistic, selfless, integral and impartial vision. Bharat of our vision [sic] is one which accepts all pluralities of the universe and is capable of presenting itself as an example of integration. (Bhagwat, 2014)

Moreover, this task – and the wider realisation of India/Bharat as *vishwa guru* placed special emphasis on the role of diaspora. Our 'Bharatiya Diaspora' and 'spiritual leaders', Bhagwat argued, 'are loved and respected' because they embody and display 'the Bharatiya ethos of love, affection and universal welfare'. 'This explains', he concluded, 'why communities and thinkers across the world see a positive hope for themselves and the world in the future of Bharat' (Bhagwat, 2014).

Soft power, public diplomacy and the diaspora

This emphasis on India as a putative 'world guru' underpinned the Modi government's simultaneous embrace of the venerable but fashionable concept of 'soft power'.[5] They were not, however, the first government to co-opt the concept or the ideas underlying it.[6] As we have seen, Nehru drew heavily on India's cultural and religious inheritance to frame its foreign policy and to try to give it influence where it lacked the economic or military power to coerce. His government made significant investments in what we now call public and cultural diplomacy in order to leverage elements of this inheritance, organising major events to promote ideas and agendas, such as the Asian Relations Conference of 1947, using bodies like the Indian Council on World Affairs (founded in 1943), the Indian Council for Cultural Relations (ICCR) (1950), and the external service of All India Radio (AIR), which dates from 1939 and which broadcasts in a number of South Asian languages, including Baluchi, Dari, Nepali, Sinhala and Tibetan (Hall, 2012, pp. 1099–100).

India began self-consciously to pursue 'soft power', as the US academic and policy maker Joseph S. Nye defined it, in the latter half of the 1990s (Thussu, 2016). Vajpayee's BJP-led government spent a great deal of effort on what became known as 'nation-branding', partly with tourism and FDI in mind, but also to try to project a new image of India in the world. Their 'Incredible India' campaign, begun in 2002, is indeed one of the most famous – and apparently successful – of such efforts (see Kant, 2009). Under Singh's UPA administration, this was followed with the 'India Everywhere' public relations blitz at the World Economic Forum meeting at Davos in 2006. Intended to emphasise India's mix of culture and high technology, it featured iPods loaded with Bollywood hits, pashmina shawls and *ayurvedic* bath oils given to attendees (Purie, 2006). Marketing campaigns aimed at foreign investors ran in parallel, aiming to present India as open for business. The 'India@60' campaign in 2007, for example, celebrating six decades of independence, involved a number of events and coordinated soft marketing in publications like *Forbes* magazine (Hall, 2012, p. 1108).

The Singh government also created a Public Diplomacy Division (PDD) within the MEA in 2006, responding in part to the establishment of similar bodies devoted to influencing foreign public opinion elsewhere in the region (Wagner, 2005).[7] The PDD organised dialogues with a range of civil society groups from Afghanistan to Mongolia, and Nepal to South Africa, and produced documentaries and books on India in Dari, Pashto, Nepali, and Tamil (MEA, 2008, 2009). In time, under then-Joint Secretary Navdeep Suri, it also embraced new digital technologies, including social media platforms like Facebook and Twitter (Suri, 2011). It also rolled out a programme intended to educate Indian domestic audiences about its work, including the regular MEA Distinguished Lectures series, delivered around the country by senior diplomats and other luminaries (Hall, 2012, p. 1098). This blurring of the lines between public relations and public diplomacy was compounded in January 2014, with the merger of the PDD and the (domestically focused) External Publicity Division, which created the External Affairs and Public Diplomacy Division (XPD).

The dying days of the Vajpayee government and the early ones of Singh's also saw a marked push to reconnect New Delhi with the Indian diaspora overseas (Rana, 2009; Thussu, 2016, pp. 94–100). In 2003, a new award was created – the *Pravasi Bharatiya Samman* (Overseas Indian Honour) – for members of the diaspora deemed to have made an exceptional contribution to their communities (Thussu, 2016, p. 95). In 2004, a Ministry of Non-Resident Indians' Affairs – quickly renamed the Ministry of Overseas Indian Affairs (MOIA) – was established. It was intended as a one-stop shop for 'information, partnerships and facilitation for all matters relating to overseas Indians' (quoted in Hall, 2012, p. 1103). It took over the organisation of events like the *Pravasi Bharatiya Divas* (Overseas Indian Day) conferences, held annually on 9 January, to commemorate the day Gandhi returned to India from South Africa. It assumed responsibility for the parallel conventions held overseas in places like New York, London, Singapore and Sydney (Thussu, 2016, pp. 95–6). And it set up a number of schemes: a 'Tracing your Roots' genealogy service, various orientation and short-stay programmes for the diaspora, and helplines and funding mechanisms to help Non-Resident Indians (NRIs) in distress (Hall, 2012, p. 1104).

Religion, dialogue and the diaspora

Given the commitment of Modi and his allies to the idea of soft power, to deeper engagement with the diaspora, and to the project of making India into a world guru, one might have expected his government to strengthen these various institutions built up for public and cultural diplomacy. His government, however, took a different approach, one that I argue was more in keeping with Hindu nationalist ideology, but which diminished or even sidelined the agencies of the state. It did not reverse the Singh administration's decision to merge the PDD with the External Publicity Division. Nor did it markedly increase its resources. Indeed, the relevant MEA budget request for public diplomacy, advertising and publicity materials actually declined between 2014–15 and 2018–19 and the volume of XPD's publications – e-books, essays and YouTube videos did not noticeably grow.[8]

In March 2018, the Modi government did however decide to deploy what were dubbed 'Acharya envoys' – essentially spiritual instructors selected by the ICCR, to teach Sanskrit, yoga and the *Vedas* at three US diplomatic missions (George, 2018). But in general, after taking office, it did not make the MEA or India's embassies central to its public diplomacy effort. In parallel it also moved to curb the autonomy of the MOIA. On taking power in 2014, it did not appoint a separate minister to run the MOIA, instead putting it under the control of External Affairs Minister, Sushma Swaraj. In January 2016, it abolished the ministry and merged some of its staff and functions into the MEA, citing the need to avoid 'duplication' of work (Bhattacherjee, 2016). And the Modi government even toyed with the idea of closing down AIR's external service, amidst a dispute between the MEA and the Ministry of Information and Broadcasting about its reach and usefulness (Ramchandran, 2018).

This seemingly paradoxical behaviour from supposed proponents of soft power makes more sense when put in the wider context of how the Modi government was conducting public diplomacy. In line with its attempt to reinvent India's foreign policy more broadly, the administration practised public diplomacy in different ways from its predecessors, using different institutions. First, it made Modi himself – and to a lesser extent his government – the focal point, and used his 'star power' as a means of marketing aspects of Indian culture, including the richness and broad appeal of its religious inheritance, the benefits of yoga and the virtues of vegetarianism, and exercising influence. Modi became, as Amit Shah reportedly put it in August 2017, 'the torch bearer of the nation's pride globally' (quoted in Karnad, 2018, p. 73). Second, it invested considerable money and time in non-state dialogues and conferences run by foundations and think tanks like Art of Living – in *samvad*, to put it in Ram Madhav's language. Third, it used the BJP and the RSS, as well as affiliates like the Vishva Hindu Parishad, to conduct a kind of parallel quasi-diplomatic effort, directed principally at India's diaspora, but also at foreign political parties and civil society organisations. Last, it sought to make the diaspora itself into an instrument for building and leveraging soft power.

Religious diplomacy

Rightly, Modi's personal commitment to religious diplomacy has been identified as one of the novel aspects of his conduct of India's foreign relations (Mohan, 2015a, pp. 180–5).[9] Other prime ministers have drawn on the country's religious traditions for their speeches; others have paid visits to religious sites or religious leaders overseas. But none has made religious texts, symbols, sites and concepts so prominent a part of their diplomacy. He began early. Modi made a point of giving the Emperor of Japan, the Japanese Prime Minister Shinzō Abe, President Xi Jinping, and President Barack Obama copies of the *Bhagavad Gita* at their first meeting, during various state visits in the first year or so of his administration (Friedlander, 2016, p. 79; see also Roy, 2014b).[10] In parallel, starting in Nepal a few months into his prime ministership, he made multiple high-profile trips to significant religious sites and engaged extensively in conferences – like the World Culture Festival – organised ostensibly for the purposes of interreligious dialogue.

In part, of course, Modi's visits to Hindu and Sikh temples, and to Muslim mosques, were driven by the desire to interact with the diaspora. When he went to the Gurdwara Khalsa Diwan and the Laxmi Narayan temple in Vancouver in April 2015, or to Mariamman temple and the Chulia masjid (also known as the Jamae mosque) in Singapore in June 2018, the principal intent was to see, and be seen by, Indians overseas, residing in those countries. Elsewhere, however, the purpose was different. Modi's visits to the Pashupatinath temple in Kathmandu, Nepal, in August 2014 and the Mukhtinath temple in Mustang, Nepal, in May 2018 were clearly motivated by the desire to highlight the common culture and religious connections with that country. The controversial donation of 2.5 metric tonnes of sandalwood to Pashupatinath reinforced that message (Parashar, 2014). Similarly, the trips to the Naguleswaram temple in Jaffna, Sri Lanka (March 2015), and Dhakashwari temple in Dhaka, Bangladesh (June 2015), were expressions of affinity with local Hindus.

More notable, in both number and intent, were the multiple visits Modi made between 2014 and 2019 to Buddhist sites across the Indo-Pacific. These included the Tō-ji temple in Kyoto in Japan (August 2014); the holy town of Anuradhapura in Sri Lanka (March 2015); the Da Xingshan temple in Xi'an, China (May 2015); the Ganda monastery in Ulan Bator in Mongolia (also May 2015); the Quan Su Pagoda in Hanoi in Vietnam (September 2016); and both the Shwedagon Pagoda in Yangon and the Ananda Temple in Bagan, both in Myanmar (September 2017). The frequency and pomp of these visits, as well as their focus, stood in stark contrast to the approach taken by the previous government. For its part, the Singh administration had taken steps to woo Buddhists, partly to attract tourists into India and partly for political expediency, as a hedge should the Tibetan issue flare in a major dispute with China (Stobdan, 2016, p. 4).[11] In 2010, it funded the construction of a temple in the historic Chinese city of Luoyang, for instance, and facilitated the refounding of the ancient Buddhist university at Nalanda in Bihar, with substantial financial assistance from a number of Southeast Asian states. But it did not go to lengths that Modi did to associate India with Buddhism, to remind the region of past religious linkages, through such overt prime ministerial interest. I will return to this point in a moment.

Notable too, not least because of Modi's past reputation and past wariness about being seen in such a context, were the inclusion on his itineraries of tours of mosques. His first visit took place in mid-August 2015 in Abu Dhabi. As part of his two-day trip, Modi went to the Sheikh Zayed Grand Mosque, where he promptly took a 'selfie' in front of the complex to post on various social media sites. In February 2018, he went to the Sultan Qaboos mosque in Oman and three months later, in May, he accompanied Indonesian President Joko Widodo to Jakarta's Istiqlal mosque, the largest in Southeast Asia. Modi also made use of India's Islamic heritage with foreign leaders, giving a gold-plated model of Kerala's Cheraman Juma Masjid to the King Salman of Saudi Arabia during his trip to that country in April 2016, and giving Shinzō Abe a tour of the Sidi Saiyyed mosque in Ahmedabad in Gujarat, as well as of Gandhi's Sabarmati ashram. These visits were driven by various demands, including by domestic electoral concerns, such as the desire to appeal to Muslim migrant workers from Bihar working in Abu Dhabi (*Deccan Herald*, 2015), and the economic imperative of building better connections with the Gulf Arab states, discussed in more detail in the following chapter.

The other motivation was to portray Modi as a Vivekanandan champion of interreligious and intercultural dialogue in the cause of conflict resolution. To that end, he was also involved in a series of high-profile interreligious conferences and events, including the Art of Living's World Culture Festival (March 2016), but also the founding of a Swaminarayan temple in Abu Dhabi dedicated, in part, to the promotion of interreligious understanding, the World Sufi Forum held in New Delhi (March 2016), and the India-Indonesia Interfaith Dialogue launched by Modi and President Joko Widodo (October 2018). The bulk of these focused on the topic of religion and political violence. The World Sufi Forum, for example, organised by the All India Ulama and Mashaikh Board, which claims to represent and promote the interests of Sunni Sufis in India (AIUMB, 2017), aimed, as Modi put it in his opening remarks, at identifying how the 'message of Sufism' could combat terrorism and 'dissolve the clouds of discord and war and spread goodwill, peace, and harmony among the people' (Modi, 2016b).

Arguably the most important of these projects, however, was the 'Samvad Global Hindu Buddhist Initiative on Conflict Avoidance and Environment Consciousness' held first in New Delhi and Bodh Gaya in

Bihar (where Gautam Buddha supposedly achieved enlightenment) in September 2015 and then at the Sitagu International Buddhist Academy in Yangon in Myanmar (August 2017). The first Samvad was hosted by the BJP-aligned think tank, the Vivekananda International Foundation (VIF), sponsored by the Japanese Tokyo Foundation, and involved representatives from India, Japan, Myanmar and Sri Lanka. Modi addressed it twice, in New Delhi and at Bodh Gaya (Vivekananda International Foundation, 2018). He spoke on the now familiar themes of the contributions that Buddhist and Hindu thought can play in devising better approaches to social conflict and climate change and at greater length on the need for philosophically minded dialogue between religions that 'produces no anger or retribution.' He concluded by arguing that Buddhism has long been the 'uniting and binding factor' in Asia and that if an Asian Century was to be realised, its truths and contribution must be recognised (Modi, 2015d).[12]

These messages were notable because while they are intended to serve the wider purpose of building and leveraging India's soft power, they run counter to another concern of Hindu nationalist ideology – criticising Buddhism and Buddhist teachings. Savarkar, the original author of *Hindutva*, argued that Buddhism and its pacifism had made ancient Indians weak; the appeal of concepts like *ahimsa*, picked up most famously by Gandhi in the modern age, did something similar. Golwalkar, as we have seen, called *ahimsa* 'perverse' and imbecilic, and castigated Buddhists as traitors to Mother India, insufficiently dedicated to her defence. Modi's involvement – and that of like-minded organisations like the VIF – in promoting Hindu-Buddhist dialogue and attempts to establish common ground between the two traditions departs from those positions. It links back to Vivekananda's supposed pluralism and Modi's professed belief in the notion that the 'world in one family', a common theme in his speeches to both domestic and foreign audiences (see, for example, Modi, 2014a and 2014b).

In international settings, Modi also appealed to Hindu beliefs or traditions as sources of wisdom for addressing climate change, among other issues, as well as launching the successful bid at the United National General Assembly for a World Yoga Day, now celebrated every 21 June (Modi, 2014b). The first idea – that ancient Indian wisdom can help manage or even abate climate change – is not a new one. Modi developed it while Gujarat Chief Minister, and published a book that touched on the subject, *Convenient Action* (Modi, 2011).[13] There he argued that the *Vedas* offered a 'whole spectrum of knowledge' applicable to climate change, which when blended with Gandhi's concept of trusteeship could yield effective public policy in this area (Modi, 2011, pp. 7–9). Exactly what lessons might be applied, however, was unclear – the bulk of the book was devoted to publicity material about agriculture and infrastructure projects undertaken in Gujarat under his leadership.

As Prime Minister, Modi's pre-eminent initiative in this area was the International Solar Alliance (ISA), outlined during another of his early addresses to a stadium filled by the diaspora, this time at Wembley in the UK (Modi, 2015e). The ISA was formally unveiled a few days later, at the Paris Climate Summit in mid-November 2015, as a treaty-based intergovernmental organisation of a large number of states located between the Tropics of Capricorn and Cancer aimed at information sharing and finding financing for major solar energy projects. Its objective is to fund $1 trillion worth of investment to build solar plants sufficient to generate 1 terawatt of power – equivalent to the entire generating capacity from renewables available globally in mid-2018 – by 2030 (Press Trust of India, 2018a). Boasting, by the end of 2018, 121 member states, the organisation is based at India's National Institute of Solar Energy in Gurugram, Haryana, north of Delhi. Modi presided over its first summit in New Delhi in March 2018, arguing that tackling climate change required a 'look at the comprehensive approach and balance of the ancient philosophy' of the *Vedas*, which understood the Sun to be the 'soul of the world' (Modi, 2018a).

Modi thus sat at the core of his government's push to generate and use soft power as what one former diplomat terms a 'strategic asset' (Sikri, 2017). His extensive travels, especially in the first two years of his government, his rousing addresses to diaspora groups, his appeals to the *Vedas* and other elements of India's cultural and religious inheritance, and of course his high-profile visits to religious sites were all designed to project an image of India as exciting, engaged with the world, equipped with wisdom that might help humankind move beyond clashes of values and beliefs, and environmentally conscious, as well as economically vibrant. The intended audience for this projection, however, was not just a foreign one. The diaspora and the domestic public were also targets, reflecting the Modi government's underlying view that, as Sikri (2017, p. 185) puts it, there is 'seamlessness between domestic and foreign policy objectives' not simply in terms of economic development or security, but also in terms of the image of India.

The object in addressing those audiences was not, however, just to generate interest or goodwill, it was also about what Madhav called *samman*: it was about boosting national pride. As Prashant Jha quotes one prominent Hindu nationalist:

> When Modi goes and prays at the Pashupatinath temple in Kathmandu, or Kedernath, or Banaras, and comes out with

tika [the mark on the forehead made with powder or paste applied after prayer], he is saying he is a Hindu and he is proud of being one. The last PM to visit temples so publicly was Indira Gandhi in her final term. Modi wears his religion on his sleeve; he is unapologetic about displays of culture. The Sangh is happy with this. Their agenda is precisely this. What else [sic] is the slogan we used in so many campaigns – Garv se kaho hum Hindu hain, say with pride we are Hindus. (Jha, 2017, pp. 236–7)

Role of the Party

Another marked feature of Modi's reinvention of Indian foreign policy was the use of lieutenants in the ruling party and *Sangh* to engage in international relations in parallel to the regular diplomacy conducted by the MEA. Especially prominent were two figures: Ram Madhav, one of the party's National General Secretaries, and Vijay Chauthaiwale, who headed its Foreign Affairs department and its so-called Overseas Friends of the BJP, a vehicle designed to tap the diaspora for political support, funds and talent. Both were given quasi-diplomatic titles by the Indian media – Madhav as 'Modi's ambassador at large' or 'outreach man' (Mohan, A., 2014; Menon, 2015) and Chauthaiwale as the Prime Minister's 'global envoy' (Verma, 2018) – though their foci were distinct. For the most part, the first had a wide-ranging role across domestic and foreign policies, as befits someone reputed to be 'far more powerful than many Union ministers', effectively the BJP's second in command, after Amit Shah (Gahilote and Sengupta, 2014); the second focused more narrowly on diaspora engagement. But both arguably did as much to articulate a narrative about the Modi government's foreign policy than Sushma Swaraj, the External Affairs Minister, or the Ministers of State within the MEA, who tended to focus on managing the everyday diplomatic and consular tasks.

Originally from Amalapuram, in Andhra Pradesh, in the Southeast of India, Madhav was very young when he joined the RSS, apparently at four years old. He became a full-time worker for the organisation at 17 (Gahilote and Sengupta, 2014). He studied electrical engineering and then political science at university. Like Upadhyaya, among others, he became an in-house journalist, contributing to RSS publications like *Bharatiya Pragna*, which first appeared in 1999. He came to public note in 2002 when he defended Modi's response to Godhra in the Indian media (Gahilote and Sengupta, 2014). A year later, when he was 39, Madhav was appointed as RSS's national spokesperson – its first ever – and he established himself as one of the organisation's key leaders. He was hailed at that time as one of a new generation revitalising the RSS (Kang, 2004). In 2011, he became involved in the RSS's new think tank, the India Foundation, discussed in more detail later in this chapter, contributing an article on 'Chinese aggression' to one of its online journals (Madhav, 2011). In 2012, he was promoted to the RSS's Executive Committee, emerging a year later as an advocate for Modi's nomination as the BJP's preferred candidate for the prime ministership (India TV News Desk, 2013).

After Modi won power, Madhav transferred from the RSS into the BJP, becoming a General Secretary in July 2014 and, according to a profile in *Outlook India*, 'arguably among the half a dozen of the most powerful men in Delhi' (Gahilote and Sengupta, 2014). That power derives in large part from proximity to Modi and to Ajit Doval, Modi's National Security Advisor, and Doval's son, Shaurya Doval, who runs the India Foundation. Madhav had cultivated a relationship with Modi long before the latter emerged as a possible national leader. They had much in common, sharing an interest in clothes, gadgets, social media and Vivekananda (Gahilote and Sengupta, 2014). After helping to manage criticism of the handling of Godhra, Madhav went on to become one of the organisers of 'idea exchanges' with the then-Gujarat Chief Minister, events that took foreign diplomats and journalists to Gandhinagar to meet Modi, then off-limits to many. This work paved the way for the restoration of communication between Modi and the Western diplomatic community in New Delhi (Mohan, A., 2014). His relationship to Doval, the founding director of the VIF, as well as the former head of the Intelligence Bureau, permitted Madhav to also cultivate relationships abroad, using think tank conferences and dialogues to build a network of contacts. Long before 2014, he established himself as 'the most influential interface for the Sangh in the international diplomatic community' (Gahilote and Sengupta, 2014).

A former RSS *pracharak*, like Modi and Madhav, Chauthaiwale grew up in Nagpur, in Maharashtra, earned a doctorate in microbiology at Savitribai Phule Pune University, followed by a postdoctoral fellowship in Knoxville, Tennessee, and rose to become a Vice-President of Torrent Pharmaceuticals in Ahmedabad, in Modi's home state of Gujarat. He took leave to help Modi with the 2014 election campaign, and then left his position to work full time for the BJP after its victory, after being offered the job of running its Overseas Friends organisation – the body that coordinates with BJP supporters in the Indian diaspora – a few months later (Ramaseshan, 2014). In November 2014, in addition to that role, he was made head of the BJP's newly constituted Foreign Affairs department in the aftermath of an Amit Shah-led internal reorganisation (Press Trust of India, 2014b).

Although formally limited to diaspora relations, in practice Chauthaiwale's role after 2014 was much broader. He played a leading role in seeking to explain Modi's approach to foreign policy, as – among other things – co-editor, with Anirban Ganguly and V.K. Sinha, *The Modi Doctrine: New Paradigms in India's Foreign Policy* (2016). He travelled extensively to outline Modi's approach to domestic and foreign audiences, including and beyond the diaspora, and was referred to by media outlets as the Prime Minister's 'global envoy' (Verma, 2018). It was Chauthaiwale, moreover, who in a quasi-diplomatic capacity helped to stage-manage some of Modi's most important appearances overseas, notably his visit to Singapore in late May and early June 2018 where he delivered his keynote address to the high-profile, security-focused Shangri-La Dialogue (Verma, 2018). Ram Madhav also accompanied Modi on this particular visit.

Chauthaiwale's involvement in that trip highlighted the major part that the BJP played after 2014 in conducting international relations beyond the MEA, and beyond simply party-level diaspora engagement. Madhav is credited with organising some of the most high-profile events of Modi's first years in office – his appearances at Madison Square Gardens in New York and at Olympic Park in Sydney – but also with persuading Modi to go to Fiji after the G20 meeting in Brisbane in mid-November 2014 (Gahilote and Sengupta, 2014). Like Chauthaiwale, he was also active in crafting a narrative around Modi's approach to foreign policy – notably the notion of the *Panchamrit* – albeit one couched in the language preferred by the RSS. The leeway granted to Madhav was significant, though it sometimes led to mis-steps, such as when he predicted in a December 2015 interview with the Qatar-based *al Jazeera* network that Bangladesh and Pakistan would one day merge back with India to restore what some Hindu nationalists term *Akhand Bharat* ('undivided India') – the greater India ruled by the British that they think forms a cultural unit (*Times of India*, 2015).[14] Although a long-standing aspiration of Hindu nationalists, such suggestions were seen as unhelpful to bilateral relations with those two states.[15]

Apart from the many domestic issues in which Madhav was involved after 2014, notably in Jammu and Kashmir, his primary international concern was China. While still with the RSS, he wrote extensively on Sino-Indian relations for the India Foundation, and published a book just before the 2014 general election titled *Uneasy Neighbours: India and China after 50 Years of the War* (Madhav, 2014a). Madhav's position on the People's Republic after the BJP came to power was complex, but broadly mirrored – as we shall see later in this book – the Modi government's China strategy. On the one hand, it holds that China constitutes a multifaceted challenge to India, economically, but also in terms of national security. This lead Madhav to deride any kind of idealism and to berate Nehru, in particular, for pursuing policies that supposedly embodied that kind of thinking (see, for example, Madhav, 2014b). But on the other hand, it sees considerable virtue in engaging China and in emulating aspects of its development model.

In any event, Madhav led a notable effort in the early years of Modi's government to reach out to the Chinese Communist Party (CCP) via the BJP. In June 2014, a month or so after winning the election, BJP leaders received a group led by Zhang Xuyi, Deputy Director General of the CCP's International Department. Two BJP delegations reportedly travelled to China for meetings with their CCP counterparts in the second half of 2014 (Mohan, A., 2014). The objective, according to Madhav, was to foster 'goodwill' at a 'party to party' level, and study the CCP's 'party structure'. To those ends, one group thus visited the Central Party School in Beijing, as well as Guangzhou (BJP, 2014b). In February 2015, Amit Shah met Wang Jiarui, the CCP's International Department chief, when he visited New Delhi, with Chauthaiwale, among others, in attendance (Press Trust of India, 2015a). And in May 2016, Modi himself received Shanghai Party Secretary and Politburo member Han Zheng. But by that point, bilateral ties had become strained, and party-to-party meetings seem to have ceased within the first year of the government, barring the BJP's participation in the first BRICS Political Parties Forum in Fuzhou in China in June 2017, where it was represented by Madhav (Madhav, 2017).

That event highlights another dimension of the Modi government's party-led quasi-diplomacy: the growing use of think tanks and so-called track 1.5 or track 2 conferences to convey the government's message to foreign interlocutors, both official and non-official.[16] The Modi government made considerable use of these mechanisms, creating its own think tanks to run them, and using the platforms provided by others, notably the Observer Research Foundation's Raisina Dialogue, first held in New Delhi 2016, and now an annual event. Modi's address to the Shangri La Dialogue in Singapore in early June 2018 arguably marked the high point of this engagement. In part, Modi and his political allies' involvement in these events is simply a reflection of their growing frequency and importance, but in part too it reflects their desire to speak to – and be heard by – audiences beyond professional diplomats.

To do so, the Hindu nationalist movement has created or strengthened a series of think tanks, as such institutions proliferate across New Delhi and further afield. Long-established institutions like the Indian Council for World Affairs (founded in 1943) or the Institute for Defence Studies and Analyses (1965) now compete with a growing number of new organisations like Observer Research Foundation (founded in 1990 with funds from the Ambani family's conglomerate, Reliance Industries) or Brookings India (founded in 2011 with donations from a range of sources within the country).[17] And within this increasingly complex ecosystem a number of think tanks aligned with the *Sangh* have also appeared, including the BJP-affiliated Dr. Syama Prasad Mookerjee Research Foundation (SPMRF), named after one of the founders of the Bharatiya Jana Sangh; the VIF (created in 2009), which has more convoluted ties; and the India Foundation (IF, created in 2011).

Of these, the VIF and IF are arguably the most important in terms of foreign policy and international engagement, though they differ in form. Run until the 2014 election by Modi's National Security Advisor, Ajit Doval, the VIF is clearly the most active in terms of research, with a relatively large team of about twenty working in a wide range of areas and a regular output of discussion papers and policy briefs. It also holds regular and high-profile events, including the Hindu Buddhist Samvad. The IF, by contrast, is smaller and its researchers comparatively junior, though it does publish its own bimonthly journal.[18] But the IF is widely considered, as the highly regarded *Hindustan Times* journalist Prashant Jha put it early in Modi's term, as 'the country's most powerful think-tank' (Jha, 2015). Its board is dominated by leading BJP politicians, including Nirmala Sitaraman, who served as Commerce Minister and then Defence Minister under Modi. The organisation is led in tandem by Ajit Doval's son, Shaurya, and Ram Madhav. As Jha points out, the IF was responsible for running the annual India Ideas Conclave, held mostly in Goa, and another Hindu-Buddhist dialogue forum (the annual Dharma-Dhamma event, first held in 2014) and major conferences on counter-terrorism and the economy (Jha, 2015).

These kinds of organisations, which expanded under Modi, formed what Jha (2015) called an 'eco-system' for generating foreign policy ideas; furnishing unofficial settings in which to interact with foreign diplomats, think-tankers and academics; serving as platforms from which to propound Hindu nationalist worldviews; and providing bases for like-minded ideologues to develop and expound their interpretations of his government's actions. They were, in other words, central to the attempt to reinvent Indian foreign policy, as well as key to the marketing of Modi's vision for world guru India.

Power of the diaspora

Central to that effort too was the diaspora, estimated at more than twenty million people (Mohan and Chauhan, 2015).[19] Here, of course, Modi, the

BJP and the RSS had mixed motives. The diaspora were a crucial source of funds for the BJP's election run in 2014, as well as for subsequent state-level efforts, and many were eloquent and influential backers of Modi himself (see Mazumdar, 2018). Some even travelled to India to help the BJP campaign (Guha, 2014). The carefully stage-managed events put on for the diaspora in Australia, Canada, the UK and the US in the 18 months after the BJP's win, at which Modi appeared and praised its vitality and ingenuity, were in part expressions of gratitude. But they were also key elements in a strategy aimed at organising and mobilising the diaspora to better serve India's interests. Two concerns were particularly salient: tapping the diaspora for talent, knowledge, and funds for investment that might be repatriated, as it were, to support various initiatives, including 'Make in India', and using it as a means of projecting soft power and exerting influence in key target states (Chaulia, 2016, pp. 59–60).

This strategy was not, of course, novel. As I have noted, the Vajpayee and Singh governments both reached out to the diaspora with similar aims, making it easier for Persons of Indian Origin (PIOs) to enter India and to bring their know-how and capital, as well as appealing to Non-Resident Indians (NRIs) to do the same. Characteristically, much of the Modi government's outreach involved extending and streamlining what had been put in place by those earlier administrations. In 2015, for example, it took the Person of Indian Origin card, first introduced in 2002, which allowed citizens of other states visa-free travel to India as well as a number of other benefits, and merged it into the Overseas Citizen of India (OCI) document, introduced in 2005, which also offers a visa-exemption but also allows OCIs to reside in the country indefinitely (MEA, 2018a).[20] In parallel, it also relaxed the rules concerning inward investment from NRIs, PIOs and OCIs, deeming that it should no longer be treated as foreign direct investment, but instead it would be considered in the same way as domestic capital (Press Information Bureau, 2015).

These reforms were not, however, just economic in intent. By extending a warmer welcome back to India to both PIOs and NRIs, the Modi government also sought their help in building what they called, in 2014, in the manifesto and elsewhere 'Brand India' (Challagalla, 2018). The 'brand' they envisaged had two components. The first was modern: the diaspora acting as an advertisement for the skill, ingenuity and diligence of Indians, especially in high-tech sectors, but also in the wider life of their host countries.[21] This meant highlighting the achievements of both Indian-origin entrepreneurs, as Modi did when he visited Silicon Valley in 2014, and Indian-origin politicians, as the Indian government did when it organised a 'PIO Parliamentarian Conference' in January 2018, inviting almost 150 individuals from across the world to New Delhi

(Bhattercherjee, 2018). The second component, however, was nominally more traditional. For Modi's BJP and for Bhagwat's RSS, the diaspora can also serve as exemplars for Indian cultural values and conveyors of key Indian ideas. They share what Vice-President M. Venkaiah Naidu, a former BJP minister, described to the PIO Parliamentarians as the 'essence of Indianness':

> ... the global vision, the holistic vision and harmonious vision. We have believed that the whole world is one family. We believe that life has to be viewed as an integrated whole. We believe that harmony and peace are at the heart of sustainable development. It is this unique world view we have collectively inherited. (Naidu, 2018)

For Hindu nationalists, in other words, the diaspora is an important transmitter of the values of what Upadhyaya identified as 'inclusive humanism' (Naidu, 2018).

To advance these values, the BJP, RSS and other Hindu nationalist organisations stepped up their attempts to organise elements of the diaspora and turn it into a more active and political influential instrument. Madhav and Chauthaiwale played important roles in this effort in 2014 and 2015, but in parallel the *Sangh* expanded their efforts (Chaulia, 2016, p. 67). The World Hindu Congresses, held first in New Delhi in November 2014 and then in Chicago in September 2018, were telling as to the nature and strength of this push. The second meeting prominently featured speeches – delivered in English – by Vice-President Naidu and by RSS *Sarsanghchalak* Mohan Bhagwat, as well as addresses from the Dalai Lama and leaders from the RSS-affiliated Vishva Hindu Parishad, alongside business and media personalities. While Naidu talked again of India as a *vishwa guru*, Bhagwat's talk was more controversial, provoking criticism for his use of the expression 'wild dogs' to allude to invaders of India, but arguing that Hindus do not seek dominance over others, and affirming the idea of the 'world is one family' (RSS, 2018).

These attempts to engage and energise the relatively wealthy diaspora found mainly in the West, were paralleled under Modi by an equally important effort concerning the relatively poorer, located largely in the Middle East and Southeast Asia. Some eight million Indians work in the Gulf states alone – many being low-paid labourers (Leveillant, 2017, p. 7). Although the country receives significant remittances in return, this part of the diaspora generates challenges for New Delhi. They regularly require consular assistance, they are commonly subject to mistreatment by their employers, recruitment agencies, or the authorities, and on occasion they need to be evacuated when conflicts erupt, as they did in Kuwait in 1991, Iraq in 2003, Libya in 2011, and Yemen in 2015 (Pethiyagoda, 2017).[22] In each of these cases, the Indian government was required to mobilise significant diplomatic and military resources, often at very short notice, and in the face of much domestic scrutiny.

Earlier governments did invest in means to try to better protect these workers and their interests. In 2009, Indian Community Welfare Funds were created in each Gulf Cooperation Council (GCC) state; bureaus and helplines were opened in Indian embassies from 2010 onwards to provide information about labour conditions and rights; and refuges for female workers have been provided (Leveillant, 2017, pp. 18–19). The Modi government extended these initiatives and focused more attention and resources on the region as a whole and the diaspora present there, partly in response to pressure from the workers themselves, their families and the states from which they come, sometimes exerted via social media, and partly for economic reasons, since this part of the diaspora is responsible for a sizable chunk of the remittances returning to India. The World Bank estimated that the country received almost $70 billion in remittances in 2017, of which more than half came from the GCC states (Duttagupta, 2018). Engaging with this group, therefore, as Modi did on successive visits to Gulf states, and trying to uphold their interests through more responsive and effective consular work by the MEA, is a key economic priority. Although External Affairs Minister Sushma Swaraj's use of Twitter, in particular, to respond to Indian workers in distress was often lampooned as well as praised (Vijaykumar, 2016), it was part of a effort to address some of the manifest shortcomings in consular support in the region (see especially Leveillant, 2017, p. 20–3).

The Modi government's work in this area also reflected, of course, political interests. Some of the diaspora in the Gulf originate from states, especially in the south, that the BJP wanted to hold or win after 2014; some also return to their communities with money and become influential (Pethiyagoda, 2017). Many are Muslims, who might not vote for the BJP, but might at least be persuaded not to actively oppose it. Public demonstrations of concern for their welfare made sense anyway for Modi and the BJP, matching the claim to be governing for all Indians, under the slogan of *sabka saath, sabka vikas*. His high-profile visits to mosques in Abu Dhabi and Oman, where large number of Indian migrant workers reside, should be interpreted partly in that context. But Modi's objectives in addressing the diaspora in these locations went further than this. As he told a crowd in Muscat in February 2018, they were about reinforcing what he called a 'feeling of belongingness [*sic*]' with India among these 'brothers and sisters', emphasising that even though his audience was overseas, they were still an element of 'New India' and the work they do in Oman was also contributing to its construction (Modi, 2018b).

Conclusion

In the aftermath of the World Culture Festival concerns soon surfaced about the impact of the event on the local environment. An expert committee acting for the National Green Tribunal, a government agency charged with environmental protection, concluded that the event had done 'extensive and severe damage' to the ecology of about 170 hectares of flood plain on which it had been held. All the local flora and fauna had been affected, and the estimated cost of rehabilitating the area was later put at about 13 crore rupees (130 million rupees or about $2 million). The remedial work would likely lasting a decade and Art of Living was fined about 5 crore rupees (50 million rupees or about $800,000) to help pay for it. The organisation rejected parts of the environmental impact assessment, however, refused to pay, and appealed the fine (*The Wire*, 2017). The issue remains in the courts, as the parties contest the various claims. That an event partly devoted to promoting ideas of environmental sustainability ended this way was unfortunate. But the episode illustrated a much wider point about the search for soft power and the project of making India a world guru – to be credible, its deeds have to match its words.

The challenge for Modi's government was that its message that India was a model of religious and cultural understanding was constantly undercut by episodes of communal violence and accusations from foreign observers that freedom of worship was under threat (McCarthy, 2015). The denial of visas to members of the US Commission on International Religious Freedom, as well as the forced closures of non-governmental organisations, compounded the impression that Modi's rhetoric was out of kilter with his government's alleged tolerance for violent acts by people affiliated with the Hindu Right (USCIRF, 2016, pp. 159–66). This impression, combined with longstanding doubts about Modi's past conduct as Gujarat Chief Minister, stymied his attempts to position India as a world guru. 'Soft power' is, of course, notoriously difficult to measure. But what gauges we have did not show a marked improvement in India's reputation after Modi came to power. The regular BBC World Service and Globescan polling, for example, reported that between 2014 and 2017 foreign perceptions remained stable, with 37 per cent of those surveyed in 2017 expressing positive views, one point down from 2014, and 39 per cent negative views, the same as before (Globescan, 2017). Other polls taken early in Modi's tenure reported positive views of India in the US, but doubt about New Delhi's ability to 'deal responsibly with world problems' (Ayres, 2015). God might have 'determined India's duty to do good in the world', as Modi once said during his days in Gujarat, but it was not clear that the world was convinced India could or should play that role (quoted in Chaulia, 2016, p. 39).

6

Prosperity and Connectivity

Before and for some time after the 2014 general election, the most widely expressed hope for Modi's government was that it might be more committed to economic liberalisation and to opening up India's markets to the world than its tentative predecessor. As Gujarat Chief Minister, it was observed, Modi had been markedly more friendly to business than many Indian leaders, as well as apparently more successful in delivering growth. The hope that Modi might bring the same approach to New Delhi were reinforced by the Bharatiya Janata Party's (BJP) overt appeals to the Gujarat model (BJP, 2014c), and promises to improve the often parlous state of infrastructure and connectivity within India, as well as with the rest of South Asia, the world's least economically integrated region (BJP, 2014a, pp. 15–16, 32–3). After Modi took office, high expectations were further fuelled by the new Prime Minister's rhetoric, his outreach to business leaders in the US and elsewhere, and his clear instruction to the Ministry of External Affairs (MEA) and India's missions to focus on economic diplomacy. They were stoked by Modi's promises to greet investors with a 'red carpet, not red tape' (Modi, 2014e), the unveiling of schemes like 'Make in India', launched with a fanfare in September 2014, and 'Startup India', announced in his 2015 Independence Day speech. The replacement in January 2015 of the old Planning Commission, with a new body, the National Institute for Transforming India, known as NITI Aayog, and the involvement of well-respected economists like Arvind Panagariya, were also widely praised (see Patnaik, 2015).[1]

Over time, however, disappointment set in among businesspeople, investors and foreign governments about the slow pace of change, as well as among many in the electorate in India concerned with the slower than expected rate of growth (Manor, 2015, p. 739). A lack of progress on domestic economic reform and on liberalising trade – notwithstanding significant changes concerning investment – undermined confidence at home and overseas. Early on, there were worrying signs. In August 2014,

Modi's government pulled out of a World Trade Organization (WTO) deal on trade facilitation, agreed at the Bali Conference the previous year, citing concerns about the effects it might have on domestic food security measures. Although this decision was reversed a month later during Modi's state visit to the United States, it was taken as a signal that New Delhi was less committed to liberalisation than expected (Wilson and Curtis, 2014). India's foot-dragging in the negotiations for a Regional Comprehensive Economic Partnership (RCEP), involving 16 major Indo-Pacific states, raised similar concerns (Cook and Das, 2017). So too did the Modi government's reticence about a number of possible bilateral free trade agreements, including those under consideration with Australia (since 2011), Canada (since 2010), New Zealand (since 2010) and the EU (since 2007), and long mooted with the US. Over time, it became clear that under Modi New Delhi was unlikely to make any substantial progress in these areas, despite all the talk from the Prime Minister of welcoming globalisation and the desire to bring in foreign capital (Gupta, 2018).

This chapter argues that the nature and outcomes of Modi's reinvention of India's foreign economic policy, with its marked shift towards a new narrative of openness accompanied by a reticence to actually realise liberalisation in key areas, were functions of a political compromise within his government and the broader Hindu nationalist movement, and of problems generated largely by China. The reinvention was, in essence, an attempt simultaneously to craft appealing messages to foreign and domestic audiences while managing the deep divisions within the BJP, and particularly between the BJP and the *Sangh*, about the merits of economic liberalisation. It was, moreover, a project intended to clothe a set of policies that were, in essence, a variety of mercantilist economic nationalism in apparently liberal garb. At the same time, it was also an attempt to cope with the multifaceted challenges that China's economic weight and dynamism present to India, especially in terms of protecting local industry and market access in South Asia and beyond. Under Modi, these challenges became acute, as Beijing has developed its 'Belt and Road Initiative' (BRI, formerly 'One Belt, One Road' or OBOR). In response, India came out – for a while, at least – as a prominent critic of the BRI and a putative competitor, seeking to forge its own connectivity projects with South Asian regional partners and with others, notably Japan, to promote *samriddhi* or prosperity not just in India, but also in its neighbourhood.

To explore these issues, this chapter begins by revisiting Hindu nationalist thinking about economic policy, noting the considerable resistance within both the BJP and the *Sangh* to liberalisation and openness, and gap between *Hindutva* and *Moditva* – and especially

'Modinomics' – in this crucial area.[2] It then turns to examine the record of Modi's government in domestic economic reform, insofar as it affects trade and investment, and in foreign economic policy. The second half of the chapter analyses India's response to China's BRI, the pressures that project exerted on Modi's 'Neighbourhood First' policy, in particular, and his government's critique of BRI and its attempts to compete with Beijing to better integrate South Asia.

Modernity without liberalism

To this day, as we have seen, the BJP remains formally committed to Upadhyaya's philosophy of Integral Humanism, which it inherited from the BJS and the wider *Sangh* (Andersen and Damle, 2018, p. 8). In practice, however, the party's policies have diverged from Upadhyaya's precepts, despite their often being cloaked in his language, generating tensions with the *Sangh*, at times, on economic issues. Until the early 1990s, the BJP remained wedded to *swadeshi* or self-reliance, defending small traders and farmers, and to opposing foreign ownership of businesses. But the reforms of 1991 – and their clearly positive effects – forced a reconsideration of the party's position and caused arguments among Hindu nationalists (Andersen and Damle, 2018, p. 11). The immediate response of the Rashtriya Swayamsevak Sangh (RSS) to Rao and Singh's liberalisation programme was to oppose and to criticise: it launched a campaign against buying foreign goods, for example, and created a new organisation – the Swadeshi Jagran Manch (SJM), founded in November 1991 to promote *swadeshi* – to help coordinate it (Nag, 2014, p. 145). RSS leaders also spoke out, with the then-*Sarsanghchalak*, Madhukar Dattatraya Deoras, criticising foreign multinational corporations as a threat to India's economic wellbeing akin to that posed by the East India Company (Blom Hansen, 2001, p. 300).

Over time, however, the BJP's response became more accommodating. After extensive discussion within the Party and between the different elements of the *Sangh*, it took a nuanced and pragmatic view. Its new economic policy, unveiled in 1992, gave a cautious welcome to the liberalisation of the domestic market, and to the use of high technology in key sectors, but retained a 'strongly protectionist posture vis-à-vis the world market' (Blom Hansen, 2001, p. 301). By the time it came into government in 1998, this vision had evolved into one of 'Bharatiya capitalism'. The BJP remained broadly opposed to foreign involvement in the economy, whether in the form of accepting IMF loans or signing up to WTO rules, or in the form of inward investment from overseas firms (Nag, 2014, p. 130). Instead, it emphasised an economic nationalist agenda that favoured growth through 'patriotic consumption' (Blom Hansen, 2001, p. 305). But that said, Vajpayee's time in government, after 1998, included some significant acts of liberalisation, including the privatisation in sectors like telecommunications and the divestment of state-owned hotels and other businesses (Nag, 2014, pp. 146–7). The regulations concerning private investment in ports and airports were also relaxed, as were those concerning roads and rail projects (Nag, 2014, p. 149).

Many analysts argue that this shift towards a more liberal economic policy at home was one of the factors that accounts for the rise of the BJP in the 1990s, alongside the *Ram Janmabhoomi* agitation concerning the supposed Ram temple at Ayodhya that energised other parts of the electorate (Nag, 2014, pp. 106–21).[3] It allowed the BJP to appeal, as Blom Hansen (2001, p. 306) puts it, to 'car *sevaks*' as well as Hindu nationalist '*kar sevaks*'[4] – to the aspiring, mostly urban, consumerist middle class for whom buying a car is a marked achievement, as well as to believers in *Hindutva*. But this shift toward more liberal economic policies did not occur without resistance or criticism from elements within the *Sangh*, which remained highly suspicious of foreign trade and investment, in particular, and protested against its manifestations, including the Western and Western-style fast food outlets springing up in towns and cities in India during the 1990s and afterwards (Blom Hansen, 1999, p. 220). To try to deter the Vajpayee government from liberalising India's foreign trade and inward investment arrangements, the SJM rallied against his government, while the RSS voiced 'grave apprehensions' about the application of WTO rules to India, calling it a 'conspiracy of developed nations' intent on undermining Indian agriculture, among other things (quoted in Andersen and Damle, 2018, p. 129).

These concerns did not, as we have seen, stem from doubts about the ability of liberalisation to bring about economic growth. Rather, they arose – and continue to arise among many Hindu nationalists today – from anxieties about its effect, and the impact of globalisation more broadly, on Indian society and culture. The arguments of the veteran Hindu nationalist and Harvard-educated economist Subramanian Swamy, a long-time member of the right-wing Janata Dal party who finally joined the BJP in 2013, and who was earlier Minister of Commerce in the Chandra Shekhar-led government in 1990–91, make this point well. Globalisation poses two risks, he asserts: one to the economy, as it can open it to attacks from 'international raiders and speculators' and the other to culture. 'Globalisation can alter values, spread disease more easily, and disrupt the family system', Swamy observes (2007, p. 81). Limits have to be placed on its reach, with India 'well integrated' into 'global markets', with appropriate 'connectivity' (Swamy, 2007, p. 90). But all of this has to be closely managed if the Indian 'renaissance' he envisages is to occur, because of the cultural corrosion that can come via globalisation. For Swamy, the proper aim should be a modernised India coupled with what he terms a 'virat [which he translates as 'virile'] Hindu identity' (2013, p. 21).

Before and throughout Modi's time in office, leading members of the *Sangh* regularly aired similar sentiments. RSS head Mohan Bhagwat, for example, repeatedly voiced his support for *swadeshi*. In September 2012, he told an interviewer that the RSS 'stand' on self-reliance had been 'strengthened' rather than weakened by globalisation:

> Our stand is that each country has its resources, its people and their aspirations. The purpose of development is to make individuals independent and self-reliant. If I can make something at home, I will not buy it. I will only bring from outside that which is not available in my country and not possible to make, yet is necessary for life. But on my conditions. In business, there are conditions from both sides. We should take knowledge and technology from everywhere. (*Indian Express*, 2012)

Echoing Upadhyaya, he argued that to ensure efficiency and to make the country 'corruption-free', India's economy ought to be what he called 'decentralised', with 'indigenous' production of goods as well as consumption (*Indian Express*, 2012).

Bhagwat did not deviate from this position after 2014, despite the tacit bargain many think was struck between the RSS and the BJP, in which the former offered not to openly criticise and to lend their volunteers – the *swayamsevaks* – to national, and later, state election campaigns, and the latter gave the *Sangh* leeway to advance their cultural agenda.[5] Nor, for that matter, did RSS-affiliates like the SJM, which attacked Modi's 'Make in India' scheme and called for indigenous technologies, funded by domestic capital, to be developed instead (Press Trust of India, 2015b). In parallel, the SJM agitated against foreign investment in India's retail sector and against the government's land reforms, intended to facilitate 'Make in India' and other programmes (Press Trust of India, 2015c). Overall, however, the *Sangh* stayed true to its bargain, and kept its doubts and criticisms to itself. Bhagwat, in particular, also showed himself willing publicly to back policies with which he (and implicitly, the RSS) agreed, despite his organisation's supposed reluctance to engage in politics. In late 2016, for instance, he was vocal in his support for Modi's controversial decision suddenly to remove from circulation all 500 and 1000 rupee notes, arguing that the move would help curb corruption (Venugopal, 2016).

This is not to say, of course, that Modi and his government had free rein, nor that the Prime Minister and his senior ministers disagreed the broad outlines of Hindu nationalist thinking on foreign economic policy, in particular. To be sure, there were disagreements and what one well-placed analyst called 'antagonisms' in this area (Manor, 2015). But the general lack of criticism from the *Sangh* – aside from the SJM – can be treated as a measure, however imperfect, of how little Modi's approach strayed from its economic thinking and that of the Hindu nationalist mainstream, despite the packaging his government gave it.

Promises

On the campaign trail, Modi famously promised to restore energy to India's economy, to ensure inclusive development ('*sabka vikas*'), and deliver *acche din* ('good days'). But although his pre-election speeches and the BJP manifesto were long on promises, only the broad outlines of an economic policy were revealed before May 2014. The avowed foci were administrative reforms, particularly in using information technology to streamline service and welfare delivery, infrastructure, skill development, combating corruption, and cutting red tape for businesses. The manifesto was tellingly vague, however, about economic reform. It promised that a BJP-led government would restore confidence and trust in New Delhi's capacity to manage the economy at home and abroad. But otherwise it promised only to 'find out solutions, which are effective in the short run and lasting in the long run', exercise fiscal discipline, allocate resources more efficiently, reform the banking sector, and 're-visit the policy framework for investments both foreign and domestic to make them more conducive' (BJP, 2014a, p. 27). Buried elsewhere was a vague reference to revisiting labour laws and land acquisition processes – two crucially important areas that needed attention if India was to boost foreign investment and employment (BJP, 2014a, pp. 28, 31).

Once in power, of course, Modi let loose a flurry of initiatives. In the first six months, his government moved to cut welfare spending and bring the budget under control, relaxed restrictions on foreign direct investment in the railways and defence industry, deregulated diesel prices, streamlined the national identification project, Aadhaar, that facilitates the payment of state benefits, and launched 'Make in India', a scheme to boost manufacturing in 25 sectors by allowing overseas interests to fully own the facilities they could build and operate. In 2015, it promoted 'Startup India', 'Digital India' and an ambitious Smart Cities programme (to build 100 new high-tech, sustainable cities), advanced plans to reform labour laws, and introduced new banking regulations. It took until August 2016, however, to finally get parliamentary and state approval for the introduction of a national goods and services tax (GST), which would sweep away a large number of local taxes and what are effectively internal customs barriers. The GST came into force – albeit with much criticism of its design and sheer complexity – on 1 October 2017.

Although frequently accompanied by the customary Modi drama in their announcements, these reforms were, as Milan Vaishnav argues, 'gradualist', reflecting an approach of 'creative incrementalism' (2015, p. 3). In part, this reflected the difficulties of obtaining support in the Rajya Sabha, which the BJP and its allies did not control. But as Vaishnav suggests, the approach may also have been a function of at least three other factors: the convictions of Modi himself about what needed to be done, and what did not; the lack of an overarching vision for reform in the government; and a 'belief that his government [had] plenty of time' (Vaishnav, 2015, p. 5). As a result – and apart from the introduction of the GST – the latter half of Modi's government witnessed little in the way of new initiatives, with one exception. In November 2016 it suddenly announced, overnight, that it was withdrawing all 500 and 1000 rupee bank notes, in an act of 'demonetisation'. This was not unprecedented in independent India – it had been done in 1978, for example – but it was generally unexpected. Modi's motives for doing this were mixed. Cracking down on the black economy, corruption and counterfeiting were the primary justification, but boosting revenues by limiting tax evasion, forcing money into banks and encouraging the use of digital payment were also cited (Chhibber and Jassal, 2017, p. 87). This was not a reform, per se, but did it have significant economic effects, pushing up deposits and tax receipts, causing substantial distress to small traders and farmers, and cutting perhaps one or two percentage points off annual economic growth, not least because new banknotes were slow to arrive.[6]

Over time, it became clear that Modi's approach to managing the economy was less neoliberal, as many in India and outside argue, and more nationalist and statist, reflecting the BJP's early promise to put 'India First' and the underlying suspicion prevalent among Hindu nationalists about liberalisation, especially of trade and capital.[7] This was also consistent with Modi's approach in Gujarat while Chief Minister, as we have seen, which was business-friendly, but sought to retain strong political and bureaucratic oversight – indeed, some have argued that 'Make in India' is simply a bigger version of the 'Vibrant Gujarat' model of business engagement (Ayres, 2018, p. 88). His economic nationalism combined a marked reluctance to open India's markets any further to international competition with a desire to try to nurture, behind existing tariff and regulatory barriers, an indigenous manufacturing industry, albeit one funded by foreign capital and underpinned by foreign know-how and technology. As Surupa Gupta argues, the Modi government did little if anything to modify long-standing protectionist positions on trade in any of the ongoing major multilateral negotiations, including for RCEP, and it took no steps toward entering into new agreements, such as the Trans-Pacific Partnership, then under discussion (Gupta, 2019, pp. 16–19).

This 'India First' economic nationalist agenda – like the ideological one of realising India's destiny as a world guru – shaped Modi's attempted reinvention of foreign policy. Because it depended on stimulating growth by injecting foreign-sourced capital, rather than wholesale liberalisation, it demanded the Prime Minister's hectic travel and enthusiastic embrace of foreign bankers and entrepreneurs, such as his trip to Silicon Valley in September 2015, where he shared a stage with Facebook founder Mark Zuckerberg (Goel, 2015). This 'nation-rebranding' exercise also required engaging and energising the diaspora, which, as we have seen, was a core focus of Modi's public, cultural and religious diplomacy, and which was perceived – reasonably – as a major source of capital and a group more likely than others to invest.[8] This was necessary to spark interest and boost flows of inward investment in the short term, adding a percentage point or two onto the GDP growth rate, in the knowledge that substantive reform in areas like land acquisition and labour reform could take the best part of the government's time in office, or run into a hoped-for second term.

Development and delivery

The Modi government came to office criticising its predecessor's failure to sustain high levels of growth, control inflation, maintain a prudent budget, manage official corruption and provide jobs. To a domestic audience, it promised instead 'inclusive' development and a 'globally competitive economy' (BJP, 2014a). To India's region, it promised – as part of the 'Neighbourhood First' approach Modi announced soon after coming to office – that India would strive to better integrate the region so that all of South Asia might grow and develop. In the colourful publicity material produced by the MEA's External Affairs and Public Diplomacy Division, it went to great pains to emphasise India's contributions to capacity building and infrastructure across the region (MEA, 2014b). These included education and training initiatives, hydropower plants, roads, and a raft of other projects. Most, however, were long-standing arrangements, dating to earlier governments, repackaged or given additional impetus by the Modi government. And over time, doubts set in about its ability to deliver on both these and other promises, both domestic and regional, as the government struggled with domestic reforms and with projects intended to improve regional connectivity.

There were successes. Foreign direct investment (FDI) inflows jumped after the Modi government's regulatory reforms and the launch of 'Make in India' during the second half of 2014. In the 2014–15 and 2015–16 financial years, there were increases in inward FDI of over twenty per cent. Some $20 billion more flowed into India in 2015–16 than had done in the last year of the UPA government – a total of $55.6 billion. But thereafter the growth in inward FDI slowed, so that by 2017–18 the total was $62 billion, only about $6.5 billion more than it had been two years earlier. And tellingly, the top three industries in which this money was invested were telecoms, software and hardware for the IT industry and services, rather than the kinds of manufacturing industries that 'Make in India' was intended to nurture (*Times of India*, 2018). Towards the end of Modi's government, the slowing pace of FDI growth led to some changes in the regulations to try to regain momentum, including a move in January 2018 to permit 100 per cent foreign ownership in so-called single-brand retail (Mohammed, 2018).

On trade, the record was even more mixed. The launch of Modi government's Trade Policy in April 2015 set impressive targets, declaring that the government wanted to see India's share of world trade rise from 2.1 per cent in 2014 to 3.5 per cent by 2020 and to see India's total exports top $900 billion (Puri, 2017, p. 1). But the policy itself, despite running to more than 150 pages, largely involved the reduction of red tape, the deployment of more officials to export promotion roles, and the development of state support schemes for Indian manufacturers seeking to export their goods (Ministry of Commerce and Industry, 2015). It did not envisage sweeping structural reform. In parallel, little progress was made on progressing towards agreement a series of trade deals under negotiation, whether bilateral (including putative deals with the EU, Australia, Canada and New Zealand) or multilateral (including RCEP). The bilateral FTAs became mired in arguments about India's desires to protect its agricultural sector and to cut special deals for migrant workers. At the same time, India's participation in talks about the RCEP – the only major multilateral process, outside the WTO, in which it is involved – was wary and cautious (Puri, 2017, p. 12), ostensibly because of fear it could open the door to low cost Chinese manufacturers able to push Indian competitors out of business.

Despite the ambition of 'Make in India' and the 2015 Trade Policy, the value of India's trade did not grow in any significant way during Modi's government. According to official figures, merchandise exports declined markedly from 2014–15 to 2016–17, from $310 billion to $275.9 billion; imports also declined, from $448 billion to $384 billion. In services, the story was brighter, at least in part, with a small increase in exports over the same period from $158 billion to $163 billion, offset by a larger increase in imports, from $82 billion to $96 billion. The trade deficit remained large, however, at $176 billion in 2017–18 compared with $214 billion in 2014–15 (Department of Commerce, 2018, pp. 6–7). These relatively poor figures were blamed on a weak global economy by Modi's government, rather than on its policies (Department of Commerce, 2018, p. 28). But they were also a function of the difficulties faced by 'Make in India', as India struggled to develop manufacturing industries producing goods for export.

The Modi government did succeed in improving India's rating in the annual 'Ease of Doing Business' survey published by the World Bank (2019) – a key aim of his government. In 2014, it was placed 142 out of 190 countries; in 2018, it had climbed to 77 (Chakraborty, 2018). But this fell short of Modi's declared objective of getting India into the top 50 by the end of his term (Press Trust of India, 2014c). Moreover, substantive progress on the domestic reforms many think necessary to attract foreign investment – in terms of complex tax regimes, antiquated rules regulating land acquisition, labour laws and banking – was also slow and uneven.[9] The Modi government did succeed in reforming India's antiquated insolvency and bankruptcy laws in 2016 (Nair, 2016). Its biggest reform, the introduction of the GST in 2017, was also a significant achievement, but it was very long in the making, and many analysts think its final version is unsatisfactory. A GST had been mooted under the Vajpayee government; it came close to been implemented under Singh. Its eventual introduction did put an end to a number of local taxes, and the so-called *octroi*, a kind of customs duty levied on goods crossing state borders, but the regime it put in place, with four different rates ranging from 5 per cent to 28 per cent, was complex and potentially problematic (Nayyar, 2018, p. 224).

The government's attempts to change laws regulating land acquisition were much less successful. Inheriting a system based on the 1894 Land Acquisition Act, which allowed the government to acquire land for 'public purpose', as well half a century's worth of legal challenges to this regime, it sought to bring about reform soon after the 2014 election with the intention, in part at least, of facilitating the realisation of 'Make in India'. In later December 2014, it promulgated a new Land Ordinance that attempted to make it easier for firms to acquire land, but which was limited to six months in duration. Early in the following year it sought to make more lasting amendments to the law concerning compensation and resettlement (Mukerji, 2017, pp. 96–7). It failed, however, to deliver reform commanding broad support. The Ordinance was heavily criticised within the BJP, and was allowed to lapse. A new Bill passed the Lok Sabha in April 2015, but could not find support in the upper house, the Rajya Sabha, and so too was set aside, and left to state governments to negotiate (Ayres, 2018, p. 89).

Modi's administration made a little more progress when it came to reforming labour laws. India has complex and stringent regulations in this area, despite the fact that because only around ten per cent of employees work in the formal sector, most of the working population are not covered nor protected by their provisions. During the 2014 election campaign, Modi promised to streamline the 44 existing codes in national law (which sit alongside dozens of parallel state regulations) to make it easier for firms to sack workers, to exempt smaller companies from some of the labour regulations, and to dilute union rights, as well as to help his drive to 'Make in India'. The objective was to try to rationalise the existing regulations into just four codes. In August 2014, this process began with an attempt to amend the Factories Act. In October 2014, a broader reform agenda was articulated (Yadav, 2014), including changes to the regulation of labour standards. A few months later, in April 2015, in the same session of parliament in which the government passed its legislation on land acquisition, a Labour Code on Industrial Relations Bill was laid before parliament, but because of ongoing disruption in the Lok Sabha, it was not read (Gopalan, 2016, p. 174). In parallel, many trade unions began a campaign against proposed new regulations, and when finally negotiations with the government unravelled in September 2015, some held a 24-hour general strike in protest.[10]

Overall, then, the Modi government fell short in crucial areas when it came to liberalising the economy in ways that would match the Prime Minister's rhetoric about openness and the need to embrace globalisation, intrinsic to his reinvention of foreign policy. In the neighbourhood, where Modi also promised *samriddhi* and more integrated and inclusive development, the government also struggled, as it came under pressure from China's fast-changing BRI, with its own set of grand promises.

Connecting the region

During Modi's first year in office, as part of the 'Neighbourhood First' approach, his government made a number of pledges to other South Asian states. At Modi's first SAARC Summit in Nepal in late November 2014, his themes were the disjuncture between 'boundless potential' of South Asia and the 'barriers of boundaries', and the need to better integrate the region. 'It is still harder to travel within our region than to Bangkok or Singapore', he observed, with good reason, and 'more expensive to speak to each other' (Modi, 2014f). He made a resounding call for better connectivity – 'We must shrink the distance between our producers and consumers and use the most direct routes of trade' – and acknowledged that 'India has to lead' (2014f). 'Infrastructure is our region's greatest weakness and its most pressing need', Modi noted (2014f), highlighting the fact that he could not travel to Kathmandu overland because the roads were so poor. He promised a SAARC development bank to support regional infrastructure projects, a push to improve the ease of doing business across the region to parallel what his government was doing at home, and an effort to try to address the large trade surplus India has with the rest of the region. And he observed both New Delhi's gift of a communications satellite for the use of SAARC members and India's hosting of SAARC's South Asian University (Modi, 2014f). In parallel, Modi also developed an even broader narrative about the need for greater integration and cooperation across the Indian Ocean. In Mauritius, he spoke about the concept of SAGAR – 'Security and Growth for All in the Region' (Modi, 2015f). He pointed to the progress made in revamping the 21-member Indian Ocean Rim Association (IORA) and the need to improve maritime security, as well as trade, across the region, and India's key role in delivering these goods.

These visions were welcomed at the time in the region and outside it, but proved difficult to realise. Making progress within SAARC was challenging. At the 2014 summit the leaders pledged to fully implement the South Asian Free Trade Agreement (SAFTA) agreed in 2004, which was meant to reduce tariffs on all merchandise trade down to zero by 2016, and lay the groundwork for a South Asian Economic Union (SAEU). But under SAFTA member states are permitted to retain tariffs on items deemed 'sensitive', and about a thousand items remain on each member's list (Weerakoon and Thennakoon, 2006). And although Modi's government cut India's list dramatically, to a couple of dozen items, others have not reciprocated, citing trade deficits, among other reasons, as a justification. In any case, the 2016 SAARC summit, set to take place in Islamabad, was cancelled after a terrorist attack in Kashmir prompted New Delhi to withdraw their involvement, followed by Afghanistan, Bangladesh and Bhutan (Jacob and Giri, 2016). Citing Pakistan's alleged continued support for terrorism, India then boycotted the 2018 summit, again scheduled to be held in Pakistan. Substantive progress on trade or connectivity was not made, and although India delivered its satellite, Pakistan refused to use it. The idea of a SAARC development bank, on the other hand, proved unviable (Mishra, 2015).

The impossibility of using SAARC to further connectivity and regional integration meant that the Modi government fell back on the tried and tested approach of using smaller, sub-regional groupings to further key initiatives or bilateral deals. These included the Bangladesh, Bhutan, India, Nepal (BBIN) working group and the Bay of Bengal Initiative for Multi-Sectoral Technical and Economic Cooperation (BIMSTEC),[11] which both date back to 1997, and the South Asian Subregional Economic Cooperation (SASEC) initiative founded in 2001. To try to deliver on its promises, it also sought to accelerate a series of existing or planned projects inherited from early governments, or to work with third parties outside South Asia – notably Japan – to develop new ones. BBIN provided the context in which the four countries to agree a deal in June 2015 to facilitate the movement of vehicles, including trucks, across their respective borders, obviating the need for goods to be unpacked and reloaded, which ought to expand cross-border trade. Getting each state to ratify the agreement took some time, however, and Bhutan decided to leave the arrangement in May 2017, ostensibly on economic and environmental grounds. In 2018, the other three moved ahead to implement it, and began to upgrade road and customs infrastructure (MRTH, 2018).

Some progress was also made, towards the end of Modi's government, with BIMSTEC, which had been slow to develop up until the mid-2010s, despite floating plans for a free trade agreement back in 2004. In 2014, however, it was given a permanent secretariat in Dhaka, and thereafter there was more activity, with regular meetings of leaders and officials (Xavier, 2018, pp. 7–8). In October 2016, Modi hosted a leaders' retreat in Goa and a joint summit with the BRICS group, injecting some energy into BIMSTEC, which he later described as a 'natural platform' for India to further its Act East agenda and improve connectivity into Southeast Asia by land and sea (Xavier, 2018, p. 10). Plans were floated for a range of road, rail, and port projects, but as an Asian Development Bank (ADB) report concluded in July 2018, only a few objectives had been achieved under BIMSTEC's auspices, mostly concerning the implementation of trade facilitation measures (Asian Development Bank, 2018, pp. 3–4).

More was achieved to upgrade cross-border roads and rail connections, develop better port infrastructure, improve regional airports, address regulatory issues concerning trade facilitation, build better energy infrastructure, and establish cross-border trade corridors under the auspices of SASEC, thanks in part to funding and technical assistance from the ADB. Between 2002 and mid-2016, SASEC delivered about 40 significant infrastructure and development initiatives, at a cost of $7.7 billion (SASEC/ADB, 2016, pp. 2, 24–8). Between 2016 and 2018, it coordinated the expenditure of another $16–17 billion on new and upgraded roads, enhanced port infrastructure and improvements to airports in Bhutan and Nepal, and an additional half a billion dollars on trade facilitation. It also laid out another $58 billion in investment in regional energy infrastructure.

Among these SASEC initiatives, one of the most important to India was the 1,360 km India-Myanmar-Thailand Trilateral Highway between Moreh in Manipur state and Mae Sot in Thailand. This promised to open up new opportunities for more overland trade with South East Asia, especially for businesses in the poor North East of the country, and to lessen India's dependence on shipping routes through the Strait of Malacca and South China Sea for moving goods into mainland Southeast Asian markets, especially in the Mekong region (Bana and Yhome, 2017). Begun in 2012 – a decade after it was first proposed – the highway was part funded by the ADB, as an integral part of the broader 'Asian Highway Network'. In August 2017, the Modi government approved more than $250 million in additional finance for the scheme, reportedly in response to competing Chinese initiatives, having earlier announced funding for the widening and improvement of the Imphal to Moreh highway linking the capital of Manipur to the border town, also in collaboration with the ADB (Chaudhary and Pandya, 2017; Dashi, 2017).

These projects, designed to aid India's development and to improve connectivity with neighbouring states, were given new impetus and in some cases new injections of funds or political commitment in the second half of Modi's government largely in response to China's evolving BRI. Over time, it became clear to New Delhi that the BRI posed a major challenge to India in the region. It promised to bind much of South Asia and some Indian Ocean states, as well as West, Central and Southeast Asia, into a China-centric economic system, one that rested on Chinese capital, access to China's market, and Chinese-set standards and regulations. New Delhi worried that the BRI could make South Asian states economically dependent on China, plunging some into debt traps, rendering them susceptible to diplomatic influence. Partly in response, Modi's government eventually decided to take a public stand against elements of the BRI and to put in place measures that might allow it to compete for economic and diplomatic advantage.

Competing with China

The 'One Belt, One Road' scheme – later rebranded by Beijing as 'BRI' – emerged in late 2013, as India's election campaign was beginning.[12] The Singh government gave it a guardedly positive welcome, reflecting a certain willingness to discuss connectivity and infrastructure projects that might be of mutual benefit. One of these emerged around the same time: the 'BCIM Corridor' linking Kunming to Kolkata via Mandalay and Dhaka, which was then conceived as a standalone (that is, non-OBOR/ BRI) project. In December 2013, New Delhi committed India to BCIM. In February 2014, when Singh met Chinese special representative Yang Jiechi, he also publicly welcomed the idea of the overland New Silk Road Initiative (NSRI) (*BRICS Post*, 2014). He would not be drawn, however, on the question of the maritime component of the BRI, the Maritime Silk Road (MSR), that Beijing also wanted him to endorse (Singh, 2014).

After coming to office, Modi's government did not change these positions, despite a public plea from the Chinese ambassador to endorse OBOR/BRI in the form of a prominent newspaper editorial published during the election campaign (Wei, 2014), and despite signs that the new Prime Minister and his team were more sceptical of Beijing's intentions than their predecessors (Panda, 2014). In late June 2014, during Vice President Hamid Ansari's visit to China, Beijing again sought India's backing for the MSR, but was met with a polite request for more detail on its plans (Singh, 2014). Another plea – this time for an endorsement of the full BRI – was made by the Chinese foreign ministry in August 2014, in interviews given to Indian journalists in Beijing, in advance of President Xi Jinping's state visit to India the following month (Krishnan, 2014). This approach was also rebuffed, with no mention of the BRI made in the lengthy joint statement issued following the meeting, apart from a reference to the two countries' shared commitment to the BCIM project (MEA, 2014c).

This refusal to endorse the BRI occurred at a time in which there was a marked cooling of bilateral relations, during the second half of 2014. In the run-up to Xi's trip to India, as Kanti Bajpai notes (2017, pp. 80–1), Beijing and New Delhi both assumed tougher stances toward one another. On the Indian side, this was achieved by way of a series of high-level visits to states with their own differences with China. Modi went to Japan from 31 August to 3 September, while Sushma Swaraj, External Affairs Minister, and then-President Pranab Mukherjee went to Vietnam. On the Chinese side, the signalling was less subtle. A week before the Xi's visit, units of the People's Liberation Army (PLA) entered Indian-controlled territory claimed by China in Ladakh, Jammu and Kashmir. This intrusion met with a sharp response from New Delhi. Modi ordered three battalions of Indian troops into the area and then – in an unusual move for an Indian Prime Minister – publicly criticised the PLA incursion during a joint press conference held with Xi during the latter's visit (Mallet, 2014). In parallel, conscious of the Modi government's hunger for FDI, Chinese diplomats reportedly dangled the carrot of $100 billion worth of investment to be agreed during Xi's time in India, only to reduce the offer down to $20 billion for the final joint statement (Chaudhuri, P. P., 2014).

In April 2015, President Xi made a state visit to Pakistan and unveiled the $46 billion China–Pakistan Economic Corridor (CPEC) project.[13] Beijing made it clear that it considered CPEC was a central component of the OBOR/BRI (Houreld, 2015). It soon became clear too that elements of CPEC, including road and rail links, were to run through territory claimed by India as part of Kashmir. Xi's announcement cast a pall over Modi's reciprocal trip to China the following month (Mohan, 2015, p. 103). In Beijing, the Indian Prime Minister reportedly lodged a formal protest about CPEC, noting its concerns about the planned route through disputed territory of some of its road and rail links (Roche, 2015). In the weeks that followed, New Delhi also began publicly to draw unfavourable contrasts between BRI and other Chinese-led initiatives that India supported, such as the Asian Infrastructure Investment Bank (AIIB), and BRICS projects like the New Development Bank (NDB). In comments made in Singapore in July 2015, for example, then-Indian Foreign Secretary Jaishankar argued that, unlike the AIIB and the NDB, which were created by multilateral negotiations, and which are governed multilaterally, the BRI is a unilateral, 'national Chinese initiative' 'devised' to serve its 'national interest' rather than any collective interest (Jaishankar, 2015a).

Despite considerable Chinese efforts to woo Indian scholars and think-tank analysts over to more positive assessments through a series of BRI-focused dialogues and conferences, New Delhi continued to resist endorsing it and to offer mild but pointed criticisms (Uberoi, 2016, p. 27). Modi, Sushma Swaraj and S. Jaishankar remaining diplomatic, but firm, advocating better 'connectivity' in South Asia and the Indian Ocean, but insisting that it be developed 'through consultative processes' not unilateral decisions, and arguing that connectivity initiatives should not become exercises in 'hard-wiring' designed to limit the autonomy of involved states (MEA, 2016).[14] Then, on 13 May 2017, on the eve of President Xi's inaugural Belt and Road Forum in Beijing, New Delhi unleashed a stinging critique. It noted New Delhi's long-standing concerns about CPEC and observed that, in India's view:

> ... connectivity initiatives must be based on universally recognized international norms, good governance, rule of law, openness, transparency and equality. Connectivity initiatives must follow principles of financial responsibility to avoid projects that would create unsustainable debt burden

for communities; balanced ecological and environmental protection and preservation standards; transparent assessment of project costs; and skill and technology transfer to help long term running and maintenance of the assets created by local communities. (MEA, 2017a)

Since these principles did not, in New Delhi's view, appear to be adhered to with the BRI – and because India believed that China was refusing to 'engage in a meaningful dialogue' on the subject – the spokesperson confirmed that an Indian representative would not attend the BRF.

Despite periodic overtures from Beijing, Modi's government thereafter refused to endorse or participate in the BRI. New Delhi repeated its preferred rules and norms for connectivity initiatives in multiple joint statements with like-minded partners, including Japan and the US (see, for example, US Department of State, 2018a). Moreover, it began to explore alternative schemes, either agreed bilaterally with South Asian states, negotiated in regional forums like BIMSTEC, as we have seen, or developed with other major powers. These included projects like the Asia-Africa Growth Corridor (AAGC), sketched out by Modi and his Japanese counterpart Shinzō Abe in their November 2016 meeting in Tokyo (Ministry of Foreign Affairs of Japan, 2016), and schemes developed under the auspices of the revived Quad – the quadrilateral consultations on Indo-Pacific security involving Australia, India, Japan, and the US.

The AAGC was outlined in more detail at the landmark India–Africa summit and African Development Bank meeting held in Gandhinagar, the capital of Gujarat, in May 2017. It promised to deliver 'development and cooperation projects, quality infrastructure and institutional connectivity, capacity and skill enhancement and people-to-people partnerships' (RIS et al., 2017, p. 2). A core aim was to improve port infrastructure, in particular, so that trade might flourish between India's West coast and East African littoral states (Kenya, Tanzania, Zambia, Zanzibar) and Indian Ocean states (Madagascar, the Maldives, Mauritius and the Seychelles). But it also encompassed Japan, a number of South East Asian states (notably Myanmar, Singapore and Thailand), as well as Bangladesh and Mongolia (Biswas, 2018). It was also conceived as an extension of long-established partnerships and projects, including India's pioneering and broad-based International Technical and Economic Cooperation programme, launched in 1964, and the Africa-India Framework for Cooperation launched at the first India–Africa Forum Summit in 2008 that also encompassed a wide range of education, health, capacity-building, peace and governance initiatives (Saran, 2012). The AAGC was conceived as means of tying these various programmes up with India's Act East policy, and Japan's

'Expanded Partnership for Quality Infrastructure', outlined at the G7 meeting in May 2016, and the latter's broader development programme, recently repackaged to fit with its Free and Open Indo-Pacific concept. The bulk of the funding, however, would come from Japan, which has promised $200 billion to the AAGC, supplemented by loans from India's Exim Bank (Pathak, 2017).

India was also involved in discussions – albeit tentative – with Australia and the US about other infrastructure projects in the region. Connectivity was on the agenda for both Modi's first meeting with President Donald J. Trump in June 2017 (White House, 2017) and the Manila meeting of the revived Quad held on the sidelines of the East Asia Summit in November 2017 (MEA, 2017b). Soon after, in February 2018, reports emerged of a putative plan for the four countries to help coordinate infrastructure funding, as well as other projects, such as the 'ASEAN-Australia Infrastructure Co-operation Initiative' announced in Sydney in March 2018 (Department of Prime Minister and Cabinet, 2018).

Conclusion

Repeatedly, Modi sought to counter long-established Hindu nationalist arguments about the dangers of foreign trade and investment, which emphasise the dangers they apparently pose to the country's social and economic development and cultural fabric, by arguing that India had a rich history of economic and cultural exchange with other parts of the world, notably East Asia, the Middle East and East Africa. On multiple occasions he observed that the Gujarati port of Lothal was 'one of the earliest seaports in the world' and that Indians had been instrumental in distributing goods and ideas throughout the Indian Ocean littoral and beyond (see, for example, Modi, 2015f). His attempt to reinvent Indian foreign economic policy was grounded in this different, more positive, outward-looking narrative, rather than the defensive one favoured by Upadhyaya and other Hindu nationalist luminaries of the past (Chaulia, 2016, pp. 84–6).

The policies of Modi's government, however, reflected an economic nationalist and mercantilist world view that reflected ongoing anxiety about the possible consequences of liberalisation, the strength of political opposition within and outside the BJP to such an approach, the institutional weaknesses of the Indian state, and significant external pressures, not least from China. 'Modinomics' proved an unstable compromise between the *swadeshi* nationalism of elements of the BJP and RSS and the demands of business, both domestic and foreign, to cut regulation and free up restrictions on the use of labour and land. It also entailed expansive promises on regional connectivity, especially in South and Southeast Asia, and uneven delivery, sometimes undermined by flare-ups in bilateral relationships, such as the 'blockade' that damaged India's ties with Nepal in September and October 2015.

That incident, which illustrated the pain that could be inflicted on regional neighbours by cutting trade routes, dissipated much of the goodwill built up in Nepal as a result of Modi's visits and religious diplomacy in 2014 and India's humanitarian assistance in the aftermath of the April 2015 earthquake. Although the blockade was nominally unofficial, organised by Madheshi people who live on both sides of the border, protesting against Nepal's proposed constitution, it showed once again the disparity in economic power between India and its neighbours, and displayed to sceptical observers in Nepal and elsewhere in the region the potential downsides of improved connectivity. In response, Kathmandu turned to China for support, in the search for transit routes that would allow it to avoid dependence on India. In September 2018, Nepal signed a deal with Beijing that will allow it to move goods to Chinese ports for sale in third countries (Nayak, 2018). In parallel, Nepal committed to China's BRI, receiving funding for roads, rail and power projects in return, as India struggled to make up lost ground with its neighbour, despite Modi's attempt to reposition India as the regional champion of prosperity and connectivity.

7

National Power and
Regional Security

The Modi government swept to power promising to deliver
'comprehensive national security', with a whole of government approach,
and 'zero tolerance' for 'terrorism, extremism and crime' (BJP, 2014a,
p. 37). It pledged that it would 'deal with cross border terrorism with a
firm hand', modernise the military and increase spending on defence-
related research and development. It also declared that it would bolster
the nuclear deterrent and 'study in detail India's nuclear doctrine, and
revise and update it, to make it relevant to [the] challenges of current
times' (BJP, 2014a, pp. 38–9). All of these pledges caused some trepidation
among both domestic and international observers. A number of analysts
expressed concern about what might be implied by a 'firm hand' in
addressing cross-border terrorism and by the apparent pledge to revise
of the nuclear doctrine, in particular.[1] They worried that Modi might
take a belligerent line towards Pakistan and that he could be prone to
unpredictable or even reckless decision making that could destabilise the
relationship with Islamabad, in particular, or indeed Beijing (see Curtis,
2014).[2] In office, however, the Modi government's approach to security
issues was more measured than expected, but arguably less robust than it
had promised, than its supporters might have hoped, and some outside
analysts feared it would be. Here, as elsewhere, the continuities in policy
and implementation from earlier governments were clearer than the
changes.

Under Modi, India did make progress on internal security in some
areas, notably in managing the threat from the Maoist Naxalite militants,
which had emerged as a major problem under Singh, and on damping
down secessionist violence in the North East. In both cases, anti-poverty
programmes, negotiated settlements, and better management of India's
porous borders, especially with Bangladesh, played roles in achieving these

ends.[3] Elsewhere – notably in Kashmir – Modi's government struggled to cope with unrest and insurgency, and security forces resorted to heavy-handed tactics that attracted both domestic and international criticism (Jaffrelot, 2017, pp. 28–9).

Equally controversially, the Modi government tried to deter Pakistan-based terrorists from carrying out attacks in India with more robust military action than its predecessors had attempted. It responded to major attacks at Pathankot in January 2016 and Uri in September 2016 with 'surgical strikes' – raids by special forces into Pakistani-controlled territory intended to destroy alleged training camps.[4] It upped the ante once more in mid-February 2019, after more than forty paramilitary police were killed in a suicide bombing carried out by Jaish-e-Mohammed (JeM). Soon afterwards, the Modi government ordered air strikes across the Line of Control in Kashmir that included an attempt to bomb the JeM camp at Balakot, just inside Pakistan proper, precipitating a crisis that ended only when a downed Indian pilot, captured by the Pakistani army, was returned to India.

Whether or not these actions achieved their objectives was hotly contested. The number of terrorist incidents fluctuated during Modi's time in office, before and after the 2016 raids.[5] There was no abatement in shooting and shelling across the Line of Control that separates the Indian- and Pakistani-administered parts of Kashmir.[6] And the 2019 air strikes prompted retaliatory action from Pakistan, leading to a messy, uncertain outcome in which both sides claimed to have gained the strategic upper hand and the moral high ground (O'Donnell and Ghoshal, 2019).

At the same time, Modi's government articulated an expansive understanding of its security interests and sought to develop the means to defend and extend them, and it used force in ways that, while not unprecedented, seemed to suggest a shift away from 'strategic restraint'.[7] Like the Singh government before it, it talked of India as a 'first responder' and 'net security provider' in South Asia and the Indian Ocean region (Mukherjee, 2014). Just how far the Modi government managed to improve India's capacity to act in these ways, however, is a matter of debate. India continued to have problems managing the process of military modernisation, especially with regard to the procurement – at a realistic cost, in a timely fashion and using processes free from suspicions of misconduct – of much-needed major new weapons systems, from assault rifles and artillery to fighter aircraft and helicopters (Joshi, S., 2018). It also struggled to transform its large but notoriously inefficient indigenous defence industry into one capable of providing what the military needs, in terms of price, timeliness and quality.[8] As a result, India under Modi remained dependent on arms imports, albeit from an increasingly diverse range of sources.[9] And although a long-planned nuclear-powered missile submarine was launched, and progress made in extending India's nuclear capabilities and constructing defensive anti-ballistic missile systems, New Delhi remains wedded to the nuclear doctrine it articulated almost two decades ago (Narang, 2018).

The security challenges Modi's government faced would be difficult enough to manage if the environment in which it found itself was benign. In practice, it was not. The rise of Xi Jinping, who became General Secretary of the Chinese Communist Party in November 2012, and the election of Donald J. Trump, who assumed the US presidency in January 2017, were highly disruptive, and New Delhi was unable to insulate India from the consequences for the country and the region. Managing the unpredictability of the Trump administration and the President himself, while seeking to drive the US-India strategic partnership forward to try to mitigate some of the effects of Chinese power and ambition, added layers of complexity to its security policy. In parallel, Chinese assertion and ambition became, under Modi, India's most pressing national security problem, partly because of the sheer scale of China's economic heft and military power and its growing influence in South Asia and beyond, and also because of Beijing's fast expanding foreign policy ambitions. In mid-2017, India came close to armed conflict with China at Doklam, a disputed area of Bhutan, where its troops engaged in a standoff with the People's Liberation Army (PLA) that lasted over two months. Despite loud and repeated threats of punishment from Beijing, the Modi government apparently stood firm, winning domestic and foreign praise, but the incident also led to questions about India's readiness for even a limited border war, should one erupt.

To explore Modi's approach to *suraksha* (security), this chapter therefore focuses largely on India's interactions with those two major powers, one an increasingly close partner and the other widely perceived as the country's principal strategic challenger. It argues that in this area – in matters of national, regional and international security – Modi's attempted reinvention of foreign policy was less ambitious that it was in the pursuit of *samman* (respect) and *samriddhi* (prosperity). In part, it suggests, this was a function of a lack of clear ideological guidance in the Hindu nationalist tradition. Put simply, the past ideologues of *Hindutva* – like Golwalkar and Upadhyaya – had much to say about securing Bharat from what they perceived as internal enemies and very little about securing it from potential physical threats from outside, concentrating instead on the problem of how to make India resilient and resistant to foreign cultural influence. In the absence of such guidance, the Modi government fell back on established concepts and approaches, some inherited from Singh's government. To be sure, it was at times bolder and more assertive than its predecessor, ordering cross-border raids in response to terrorist attacks, for example, but the narrative it wove around its management of security was less novel and less clearly ideological than those it spun in other areas.

Like the others, this chapter first explores elements of Hindu nationalist ideology, looking closely at the curious lack of any definitive advice on managing international – as opposed to internal – security. Next it examines the expansion of India's 'strategic space' in the past two decades and the concepts and approaches that have evolved that underpin New Delhi's aspirations and behaviour. It then turns to analyse the Modi government's handling of the source of its biggest external security challenges: China. This third section explores the development of the US–India strategic partnership after 2014 – a partnership that some thought, because of Modi's past troubles with Washington lawmakers, and because of the Trump factor, might not flourish under the two leaders. The last looks at the government's management of regional security, particularly India's vexed relationship with Pakistan.

The power of the *Rashtra*

Hindu nationalist thought about power and security displays a curious combination of concern and ambivalence, caught as it is between two convictions that ostensibly lead in different directions.[10] On the one hand, as have seen, it holds that the principal reason that India became subject to what Hindu nationalists regard as foreign rule, by Muslims and then by the British, is that Hindus let themselves become soft and 'unmanly'.[11] To be able to resist further invasions, they must, as Golwalkar put it (1996, p. 435), 'be Men with capital "M"'.[12] This thinking could lead to the advocacy of a kind of political realism that emphasises the acquisition of material power and an amoral attitude to its use. Golwalkar certainly flirted with that kind of thinking, arguing that '[c]onflict is in the very nature of mankind as it is constituted today' and that 'To be strong is the real path to peace' (1996, pp. 257, 262). Upadhyaya expressed similar views – in his journalism, he repeatedly argued that India needed to shed Nehruvian idealism, acquire military power, including nuclear weapons, and, if necessary, fight wars (Upadhyaya, 1968, p. 50).

On the other hand, however, Hindu nationalists hold that what matters fundamentally, in the final analysis, is not physical strength, but cultural resilience. The 'feeling of burning love for Bharat Mata', Golwalkar insisted, 'alone shall bring into full play the invincible potency of our people ...' (1996, p. 338). And for them, military power will one day become redundant, as the world comes to acknowledge the truth of the *sanatana dharma* ('true religion'). Golwalkar made it clear that acquiring power was a means to an end, and only a temporary expedient, necessary so that Bharat can be heard:

> Let us ... recognise the truth that for real national honour and peace, there is no way except the building of invincible national strength. It is only then that the great principles that we preach to the world will carry weight and prestige. The world is not prepared to listen to the philosophy, however sublime, of the weak. (Golwalkar, 1996, p. 270)

Hindus should become strong and 'manly' once more, in other words, but cultural strength is ultimately what is required to realise what the Rashtriya Swayamsevak Sangh (RSS) refers to as India's *param vaibhav* (or 'ultimate glory') as a world guru. Golwalkar saw this as a necessary blend (his word) of realism and idealism – necessary because India had to survive and thrive in the world that we have, if it was to create the world it was destined to foster. But for all that, Hindu nationalist thinkers have tended on the whole to neglect questions of *international* security, beyond rejecting Gandhian *ahimsa* or non-violence, which Golwalkar famously called 'imbecilic' (1996, p. 272). Instead, beyond providing a systematic explanation for India's past subjection by invaders and the lessons that might teach, they tend to focus on those internal matters that they perceive as greater and more pressing threats to *national* security and the measures that can be taken within the state to address them.

At the same time, Hindu nationalist thinking – especially within the RSS – is also profoundly ambivalent about the state and its role. As we saw in Chapter 3, they see the sovereign state for what it is – a European contrivance underpinned by social contract theory and designed for what they believe to be a different kind of world, one of competition and combat, to the one that they envisage. 'Our existence as *Rashtra* is based on *Sanskriti* [that is, culture] and people', as Mohan Bhagwat has put it, 'which is unique and entirely different from the nation-state concept rooted in power' (Bhagwat, 2017). Both Golwalkar and Upadhyaya implied that there was no need for the state once the Hindu *Rashtra* was established as a world guru and the *sanatana dharma* was recognised by all. As a consequence, Hindu nationalists and their followers devoted little time to systematic thought about state policy, believing since the present order was transitory, and epiphenomenal, it need not be done.

All of these beliefs are apparent in the annual speeches delivered by RSS chief Mohan Bhagwat to coincide with Vijayadashami or Dussehra, which concludes the Navaratri festival in the Hindu calendar. In his 2014 address, for instance, he opened with the familiar arguments about India's destiny, contrasting its 'genuine efforts' to bring about a 'happy and beautiful world' through 'truth and non-violence' with '[t]hose forces which focus only at achieving the economic interests of their own groups in the name of globalization; want to expand their own empires in the name of establishing peace or; compelling all other countries to remain weak and helpless in the name of non-proliferation of weapons' (Bhagwat, 2014).[13] He observed that the new Bharatiya Janata Party-led government was doing good work at home and abroad, but soon turned to another key theme – national disunity and the need to remedy it socially, and not to wait for government to act. Many internal and foreign forces are still active in Bharat, whose only aim is to 'exploit the system for their petty gains'. He pointed to jihadis, illegal migrants and Maoists, and argued that while the state could take measures to combat them, society had to play its role. 'We need a vigilant government, a strong defence policy and brave and efficient defence force to ensure the security of our nation', Bhagwat argued, 'but we equally need a society of people who are patriotic, vigilant and of a high moral character' (Bhagwat, 2014).

Bhagwat said more about international relations and foreign policy in later addresses. In 2015, for instance, he complained in passing of Pakistan's 'hostilities', China's 'expansionism', 'unfair international diplomacy', and the iniquities of foreign development models, but concentrated mostly on domestic social issues and how 'Bharat's esteem in the world has gone up many-fold' in recent years (Bhagwat, 2015). Two years later, in the aftermath of the Doklam standoff between China and India in Bhutan, he noted that the world now recognised the 'strength' and 'international standing' of Bharat, but spent far more time discussing Kashmir and 'anti-national forces' supposedly fostering division, and more still on social and economic problems (Bhagwat, 2017).

It was only in Bhagwat's 2018 speech, however – the last before the 2019 election, and one quite different in tone and content from the previous ones – that he focused on international relations and national security at any length. Obliquely, he praised the government's work on securing India's borders and its efforts to 'entwine the web of international relations by appraising the nations with our security concerns and getting their backing and cooperation'. He praised too past 'bold actions' to respond to threats in the region. More significantly, Bhagwat concentrated on military matters, arguing that the Modi administration's military modernisation programme was 'one of the reasons that the prestige of Bharat is rising in the world'. He criticised, however, the 'amenities' available to members of the armed forces and their families, the security of military bases, and slow progress towards 'total self reliance in the field of defense production'. Moreover, he called for more progress on poverty alleviation, arguing that deprivation caused division and violence, and pointing to Maoism, in particular, as well as so-called 'urban Naxals' – that is, alleged supporters of Naxalism found in the media and universities. Bluntly, Bhagwat stated that in his view 'The administrative sensitivity, alacrity, transparency and totality in the implementation of good policies of the Government', in these and other areas, 'are still not up to … expectations' (Bhagwat, 2018).

Bhagwat's arguments, in other words, illustrate both the core preoccupations and inherent tensions of Hindu nationalist thinking about national security. Internal security is the preeminent concern, to be addressed by robust responses to forces that might bring about social division and by a combination of moral uplift and economic development. International relations – still less international security understood as a public good – is a marginal issue and a matter of pride, recognition, and prestige. The approach of the Modi government, as we shall see in what follows, was prone to this ordering of priorities and conception of foreign and security policy. Its attempted reinvention of India's security policy reflected elements of this Hindu nationalist worldview in its management of the relationship with China, for example, though it also showed signs of engaging more substantively with the challenges of national and international security than the ideologues of that movement, including Bhagwat, have done.

Expanding horizons

Three aspirations defined the Modi government's security policy: becoming a 'leading power', behaving as a 'net security provider', and delivering what the Prime Minister called, borrowing the Hindi word for 'ocean', 'SAGAR' – 'Security and Growth for All in the Region'. None was clearly linked with Hindu nationalist thought, at least as Golwalkar or Bhagwat outline it. The first – the idea of India as a leading power – originated with Jaishankar, Modi's Foreign Secretary from early 2015 to early 2018. The next originated in Washington, in a speech by President Obama's then-US Defense Secretary Robert Gates in which he described his understanding of India's place in the Indian Ocean region to be one of 'net security provider', rather than a state concerned with merely defending its own citizens, interests, and values (quoted in Mukherjee, 2014, p. 1). It was embraced by Singh's government (Singh, A., 2013), and then by its successor. The last was Modi's own invention, involving his characteristic play on words and fondness for acronyms, first appearing, as we have seen, in a landmark speech given in Mauritius in March 2015 (Modi, 2015f).

All three concepts reflected broadening understandings of what we might call India's strategic space and its role within it. Twenty years ago, as Shashank Joshi (2015a, p. 6) observes, it was commonplace to conceive of that space as stretching from Aden to Malacca, and north into Central Asia. Already encompassing a large area, including South Asia and the Indian Ocean littoral, it has since grown even bigger, to include the Horn of Africa, West Asia (that is, the West's Middle East), East Africa, Central Asia and East Asia (Brewster, 2018, pp. 500–10). Obviously, India's interests and capacity to defend and extend them vary throughout this space, being more intense in the inner circle, as it were, of what the ancient strategist Kautilya called the *raja-mandala* ('circle of states'), and less so as one moves out to the periphery (Kautilya, 2000). But New Delhi's strategic partnerships, especially those focused on security cooperation, with Australia, Japan, Singapore, Vietnam and the US, as well as its ties with Israel and Saudi Arabia, among others, are helping both to shift its priorities and its capabilities.[14] In 2014, at a conference of senior military officers, Modi even spoke of India becoming an 'anchor' of 'global security', not just a player in its region, however defined (Modi, 2014g).

In parallel to this shift in perceptions of strategic geography, India changed its understanding of its role. Under Singh and then Modi, it embraced the idea, central to being a 'net security provider', of being a 'first responder' in times of crisis or emergency. Its armed forces were understood not simply as defenders of India's territory, citizens and interests, but also as deliverers of humanitarian aid and disaster relief across the South Asian and Indian Ocean regions. In 2004, the Indian air force and navy provided assistance not just to Indian victims of the Boxing Day tsunami on its east coast and on the Andaman and Nicobar islands, but also to the Maldives and Sri Lanka. The military acted in a similar capacity after Cyclone Nargis damaged large parts of Myanmar in May 2008 (Mohan, 2014b, pp. 7–9). And under Modi, they mobilised again in April 2015 to assist in Nepal after an earthquake, deploying its large C-17 Globemaster transport aircraft and many helicopters, as well as allocating more than $1 billion in funds for reconstruction (Chand, 2017).

Beyond South Asia, new understandings of wider roles for India also emerged. Implicit in the moves to integrate the country into East Asian institutions – beginning in the mid-1990s with its inclusion in the ASEAN Regional Forum, and then its membership of the East Asia Summit – was the notion that it could be a kind of counterweight to rising China. It was not conceived as a balancing force, in a military sense, but the hope was that it might soon emerge as political and economic leader with sufficient heft to help ensure that Beijing did not dominate the region (Almonte, 1997). Similar thinking underpinned Washington's engagement of New Delhi during and after the Talbott-Singh talks that followed the nuclear tests. By 2005, the Bush administration had determined that aiding India's aspiration to become a 'major world power' was a key foreign policy objective (quoted in Tellis, 2015, p. 490). The advent of the notion of the 'Indo-Pacific', which emerged in 2012 and evolved thereafter in the strategic thinking of Australia, Japan, and the US, in particular, also shifted understandings of the role that India might play.[15]

Under Modi, these ideas and others shaped New Delhi's self-perceptions. Jaishankar's notion of India as a 'leading power' responded to these expanding conceptions of its role and capacities. Fuelled by 'greater self-confidence' and involving Modi's 'energetic diplomacy', this idea implied an India with a 'willingness to shoulder greater global responsibilities', especially in the areas of humanitarian assistance and disaster relief, peacekeeping, policing the oceans, and 'active participation in important global negotiations' (Jaishankar, 2015b). It also positioned India within the broader context of the so-called rules-based order – a concept that became central to US, Australian and Japanese approaches to securing the Indo-Pacific. From September 2014 onwards, one version or other of 'rules-based order' crept into a series of official statements issued by the Ministry of External Affairs, beginning with the US-India 'vision statement' issued during Modi's visit to Washington (MEA, 2014d).[16]

Modi's SAGAR concept, outlined initially in Mauritius in March 2015, appropriated this idea of a rules-based order and wrapped it into a broader story about India's maritime past, ancient civilization linkages, and the economic ambition of his 'New India'. It built too on the Singh government's efforts, in partnership with other regional powers, including Australia and Indonesia, to revitalise Indian Ocean regional forums, including the Indian Ocean Rim Association for Regional Cooperation (renamed the Indian Ocean Rim Association in 2013) and the Indian Ocean Naval Symposium (created in 2008). And it recognised the importance of seaborne trade for India, as well as the need not just to better engage regional states, but also to upgrade India's port facilities under the so-called *Sagarmala* initiative, begun under Vajpayee in 2003 (Chaturvedy, 2017, pp. 167–71). Yet on the whole, it did not offer anything particularly novel in terms of ideas.

Nor did Modi's keynote address to the Shangri-La Dialogue on 1 June 2018. The event offered the Prime Minister a chance to outline his vision for regional security in detail to an audience of policy makers and analysts from across the Indo-Pacific, but the speech he delivered underwhelmed. It was narrowly focused – aimed at a Southeast Asian audience, in particular, reassuring ASEAN member states of their much-vaunted 'centrality' to regional security architecture. With an eye on China, it emphasised the need to ensure that all states in the region remain '[f]ree and fearless in their choices'. It implied that this might be achieved by ensuring that a 'strong multipolar world order' prevailed. It made reference – uncharacteristically, since Modi generally avoided the term – to the importance of India maintaining 'strategic autonomy'.[17] It warned of the risk of a 'return to the age of great power rivalries' and said that India stood for partnerships and cooperation rather than alliances and containment. But at the same time, it made clear the values for which Modi would like New Delhi to stand, observing that it sought to 'promote a democratic and rules-based international order, in which all nations, small and large, thrive as equal and sovereign' (MEA, 2018c).

The Shangri-La speech was thinly cloaked in by now familiar Hindi and Sanskrit terms, with Modi calling for *samman* (translated in the official transcript as 'respect') *samvad, sahayog* ('cooperation'), *shanti* ('peace'), and *samriddhi*. But the underlying vision of regional order, and India's place within it, did not clearly derive from any Hindu nationalist ideology. Instead, as with the Modi government's understanding of international security and security policy as a whole, it borrowed heavily from its predecessors', and from others' – especially Washington's – approaches.

Movement and inertia

To be a 'net security provider', a 'pole' in a new multipolar order, or a 'leading power' requires resources and a robust strategy about how to use them and how to acquire more of what one needs. Early in the Modi government there were signs that this was understood in New Delhi. Ajit Doval, the National Security Advisor, was quoted as saying that India needed to stop punching below its weight, and devote itself to gathering the resources to compete more effectively (in Pant, 2015, p. 110). But the administration struggled to deliver what was needed. Despite repeated hints that it would shake up the command structure for the armed forces, for example, with the creation of a post of Chief of the Defence Staff, this did not eventuate (Joshi, 2015b). The Modi government toyed also with the notion of creating a series of joint commands, in which a single officer would be put in charge of resources from all three services, either for particular theatres, akin to the Andaman and Nicobar Command created in 2001, or in charge of joint operations in key areas, such as cyber security or special operations.[18] The idea of a national security strategy was floated, and drafts apparently written, but one was never published (Gokhale, 2018). The nuclear doctrine was not amended (Narang, 2018). Changes were made to bureaucratic processes for supporting the armed forces and acquiring equipment, but as Arvind Gupta, the deputy National Security Advisor between 2014 and 2017, observed: the 'efforts so far have been half-hearted and had partial success' (Gupta, 2018, pp. 354–5).

Moreover, the Modi government did not markedly increase India's defence budget – indeed by mid-2018 informed observers were arguing that the military faced a 'severe resource crunch' (Joshi, M., 2018, p. 1). As a proportion of gross domestic product, the defence budget actually declined during Modi's time in office, from just over 2 per cent in 2013–14 down to about 1.5 per cent in 2018–19 (Bedi, 2018). Much-needed modernisation was sluggish as a consequence, despite one senior officer telling a parliamentary committee that more than two thirds of equipment was 'in the vintage category' (Joshi, M., 2018, p. 2). Moreover, the government struggled to take control of the costs of personnel, in particular. By 2018–19, personnel costs accounted for fully 58 per cent of the defence budget, up from 44 per cent in 2010–11 (Joshi, M., 2018, p. 4). Committed to implementing a so-called One Rank, One Pension arrangement for serving and retired members of the armed forces, it was faced with significant additional liabilities. In 2018–19, the pension budget grew to exceed the sum allocated to capital investment in new equipment (Pubby, 2018). This alone made it difficult to acquire and induct the modern rifles, tanks, artillery, aircraft, ships and other materiel badly needed by the armed forces.

What made things worse is that the Modi government fumbled a series of defence procurement deals – above all the acquisition of 126 new multi-role combat aircraft, despite a rigorous process recommending a product (the French Rafale) that met the stated requirements and that the air force wanted. When negotiations faltered over who was to manufacture them and where, Modi resolved, during a visit by French President François Hollande, to order only 36 aircraft made in France, rather than in India (Bitzinger, 2015, pp. 536, 548). More progress was made with the purchase of much-needed helicopters for the air force and navy, and a new artillery system, albeit in a piecemeal fashion. In September 2015, it succeeded in finalising long-awaited deals, held up under the previous government, to buy Chinook and Apache helicopters from the US at a cost of $3.1 billion (Gokhale, 2017b, p. 161). In August 2018, New Delhi authorised the acquisition of 24 MH-60R helicopters – also from the US – for $1.8 billion and opened a process for more than 100 more, but this fell well short of providing the more than 200 such aircraft some think the navy needs (Gady, 2018).[19] The larger deal came, however, under the auspices of the government's 'strategic partnership' programme, rolled out in the 2016 Defence Procurement Procedure, requiring foreign entities to agree to manufacture elements in India and transfer technology to their local partners (MoD, 2018).

Overall, however, the Modi government made heavy weather of modernising the military and reforming India's defence industry. It struggled, for example, to raise foreign direct investment (FDI) in defence manufacturing, despite regulatory changes and political will. In March 2018, it was reported that only about $160,000 of some $54 billion in total inbound FDI had gone to the defence sector between May 2014 and December 2017 (Banerjee, 2018).[20] It struggled too to extract good-quality products from state-owned facilities in a timely way. The much-vaunted Tejas Light Combat Aircraft, for example – a platform that took fully thirty years to develop – was finally inducted into service in 2016. But the company producing it, the state-owned Hindustan Aeronautics Limited (HAL), failed to keep up even with the agreed schedule of producing eight aircraft per year in 2017–18, delivering only six of the 200 or so required (Singh, R., 2018). The Modi government did preside over some successes in other areas, notably in the induction of the nuclear-powered missile submarine, INS Arihant, into the navy, and the launch of a second, INS Arighat, but overall, modernisation was uneven and slow.

Renewing strategic partnerships

Somewhat against the odds, the Modi government was markedly more successful in managing New Delhi's relationship with Washington. The strategic partnership broadened and deepened after 2014, even after Donald J. Trump brought a radically different, capricious, and openly transactional style to the White House in January 2017. That partnership had first emerged in the early 2000s, catalysed by significant pledges of good faith on both sides in the wake of India's nuclear tests, including Bill Clinton's unequivocal condemnation of Pakistan's provocation of the 1999 Kargil War, Vajpayee's famous declaration in September 2000 that the two countries were 'natural allies', and the latter's promise of material support to the US after 9/11 (Bajpai, 2005, p. 3578). The Talbott-Singh dialogue under Clinton helped clear mutual suspicions; counterterrorism cooperation, ideological commitment from the Bush administration, as well as concern about China's future impact on the region, laid the foundations for a partnership. In November 2001, Vajpayee and Bush declared themselves committed to completing 'the process of qualitatively transforming US-India relations in pursuit of their many common goals in Asia and beyond' (White House, 2001).

Two years of intensive negotiation followed, leading to the January 2004 announcement of the 'Next Steps in Strategic Partnership' (NSSP), which effectively swept away thirty years of American sanctions and restrictions on India concerning its access to civilian nuclear technology in exchange for a promise from New Delhi not to use it for its weapons programme (Tellis, 2005, pp. 4–5). With NSSP and the civilian nuclear deal that followed, India secured recognition of its status as a de facto nuclear weapons state, and a pathway to obtaining technology for its space and missile programmes. NSSP also opened the door to a ten-year Defence Framework Agreement, signed in July 2005, which gave New Delhi better access to US military technology. Major arms deals followed for various systems, including an amphibious ship, the former USS Trenton (in 2007), P-8 Orion maritime surveillance aircraft (2009), C-130J Hercules transport aircraft (2009), C-17 Globemaster III heavy lift aircraft (2009) and AH-64 Apache attack helicopters (2010) (Cohen and Dasgupta, 2011, p. 24).

In the late 2000s, however, momentum was lost. The management of ties with some third parties, including India's with Iran and Washington's with Islamabad, caused irritation. The ratification of the US-India Nuclear Deal almost brought down Manmohan Singh's government in July 2008, and drew unwelcome attention from the Indian Left, in particular, to the strategic partnership. The onset of the global financial crisis and the advent of Barack Obama's presidency exacerbated matters. Both sapped Indian confidence in its new partner, as Washington wrestled with recession and attempted a reset in relations with Beijing, raising the spectre of a US-China G2 – a perennial concern in New Delhi. A series of blows to the partnership followed during 2009. In April, India announced it would not buy either of the US aircraft offered to meet its multi-role fighter needs; six months later its parliament passed a Civil Liability for Nuclear Damage Act that made it difficult for US firms (and indeed others) to bid for contracts to build nuclear reactors. In December, India sided with China in Copenhagen to scupper a climate deal brokered by Obama. The following year, New Delhi responded with ambivalence to the Washington's so-called 'Rebalance to Asia' (originally the 'Pivot', involving a refocusing of US strategy towards the Asia–Pacific region).[21] Thereafter, differences emerged elsewhere, notably in the management of the crisis in Libya in 2011, as New Delhi loudly criticised NATO-led military action against Muammar Gaddafi's regime.[22]

Modi's election did not bring about an immediate change in the relationship, beyond creating a sense that a fresh start might be possible

(Pant and Joshi, 2017, p. 137). It took until the September 2014 summit with Obama, however, before this became clear. Apart from the overarching 'vision statement' they articulated, the two sides agreed to renew the Defence Framework Agreement for another decade – something that Singh's government had been reluctant to do. They also promised to 'reinvigorate' their bilateral Political-Military Dialogue, to revive the US-India Defense Technology and Trade Initiative (DTTI) started in 2012 to boost industrial collaboration, and to upgrade the trilateral naval Exercise Malabar.[23] The US also vowed to help India with its new National Defence University (White House, 2014). Soon after, Modi extended a highly symbolic invitation – via Twitter – to Obama to become the first US President to be the guest of honour at India's Republic Day celebrations on 26 January 2015.[24] When the President arrived in New Delhi, he was greeted with a signature 'Modi hug'. The two countries issued a broad 'joint vision statement' during the visit, prefiguring a number of further deals, particularly in the area of defence research and technology. An agreement to form a working group to explore avenues for cooperation on aircraft carrier and jet engine technology soon followed (US Embassy, New Delhi, 2015).

In 2016, the last full year of Obama's presidency, the partnership was broadened even further. When Defense Secretary Ashton Carter went to India in April, the two agreed to establish a Maritime Security Dialogue. In August, Modi's government agreed to finally sign a military logistics agreement over which New Delhi had long procrastinated.[25] Joint military exercises were stepped up: the Indian air force was involved in the Red Flag exercise in Nevada and the Indian navy took part in the annual Rim of the Pacific Exercise. At the end of the year, formal Congressional approval was secured to designate India a 'major defense partner', a *sui generis* category that allows it a similar level and speed of access to US military technology as a treaty ally.[26] When Ashton Carter returned to New Delhi in December, India announced the purchase of M777 howitzers from the US, at a cost of $700 million (Unnithan, 2016a).

The election of Donald J. Trump in November 2016 surprised and worried New Delhi as it did other governments, but did not derail the relationship. Key parts of Trump's platform, especially the promises to rebalance trade and restrict immigration, potentially ran counter to India's interests. Although early phone conversations were reportedly courteous, there was trepidation before Modi's first meeting with the new President in June 2017 and limited expectations about what might be achieved. The joint statement issued afterwards did pledge, however, to deepen defence and security ties (White House, 2017), and the Pentagon announced at the same time that the US was keen to sell the unarmed maritime surveillance variant of the MQ-9 drone to India (Schaus, 2017). Although it took some time for Trump to nominate a new ambassador to India, Washington did step up its defence diplomacy with New Delhi. Defense Secretary James Mattis met both Modi and his new Defence Minister, Nirmala Sitharaman, in September 2017. In public comments, Mattis made a point of referring to what he called the 'strategic convergence' between the US and India, as well as their shared commitment to uphold the 'rules-based order' (Cronk, 2017).

Modi's government proved receptive to these overtures, despite hints that Trump was displeased with India's trade surplus with the US, threats that sanctions might be imposed on New Delhi over a deal to buy a Russian air defence system and over continued trade with Iran, serious misgivings among some Hindu nationalists about US influence, and diplomatic gaffes by the President, which included mocking Modi's marital status.[27] Of these issues, the question of potential sanctions over Russian arms was the most serious and the most revealing about the state of the strategic partnership. New Delhi badly needed to upgrade its air defence systems and it judged that the tried and tested Russian S-400 system fitted its requirements. The Modi government agreed an in-principle deal during the October 2016 BRICS Summit in Goa. In July 2017, however, the US Congress passed the Countering America's Adversaries Through Sanctions Act, targeted at Iran, North Korea and Russia, and it was signed into law by Trump, despite public reservations. In October 2018, India went ahead with the S-400 deal, signing a $5.4 billion contract, but only after tacit assurances were given by Washington that sanction would not be applied, apparently in return for promises to consider buying US fighter aircraft (Singh, S., 2018). Throughout Trump's presidency, indeed, Modi's allies – notably Ram Madhav – have been keen to assure the US of New Delhi's good intentions, especially when it cut deals with Moscow or Beijing (see Press Trust of India, 2018).

This level of sensitivity to each other's concerns is testament to the robustness of the strategic partnership under Modi and to the limits of the push to infuse inherited ideology into Indian foreign policy. Traditionally, Hindu nationalists have oscillated between deep mistrust of the US arising from suspicion of its cultural influence and the American way of life, as Golwalkar and Upadhyaya made clear, and the advocacy of an expedient alliance with Washington to deal with bigger threats, especially Chinese communism. Bharat Karnad, in the process of an extensive exercise in amateur psychoanalysis, has speculated that a personal admiration for the US on Modi's part has overridden these preferences (Karnad, 2018, p. 73, p. 96, and p. 101). Just as plausible, however, is the argument that a combination of sustained and adroit engagement by the US, led by the Pentagon, together with mounting concern about the challenges China poses for India, moved Modi's New Delhi to strengthen ties with Washington, despite a lack of ideological affinity with Obama and despite Trump's manifest capriciousness.[28]

This second factor also helps explain the Modi government's moves to deepen India's strategic partnerships with a number of other states, notably Australia, Singapore, Vietnam, and of course, Japan, as well as to build closer defence and security ties with Indonesia, the Philippines and Taiwan.[29] Moreover, it helps to account for its decision to agree to revive the Quad (in its original incarnation, titled the 'Quadrilateral Security Dialogue') in November 2017, together with the US, Australia and Japan.[30]

Managing China

By the time Modi came to power in 2014 the majority of India's political elite had come to the conclusion that China presented the most serious and pressing potential security challenges to the country. Within the Congress Party and its supporters in academia and think tanks, the notion that China and India had substantial overlapping interests and could work together to realise them, as well as to refashion the architecture of global governance and balance – albeit softly – US power, had lost favour. Concepts like 'Chindia', which rested on optimistic assumptions about the ways in which the two could work together (see Ramesh, 2005), had fallen by the wayside. By 2012, what might be called the 'Establishment' view – expressed, for example, by a series of leading thinkers in an important report from the Centre for Policy Research, *NonAlignment 2.0* – was that China was 'the one power which impinges directly on India's geopolitical space' and that its intentions toward India and the wider region were uncertain. It recommended that New Delhi carry on building partnerships with the US and other regional powers, and improve its military capabilities and cyber defences, to hedge against Beijing acting in ways that directly threatened India's interests and security (Khilnani et al., 2013, p. 13).

Under Singh, that approach had been followed, at least to a point. From the mid-2000s onwards, as we have seen, New Delhi built strategic partnerships with the US, Japan, Vietnam, Singapore and others, and involved itself in the first iteration of the Quad. But as we have seen, during Singh's second term in office, New Delhi became more tentative after 2009, slowing progress in building security and defence ties with Washington, in particular. Partly this was due to doubts about the wisdom of closer engagement with the US seemingly in relative decline. But partly too this was a product of the worry that New Delhi might antagonise Beijing if it was seen to be too close to Washington and its allies. This official anxiety was neatly captured in the non-official *NonAlignment 2.0*: 'If China perceives India as irrevocably committed to an anti-China containment ring', its authors observed, 'it may end up adopting overtly hostile and negative policies towards India, rather than making an effort to keep India on a more independent path' (Khilnani et al., 2013, p. 14).

From the start, it was clear that the Modi government believed that this kind of thinking was too timid.[31] The new Prime Minister sought to make clear at the outset that India's foreign and security policy choices would not be circumscribed by Beijing or by worries that it might be upset by this or that action. This was the message sent by his invitations to the representatives of Taiwan and the Tibetan government-in-exile to his inauguration. Another – that India was concerned about China's intentions and would act, alone and in conjunction with others, if its interests were threatened – was conveyed during Modi's visit to Japan in August 2014, when he warned those states that believed in what he called 'expansionist policies' that it would better to return to 'the path of development' (quoted in Gokhale, 2017a, p. 120). Together, the aim was the make clear that New Delhi had options to complicate China's calculations and that it was concerned about its behaviour. None of this, however, precluded good relations – provided both sides understood where they stood and Beijing was attentive to New Delhi's interests.

Having dispatched these messages, Modi reached out to Xi Jinping in an effort to reset relations, establish a personal rapport with the Chinese leader with two bilateral summits and a number of meetings at mini-laterals like the BRICS Summit, and attract inward investment from the People's Republic. China's responses were not wholly positive, however. Xi visit to Gujarat in mid-September 2014 was a lavish production, but produced less in the way of promised investment than hoped; stories of a commitment of up to $100 billion circulated prior to the meeting were not borne out by what was actually put on the table, which was about $20 billion. India's burgeoning trade deficit with China was discussed, but little progress was made on addressing its causes. Most worrying of all, a major incursion of about a thousand PLA troops across the Line of Actual Control (LAC) occurred at the same time as the summit,[32] leading Modi to depart from past diplomatic practice and publicly criticise the action while standing alongside Xi in a carefully controlled press conference (Bajpai, 2017, p. 81).

This set the tone for Sino-Indian relations under Modi, as he tried to 'stand up' to Beijing (Gokhale, 2017a, pp. 111–40). On the LAC and elsewhere, China pushed and probed. It stepped up its support for Pakistan, not least with the China–Pakistan Economic Corridor (CPEC), announced in April 2015 during Xi's visit to Islamabad. It blocked a series of New Delhi's moves in international forums, including the effort to have India become a member of the Nuclear Suppliers' Group (NSG) and to have Pakistani-based alleged terrorists listed as such by the UN. The most serious crisis in bilateral relations occurred, however, in Bhutan, over eight weeks in June, July and August 2017, when the Indian army confronted PLA units building a road through territory contested by Bhutan, to which New Delhi has treaty obligations, and China. The standoff triggered a wave of criticism from the Chinese foreign and defence ministries on New Delhi's behaviour, as well as threats of dire punishment to be inflicted on India, and a torrent of abuse from Chinese state media outlets.[33]

The Modi government's approach to the Doklam crisis – named after the contested area of Bhutan in which the standoff occurred – fitted the general pattern established early, in mid- to late 2014 (see especially Bajpai, 2017). It publicly criticised China's conduct, as it perceived it. New Delhi showed itself willing – at least for a period – to tolerate the risk of conflict and to withstand Beijing's implicit and explicit threats. It reinforced the troops on the ground and deployed other significant military assets closer to the border or to positions from which they could strike the PLA. But it also continued to try to cut some kind of deal with China to reduce tensions and establish a modus vivendi that implied tacit respect, on Beijing's part, of India's status, concerns and interests (Small, 2018). To that end, Modi travelled to Wuhan to meet Xi for a so-called informal summit in late April 2018 to 'review', according to the opaque joint statement issued after the meeting, 'developments in India-China relations from the strategic and long-term perspective' (MEA, 2018d). In effect, the two sides agreed to temporarily suspend behaviour that the other might consider problematic, as Modi entered the long campaign for re-election in 2019 and Xi tried to manage pressure from Trump's Washington over trade and security issues.

In the background, throughout Modi's government, New Delhi sought also to reinforce India's defences against China and bolster deterrent capabilities. It pressed ahead with long-range missile programmes, including the development of the nuclear-capable Agni-V, first tested in 2012, which has the range to strike Beijing, as well as the nuclear missile submarines. It pushed on with modernising the navy to give it enhanced capabilities to deal with Chinese submarines, which began to venture into the Indian Ocean in late December 2013. In other areas, however, it struggled. Most obviously, it failed to find the funds to raise a Mountain Strike Corps, promised in 2013 by the Singh government (Dutta, 2018). This led to accusations that the Modi government lacked the will and strength, as well as a coherent strategy, to manage Chinese pressure (Karnad, 2018, p. 173).

Persuading and punishing Pakistan

Modi's track record of dealing with the various security challenges emanating from Pakistan was similarly mixed. Immediately prior to the election, he vowed to follow in Vajpayee's footsteps, promoting economic development in Kashmir to address local disquiet and avert unrest, as well as dialogue with Pakistan (Tremblay and Kapur, 2017, pp. 190–5). Early on, he unexpectedly attempted diplomacy, inviting Nawaz Sharif to New Delhi for the swearing in, and making a show of shaking the Pakistani Prime Minister's hand. But little progress followed. A meeting between Kashmiri separatists (the *Hurriyat*) and the Pakistani High Commissioner to India prompted the Modi government to call off talks between foreign secretaries Sujatha Singh and Aizaz Ahmad Chaudhry, due to take place in August 2014. Thereafter, the approach hardened for a time, as India tried to bring international pressure to bear on Pakistan over its alleged sponsorship of terrorism. That threat featured prominently in Modi's first address to the UN General Assembly in late September 2014 (Modi, 2014b), which heralded a new push for a Comprehensive Convention on International Terrorism, first proposed by India almost twenty years earlier (Sasikumar, 2010). In early 2015, however, India signalled that it was ready once more to talk, and at the SCO Summit in July the two sides agreed to a meeting of National Security Advisors later in the year (Bajpai, 2017, p. 74). Two cross-border terrorist attacks swiftly followed, as did a dispute over including Kashmir in the talks, and the meeting was cancelled.

This 'cooperation–defection cycle', as Bajpai (2017, p. 72) calls it, continued until September 2016. Modi reached out to Sharif personally in late December 2015, making an impromptu visit to Lahore to wish the latter happy birthday; another foreign secretaries' meeting was arranged, but a terrorist attack at Pathankot in Punjab on 2 January 2016 put paid to that initiative.[34] Instead, the Modi government stepped up its efforts to isolate Pakistan on terrorism, at the UN and elsewhere. It succeeded in getting a number of Middle Eastern states, including Saudi Arabia and the United Arab Emirates, which both have deep ties to Islamabad, to include condemnations of support for terrorism in joint statements (Bajpai, 2017, pp. 76–9). A further attack, this time at Uri in Kashmir, on 18 September

2016, claimed the lives of 19 members of the Indian security forces and four terrorists, and put paid to any further diplomacy. Eleven days later, Indian commandos conducted a raid – framed by New Delhi as 'surgical strikes' – across the Line of Control into Pakistani-controlled Kashmir and destroyed a series of camps, killing an unknown number of people.[35] In parallel, New Delhi denounced Islamabad's alleged support for terrorism and treatment of minorities to the UN Human Rights Council (Press Trust of India, 2016).

This impasse persisted until the end of Modi's term. The flaring of serious unrest in Kashmir in 2016 after the killing by security forces of a 22-year-old local militant belonging to the Hizbul Mujahideen group, Burhan Wani, did not help matters, and nor did the heavy-handedness of New Delhi's response. Rioting led to dozens of deaths and hundreds of injuries, some from the use of 'pellet' guns by the police and armed forces. In turn, this attracted – for New Delhi – the unwelcome attention of international organisations and human rights advocates, and undermined India's attempts to contrast its behaviour with Pakistan's, despite widespread acknowledgement of Islamabad's support for militancy and terrorism within Jammu and Kashmir (see especially Office of the United Nations High Commissioner for Human Rights, 2018).

As with China, then, the Modi government attempted to change New Delhi's approach to Pakistan, but with very mixed results. Wittingly or not, Islamabad stymied, as we have seen in the previous chapter, its attempts to use SAARC as a means of realising a more integrated region, leading to a resort to sub-regional mechanisms. With CPEC, Islamabad also brought Chinese economic muscle to bear in a different South Asian theatre. Continued relationships with militant groups allowed Modi to try to isolate Pakistan both rhetorically – not least with the memorable line that 'While India exports software, Pakistan exports terrorism' (quoted in Tremblay and Kapur, 2017, p. 185) – and diplomatically, but success here was only partial. While New Delhi did succeed in ensuring that interlocutors in South Asia and the Middle East spoke out against terrorism, the practical effect of these statements was debatable. Equally, the deterrent effect (if any) of the September 2016 and February 2019 strikes were unclear, despite the political capital the Modi government sought to extract from them.[36]

Conclusion

To be sure, the 2016 surgical strikes and the 2019 air strikes resonated positively with Modi's Hindu nationalist constituency and, to a considerable extent, with the broader community. The first action was much praised by the RSS and others: Mohan Bhagwat declared that '[w]hat we were waiting for in our hearts has happened' (Ramachandran, 2016), deemed the attack as a 'firm and fitting reply' (Bhagwat, 2016). Modi's government extracted as much political capital as it could from the Uri strikes, holding a three-day celebration, dubbed *Parakram Parv*, to commemorate 'Surgical Strike Day', in 2018, apparently to the irritation of some in the armed forces (Sagar, P. R., 2018). They made much of a blockbuster movie dramatizing the action, released just before the Pulwama bombing in the run-up to the election in 2019. The air strikes that followed reinforced this narrative about the Modi government's tough stance towards both terrorism and Pakistan.

This drumbeat did not, however, dispel the perception among critics that in its pursuit of *suraksha*, as with *samriddhi*, it had struggled to establish a clear plan linking ends to means, and to realise its objectives.[37] No grand strategy was unveiled, still less one that clearly linked aspirations to a Hindu nationalist agenda (Sridharan, 2017, p. 60), notwithstanding the intrinsic weaknesses and apparent contradictions of Hindu nationalist thinking in this area. Instead, the Modi government changed some of the language of policy, introducing ideas like becoming a 'leading power' and SAGAR, and modified some diplomatic settings, but not in ways that suggest the emergence of a markedly new, fully developed approach, underpinned by a set of clearly articulated principles. It doubled down on the strategic partnership with the US, took a more robust line with China, at least until the Doklam standoff, and oscillated between outreach and punishment with Pakistan. In the background, however, it struggled to modernise the military and reform the defence industries. In both cases, there was a clear lack of follow-through, beyond an initial spate of activity, such as the clearing of a substantial inherited backlog of acquisitions (Gokhale, 2017a, p. 161), and grand declarations of intent.

It is tempting to suggest that the mixed record of the Modi government on national security was a function of its ideology – of its underlying ambivalence in Hindu nationalist thought about the acquisition and use of military power. Some have indeed made a similar argument (see especially Karnad, 2018), and Modi's major speeches on foreign and security policy – such as those he gave at Raisina in 2017 and the Shangri La Dialogue a year and a half later – invite that conclusion. Those addresses, aimed principally at international audiences, emphasised globalisation and connectivity, development and cultural diffusion, the need for 'inclusive' security architecture and dialogue grounded in respect (MEA, 2017a; MEA, 2018c). But it is clear too that the Modi government struggled with sheer scale of the challenge of overhauling the institutions that needed reform, prioritised other areas of both domestic and foreign policy, and lacked the resources necessary to bring about the change required. It invested surprisingly little, with the defence budget declining to 1.5% of GDP in the government's 2019-20 budget, failed to bring about major reforms, such as appointing a Chief of the Defence Staff, and did not succeed in reforming a defence industry crying out for change. In so doing, it arguably left India exposed to both Chinese and Pakistani pressure, and to criticism from sceptical voices within putative partner states across the Indo-Pacific, keen to discount New Delhi's capacity to be the 'net security provider' it promised to be.

8

Conclusion

Narendra Modi need not have invested so heavily in foreign policy after coming to power in 2014, in terms of either time spent on foreign visits and summits or on trying to recast it into a different – broadly Hindu nationalist – idiom. His government faced considerable domestic challenges and the approach to international relations Modi had inherited from his predecessor – while perhaps not optimal – was at least serviceable. The fact that Modi devoted scarce resources to trying to reinvent Indian foreign policy demands some explanation.[1]

That this activity did not result in major shifts in Indian strategy makes his attempt at reinventing foreign policy even more puzzling. Modi might have had a 'transformative agenda' and even a 'fluid, dynamic multilevel alignment cognitive script', as sympathetic analysts have suggested (Tremblay and Kapur, 2017, pp. vii, viii), but it is not clear that India's basic approach to managing key relationships and challenges changed. I have argued here – as others have done elsewhere – that the 'fundamentals', as Rajesh Basrur calls them (2017), were not modified. India continued to prioritise domestic economic development. New Delhi drew closer to the US, as it has since the early 2000s, and hedged between engagement and pushback in the face of China's growing power. It deepened strategic partnerships with states and slowly augmented its engagement with regional institutions. It continued to pursue soft power and status, while struggling to pursue hard power and leverage. To be sure, Modi showed more muscularity toward Pakistan, in particular, but his government was unable to translate tactical wins, such as they were, into lasting gains.

So why did Modi try to reinvent Indian foreign policy and why did this project fall short of its objectives of making India 'a force for peace, a factor for stability and an engine for regional and global prosperity' (MEA, 2017a)? The answers to these questions are, I argue, interlinked. The reinvention was driven by a mix of ideological conviction and electoral calculation – calculation that, in the event, helped deliver electoral dividends, especially in 2019. But because of inherent weaknesses in the ideology and the domestic political focus of the effort, as well as in those parts of the Indian state charged with managing Indian foreign policy, it did not succeed in bringing about the transformation that it promised.

In part, Modi and his allies pursued their reinvention because some of them, at least, believe that Hindu nationalist political thought offers a better foundation for policy making at home and abroad than the Nehruvian thinking that shaped the original invention of India. In part too, it is clear that Modi and his allies were convinced that recasting Indian foreign policy in Hindu nationalist language, and energising and personalising Indian diplomacy, would prove electorally advantageous. They perceived that reinventing foreign policy allowed Modi to portray himself, and be portrayed, by key supporters like Bhagwat and Madhav, as a 'transformational leader' on the par even with Nehru, equipped with his own distinctive philosophy of politics and foreign affairs (Chhibber and Verma, 2018, p. 139).[2] It aimed – quite successfully – at consolidating the idea of Modi as the embodiment of resurgent national pride.[3]

Reinventing foreign policy delivered less, however, in terms of building India's power and influence. Conventionally, scholars of Indian foreign policy assume that the dominant position occupied by prime ministers in the policy-making and implementation processes makes it relatively straightforward for those in the post to realise at least some of their ambitions. The 'personality factor', as Jayantanuja Bandyopadhyaya called it (1991, pp. 283–344), also often looms large in explanations of decisions and directions, especially when prime ministers are strong-willed and in advantageous political positions. In Modi's case, however, we see evidence to suggest that despite his ideological equipment, his energy and his centralisation of control over the government, he did not succeed in achieving all that he said he wanted to achieve, in terms of reinventing the foundations, objectives and methods of Indian foreign policy, during his first term in office.

That failure, I argue, is suggestive of the limitations of Hindu nationalist political thought, as well as of the character of his government, and of the broader lack of capacity in the institutions of foreign and security policy making in contemporary India. It points to inherent problems with using Hindu nationalist ideas – with Integral Humanism and associated approaches – as a foundation for policy. It also points to weaknesses in the Modi style of government – weaknesses that have been observed elsewhere, concerning a lack of process and consultation in decision making and a lack of focus on implementation. And it highlights deeper problems within the Indian state that Modi will have to confront in his second term, if he wants to realise his reinvention.

Foreign policy and domestic politics

The energy that Modi displayed in his personal diplomacy in the early months of his government, his embrace of a strategic partnership with the US, his noticeably more robust management of China, and his apparent grasp of the need rapidly to improve connectivity and economic integration in South Asia together gave rise to the impression that his government would pursue a more pragmatic, less ideological foreign policy. If there was such a thing as a 'Modi doctrine', many analysts – including the current author – concluded in 2014 and 2015, it lay in this apparent shift towards a kind of realism, coupled with a focus on efficient and effective implementation.[4]

In this book, I have suggested that this conclusion was hasty. The Modi government's foreign policy was, I have shown, more infused with Hindu nationalist ideology than its initial behaviour indicated. Its prioritisation of the pursuit of soft power, and the manner in which it pursued it, reflected deeply held views on the Hindu Right about the role that India is destined to play as a world guru, bringing peace and enlightenment through its ancient wisdom. Its trade and investment policies, and indeed its broader economic strategy, aligned with long-standing Hindu nationalist preferences and was shaped by deep-seated concerns about the pernicious influences on Indian society and culture that greater liberalisation and openness might bring. Even its security policies, I have suggested, betrayed some of the ambivalence inherent in Hindu nationalist ideology about the pursuit and use of hard power, as well as better-known shortcomings in state capacity. As Manjari Chatterjee Miller and Kate Sullivan de Estrada have rightly argued (2017, p. 29), the Modi government's policies were clearly 'constrained by both ideology and institutionalised ideas', for all its pragmatism in some areas of implementation.

At the same time, Modi himself, and his allies, were also enabled by the reinventing of Indian foreign policy in a Hindu nationalist idiom and conceptual language. Casting foreign policy in terms of *samman*, *samvad*, *sahayog*, *shanti*, and *samriddhi*, and using Hindi and Sanskrit words unfamiliar to most foreigners to do it, as Modi did in his speech to the Shangri La Dialogue (MEA, 2018c), was part and parcel of a broader effort to use foreign policy and prime ministerial diplomacy to strengthen his government's appeal to Indian voters at home and BJP supporters overseas.

The principal target of this messaging was domestic, not international. Indeed, if there is one major difference between the Modi government and its immediate predecessor, it lay in its appreciation of the potential value of foreign policy for domestic electoral politics. Self-consciously and deliberately, it politicised foreign policy – albeit not for the first time in Indian politics. Like Jawaharlal Nehru, Indira Gandhi, and Atal Bihari Vajpayee, Modi sought to generate an image of himself as a respected player on the world stage as a means of bolstering his standing in the eyes of Indian voters and potential donors within and outside the country. He aimed to create the impression that if he, as India's representative, was lauded and listened to by world leaders, then India itself must also stand tall, and that ordinary Indians should take pride in this achievement.

The restoration of *samman* – pride and dignity – was crucial to this effort. The Bharatiya Janata Party's (BJP) made this clear from the outside. 'Our national ambition', declared its 2015 resolution on foreign policy, 'is Bharat's rise as a strong and *respected* world power' (my italics). During the 'lost decade' of the previous Congress-led government, it observed, 'New Delhi had punched substantively below its weight in pushing through its foreign policy objectives, while often appeared side-lined in the international arena'. Its foreign policy 'tended to weigh the nation down', instead of being a source of pride and an instrument for realising India's development and destiny (BJP, 2015). The BJP's promise – and Modi's, in particular – to voters was that it would restore India to its rightful standing, for once that was achieved, they implied, strategic partners and investors would flock to the country, and rivals would accommodate its interests. But above all, it would allow Indians to hold their heads high once more – and continue to elect a leader and a government that gave them that chance.

Modi's frenetic globetrotting, summitry and photo opportunities with world leaders, tech entrepreneurs and Hollywood actors were designed for this purpose. This high-profile personal diplomacy, sometimes interpreted as egotistical self-indulgence,[5] allowed Modi to project a new version of himself, as a statesperson rather than a mere politician, lately a Chief Minister, by definition provincial, without great experience of international affairs. And it provided the opportunity for him to claim that his actions had decisively shifted foreign perceptions of India. 'In this era of global economy', Modi declared in his Independence Day speech in August 2018, 'the entire world is looking at every development in India – big or small, with deep interest and hope and expectations':

> There was a time when the world used to comment about red
> tape in India but now they talk about Red Carpet. We have

reached the 100th spot in Ease of Doing Business ranking. Today, the entire world is looking at this achievement with pride. There was a time when the world perceived India as a country with 'policy paralysis' and 'delayed reforms'. Old newspaper clippings confirm this view. However, today the world opinion about India has changed and they talk about our focus on reform, perform and transform. ... There was a time when the world counted India among the 'fragile five'. They were concerned that India was pulling down the world economy but now their tone has changed as India has become a multi-trillion dollar investment destination. (Modi, 2018c)

In other areas too, Modi claimed, India was now perceived very differently. 'India's stature at International fora has risen greatly', he argued, and 'India is playing a crucial role in shaping up the discourse', he insisted, 'and providing leadership to these organizations'. Moreover, he claimed, 'India offers a ray of hope for those who are concerned with environmental issues and global warming'. Above all:

Today, every country of the world is keen to welcome any Indian stepping on its soil. A new consciousness is visible in their eyes, when they look at an Indian. The strength of the Indian passport has multiplied manifold. This has instilled a new self-confidence, fresh energy and a resolve in every Indian to move ahead with new hope. (Modi, 2018c)

Whether or not these claims could be substantiated, they spoke directly to key motivations of Modi's reinvention of foreign policy, to the desires to restore *samman* to Indians, and for the Prime Minister and the BJP more broadly to be seen as its deliverers. This became clear during the 2019 election campaign. A year out from the poll, the Modi government looked to be facing significant losses, with some speculating – not unreasonably – that it might lose office altogether, or perhaps limp on with the support of additional coalition partners (Vaishnav, 2018). The state of the economy, battered by demonetisation in late 2016, suffering from low prices for agricultural goods, failing to generate new jobs, experiencing little boost in industrial output from 'Make in India', and facing a potential banking crisis, was not good (Soz, 2019, pp. 131–206). The Congress Party, led by Rahul Gandhi, was making some inroads, highlighting the apparent disparity between the *acche din* Modi had promised in 2014 and what his government had delivered, and accusing the Prime Minister of impropriety as well as incompetence, not least over the purchase of

French Rafale fighter aircraft. *India Today*'s 'Mood of the Nation' poll, published in August 2018, found Gandhi's personal popularity growing and the Modi government's chances of returning to power with a majority diminishing (Virk, 2018).

The Modi government's prospects picked up in early 2019, initially due to a characteristically strong campaign from the Prime Minister himself. But it was the Pulwama terrorist attack on 14 February, and the Modi's decision to respond with air strikes across the Line of Control in Kashmir, and into Pakistan proper, that provided his campaign with the fillip it needed. Thereafter he and his allies shifted the contest into one about who could best be trusted to manage India's national security. Rebranding themselves as *chowkidars* ('watchmen'), the BJP argued that the opposition parties were too weak effectively to address terrorism and implied that Modi was the one leader capable of standing up to the various threats facing the country, from both within and outside its borders.[6] In stark contrast to 2014, the party's manifesto opened with a discussion of national security policy rather than economic or social issues (BJP, 2019b). As much political capital as could be garnered was squeezed out of the retaliatory air strikes, and the surprise anti-satellite missile test that followed a few weeks later, with the Prime Minister on one occasion even calling on first-time voters to dedicate their ballot to Balakot, the alleged location of the JeM camp bombed by the Indian Air Force (Press Trust of India, 2019). In another speech, Yogi Adityanath, the controversial Hindu nationalist Uttar Pradesh Chief Minister went even further – falling foul of Electoral Commission rules in the process – in referring to the armed forces as 'Modi's army' (*Modi ki Sena*) (Bhaumik, 2019).

Using foreign and security policy in this way, for domestic political purposes, was not of course unprecedented. Nehru used it to sustain his image as a statesman; Indira Gandhi played on fears of US interference in India to consolidate her power. As Kanti Bajpai has argued, one element in the decision-making process that led to the Vajpayee government's nuclear tests in May 1998, just weeks after coming to power, was the desire to address the perception among Indian voters that the then-Prime Minister was a 'weak, rather ineffectual leader' (Bajpai, 2009, p. 40).[7] Political survival was a consideration in the determination to test, alongside a number of others, including the belief that nuclear weapons would deliver 'power and status' to India (Bajpai, 2009, p. 38). Ordering the tests and following the order with a voluntary moratorium on further iterations would, Vajpayee calculated, 'project him as a strong, nationalist, and rational leader' – all at the same time (Bajpai, 2005, p. 46). In the event, this tactic worked: Vajpayee was seen in a new light, as a 'national hero' but also as a kind of Nehruvian philosopher-king (Bajpai, 2005, p. 52).

In 2014, of course, Modi did not need to create an impression of strength – he was already well known, and indeed feared and in some cases reviled, as a hardliner and a firebrand. Instead, he needed to soften his image abroad and reconfigure it at home. Just as he did in the second half of his tenure as Chief Minister of Gujarat, when he took pains to recast himself as an inclusive 'development man' (*vikas purush*) rather than a divisive communalist in the aftermath of 2002, after he became Prime Minister, he set about transforming his image once more. This time Modi sought to become an embodiment of India's values and inherited wisdom for foreign audiences, and a statesperson, elevated above the normal political fray, for domestic ones (Sen, 2016). Promoting yoga and sharing stages with celebrities like Hugh Jackman were elements in the former strategy, as well as advocating concepts like *vasudhaiva kutumbakam* and environmental consciousness. Summits and bear hugs for world leaders – walking the world stage, shoulder-to-shoulder with his foreign peers – were elements of the latter.

There continues to be little concrete evidence to suggest that Indian voters, like voters in other democracies, choose their representatives purely or even predominantly on the basis of foreign policies or international issues.[8] Yet it is equally clear, not least from the 2019 election campaign, that Modi and his allies believed that if the public perceived that foreign policy was in good hands, and that India was respected in the world, these impressions would rebound to their advantage. Certainly, they were quick to modify behaviour when public opinion about Modi's travels turned sceptical in the second half of 2015, and threatened to rebound. Thereafter, the pace of his globetrotting slowed (Gupta, 2015). On the whole, the calculation that foreign policy could be used as a means of burnishing Modi's appeal to voters appears to have been well founded, if opinion polls are to be believed. In February 2015, an *India Today* poll found that respondents ranked 'improving India's international image' as the Prime Minister's biggest achievement during his first year in office (Mail Today Bureau, 2015). In August 2016, a survey for the same outlet reported that 57 per cent of those polled believed that India's foreign relations had fared better under Modi's government. Indeed, as *India Today* reported the results, its 'primary claim to success appears to be the robust foreign policy espoused by the prime minister' (Unnithan, 2016b). Even more impressive were the results of a *Times of India* poll in May 2018, which found that almost 63 per cent of respondents rated Modi's foreign policy as 'very good', 17 per cent as 'good', and only about 16 per cent as 'poor' (*Times of India*, 2018). Exactly how these public perceptions translated into electoral outcomes is not clear. But they suggest that Modi's attempted reinvention of foreign policy did succeed as intended in one area, at least: in shaping positive perceptions of the Prime Minister in domestic public opinion and in creating the impression that the nation was well represented, internationally, on his watch.

Ideological and institutional weaknesses

There are, of course, no clear metrics for measuring foreign policy success. At the same time, however, it is hard to argue that Modi's attempt to reinvent India's international relations achieved all or even most of its objectives. Although several sympathetic and ingenious analysts have tried to tease out a 'Modi doctrine', his government did not overtly articulate any kind of national strategy, still less one that clearly relates ends and means to the Hindu nationalist ideology it claims as inspiration.[9] It issued no foreign or security policy White Papers, or anything resembling such a document.[10] What passed for strategic thinking in Modi's statements, as Karnad (2018, p. 54) and others suggest, was generally vague and unhelpful. And there is evidence that as they have faced different challenges, Modi and his core team picked and chose from a range of ideas to be found within the *Hindutva* tradition, in line with long-established BJP practices. Attempts from within the BJP to articulate a coherent, integrated vision for foreign policy grounded in elements of Hindu nationalist thinking – such as Madhav's *Panchamrit* – were not taken up in clear and consistent ways by Modi or his senior ministers. There are family resemblances, at best, to Madhav's ideas and to those expressed in, say, Modi's Shangri La address in June 2018, but even there, terminology and concepts have been chopped and changed, and they are not consistent with other significant statements (for example, MEA, 2017a).

What Modi's attempted reinvention has shown is that replacing inherited, mostly Nehruvian, language and concepts of foreign policy with one drawn from Hindu nationalist political thought is extremely challenging, if not simply impossible, because of its inherent flaws. Confined as it is to a relatively small number of key texts – Savarkar's *Hindutva*, Golwalkar's *Bunch of Thoughts*, and Upadhyaya's *Integral Humanism* above all – and to texts that range very widely across topics, the tradition lacks specific guidance on a swathe of political issues. In part, as we have seen, this is due to its flat rejection of modern politics as a practice – of its institutions, rules and norms – in preference for a supposedly apolitical and autochthonous kind of social order governed in some way by *dharma rajya* and Integral Humanism. The tradition has also lacked the kind of intellectuals that conventionally translate political philosophies into policies, and although the BJP and Rashtriya Swayamsevak Sangh have taken steps to create think tanks like the Syama Prasad Mookerjee Research Foundation or the India Foundation, the output frequently relies on outside rather than homegrown talent.[11] As a consequence, the Hindu Right – including Modi's BJP – remained (and remains) intellectually 'malnourished', as Sagar (2018) memorably put it, without a steady diet of new policy ideas faithful to the Hindu nationalist tradition.

This problem was arguably compounded in the Modi government by its highly centralised – even personalised – nature. The Prime Minister took the lead in all of the major foreign and security policy decisions: in the settlement of India's border with Bangladesh in May 2015, for example, which involved a reversal of his party's earlier opposition to a deal; in the agreement to buy only 36 Rafale aircraft from France in January 2016; in the use of a 'surgical strike' to punish Pakistan for its alleged sponsorship of terrorists and militants in September 2016; in the signing of a secure military communications agreement with the US in September 2018; and in the air strikes of February 2019 and the controversial anti-satellite missile test a month later. It is widely claimed that Modi and the Prime Minister's Office side-lined and downgraded both the External Affairs Minister and the Ministry of External Affairs (MEA), refocusing their work on consular issues and economic diplomacy.[12] It is suggested that the MEA was not as involved as it might have been in the preparation of Modi's foreign visits or the work needed afterwards to ensure that promises are met (Tharoor, 2018, pp. 396–7). We have seen too how Modi used unofficial channels for quasi-diplomatic missions and dialogues, leaning on individuals like Madhav or non-governmental institutions like the Vivekananda International Foundation or even the Art of Living Foundation.

The centralisation of decision-making was consistent with Modi's practice in Gujarat, but it came at a cost. Rendering ministers into subordinates and ciphers, tasking with carrying out instructions rather than engaging in policy making, as some have suggested he did, deprived him of potentially useful advice and alternative perspectives (Manor, 2015, pp. 738–9). That tendency, combined with a desire to take credit for government successes, also disincentivised timely and effective implementation of policies. Relying on a small coterie of officials rather than reaching out to a wider group of experts and analysts, as some leaders do, and as Modi manifestly did not, generated a similar problem (Karnad, 2018, pp. 26–7). It is striking, indeed, that his government made little use even of official bodies like the National Security Advisory Board (NSAB), which reports to the National Security Council, let alone non-governmental organisations. The NSAB reportedly met only once during Modi's first year in office, and its membership, which came up for renewal in January 2015, was then allowed to lapse. When it was eventually reconstituted, in July 2018, it had only four members, including three former senior officials, and only one from outside government (Kartha, 2018).[13]

In part, of course, Modi's centralisation of power was a function of his reservations – some quite reasonable – about the skills and commitment of both his fellow ministers and the New Delhi bureaucracy and about their willingness to realise his agenda. And there is no question that India's lack of 'state capacity' (Ganguly and Thompson, 2017) affected his ability to see through a reinvention of foreign policy. The government's seeming inability to bring about substantive change in the country's defence industry was a function of poorly crafted policies and a lack of clear incentives for change, especially in the state-owned enterprises that dominate the sector. Its inability to deliver quickly and effectively on promised connectivity projects linking underdeveloped parts of India to neighbouring states was another example of the challenges the government faced in mobilising resources to realise policy objectives.

Of course, Modi's attempt to reinvent Indian foreign policy was not helped by the international circumstances in which his government found itself. An increasingly confident and nationalistic China, keen to extend its influence not imply into Southeast and Central Asia, but also into South Asia and the Indian Ocean, and further afield into the Middle East and Africa, loomed increasingly large after Modi came to office in 2014. Its new assertiveness made bilateral relations more difficult to manage and forced New Delhi into a series of reactive or pre-emptive moves, especially in the immediate region, to try to retain its own sway and interests. The advent of the Trump era in Washington imposed additional pressure, especially on the diaspora and trade, even if it also opened up more possibilities for arms acquisitions and security cooperation, and damped down criticism of New Delhi's handling of human rights and religious freedoms. The continued tussles between civilian and military authorities, in Pakistan, as well as between traditionalist and Islamist elements, made dealing with Islamabad challenging and frequently unrewarding. And in the background, economic instability, technological change and fluctuating oil prices meant that it was hard to bring in the investment the government wanted in the areas they desired, provide much-needed jobs, and sustain higher rates of growth.

But all this said, important aspects of Modi's attempted reinvention of foreign policy were undermined not by external pressures, but by internal contradictions. The push to realise India's destiny as a world guru and to convince others of the fundamental truth of *vasudhaiva kutumbakam* sat very uneasily with the upsurge in communal violence many argue occurred on Modi's watch, and which he was allegedly slow to condemn or to address. Attacks on Muslim and Dalit butchers, pushes to 'reconvert' Muslims and Christians back to Hinduism under the banner of *ghar wapsi* ('homecoming'), the beatings of young men for supposedly engaging in a 'love jihad' to turn young Hindu girls to Islam, and the burnings of Christian churches undercut, in the eyes of many, messages about religious tolerance and harmonious coexistence.[14] The re-emergence of the movement to built a Ram temple at Ayodhya, led by the Vishva Hindu Parishad and hard-line Hindu chauvinist politicians like the Yogi Adityanath, the Uttar Pradesh Chief Minister, which gathered pace in the latter half of 2018, had similar effects (BBC, 2018).[15] And so too did the Modi government's attempts to control criticism and dissent, especially by foreign non-governmental organisations, through the courts and the use of the Intelligence Bureau, and its efforts to extend its ideological influence through the education system, including the universities (Chacko, 2018).

These acts of omission and commission could not but affect any project to reinvent Indian foreign policy that lent so heavily on building and using soft power, provided, of course, that project was primarily aimed at the outside world. But as I have argued, this was not Modi's only, or even principal, purpose. His strenuous efforts, his far-flung trips, and his keenness to be seen in the company of world leaders was directed more at Indians, at home and abroad, as it was at anyone else – at restoring Indian pride and Indian confidence, and at entrenching Modi himself and the BJP as the symbols of the 'New India' they promised.

Notes

Preface

[1] The notion of an 'idea of India' comes, of course, from Sunil Khilnani's (2012) well-known book, *The Idea of India*, first published in 1997 to coincide with the 50th anniversary of independence.

[2] On the track record of the Vajpayee governments in general, see Blom Hansen and Jaffrelot, 2001; and Adeney and Sáez, 2005; and on the ideological disputes more broadly, see Chhibber and Verma, 2018. On its pragmatic foreign and security policy, see Ogden, 2014.

[3] 'Transformation' was, indeed, a key theme of one of Modi's most important foreign policy speeches, given to the Raisina Dialogue in New Delhi in January 2017 (MEA, 2017a).

Chapter 1

[1] All monetary conversions are in US$.

[2] The Lok Sabha has 543 seats for elected members and a further two seats reserved for the Anglo-Indian community, filled by nomination by the President of India.

[3] For analysis of the election – the campaign and the results – see Chacko and Mayer, 2014; Sridharan, 2014; Heath, 2015; Jaffrelot 2015a; Sardesai, 2015; Torri, 2015; Chhibber and Verma, 2018.

[4] For a detailed account of these events, see Mitta, 2014.

[5] On corruption and politics in India, as well as the links between politicians and organised crime, see Joseph, 2016; and Vaishnav, 2017.

[6] For a brief but insightful contemporary assessment of the manifesto, see Mohan, 2015a, pp. 37–9).

[7] See, for useful discussions, Panda, 2013; and Madan, 2014.

[8] Grare (2014) provides a perceptive contemporary assessment of Modi's initial impact on India-Pakistan relations.

[9] For a useful set of essays exploring 'neighbourhood first', see Bhatnagar and Passi, 2016.

[10] Obama was not the first president to receive such an invitation. Bill Clinton was asked to be the guest of honour by then-Prime Minister P.V. Narasimha Rao, in 1994.

[11] On this idea of India as a 'leading power', see also Mohan, 2015a, pp. 201–14.

[12] This was not the first time this term had been employed by the BJP. Modi himself used it while Gujarat chief minister, but not to refer to principles of foreign policy. Instead, he used *Panchamrit* to refer to the five parts of his 'development vision' for the state, which included *Jal Shakti* (water power), *Urya Shakti* (electricity), *Gyan*

Shakti (the power of education), *Raksha Shakti* (defence), and *Jan Shakti* (literally, 'people power') (Verma, 2014, p. 189).

[13] See, for example, Abhyankar, 2018; Bajpaee, 2016; Basrur, 2018; Chatterjee Miller and Sullivan, 2017; Chandra, 2014; Mohan 2015a; Ogden, 2018; Panda, 2016; Pant and Joshi, 2017. Realism, in this context, refers to that philosophy of international relations that conceives the relations between states to be inherently conflictual, demanding that they build and use military and other forms of power to secure their interests.

[14] On Modi and transformational leadership in India's domestic politics, see Chhibber and Verma, 2018, pp. 139–40, and on the distinction between these two leadership styles, see Burns, 1978. On Modi's self-portrayal as a transformational leader, see especially MEA, 2017a.

[15] For critical treatments of Modi's track record in government between 2014 and 2019, see inter alia Mehra, 2019; Soz, 2019; and Tharoor, 2018.

[16] The classic – and still very useful study – is Bandyopadhyaya, 1991, first published in 1970. But see also Malone, 2011; and Malone et al., 2015.

[17] For the view of one former diplomat of these directives and how they form the 'crux of India's global mission', see Abhyankar, 2018, p. xix.

[18] This is not to say that Nehru faced no opposition, even in the early years. See, for an insightful account of early foreign policy debates, Sagar and Panda, 2015.

[19] For a useful view of how this functions (or does not) provided by a parliamentarian with extensive experience of foreign policy, see Tharoor, 2012, pp. 354–63.

[20] Prime Ministers Lal Bahadur Shastri, Indira Gandhi, Rajiv Gandhi, V.P. Singh, P.V. Narasimha Rao, I.K. Gujral, Atal Bihari Vajpayee and Manmohan Singh all combined the roles at some point in governments, but none for longer than 18 months.

[21] On the relationship between Indira Gandhi and P.N. Haksar, see also Ramesh, 2018.

[22] Whether or not public opinion is becoming a more significant factor in foreign policy making is a subject of some debate. See especially Kapur, 2009; and Kapur, 2015.

[23] See, for example, the work of the former BJP-led government's EAM, Jaswant Singh, including his *India at Risk: Mistakes, Misconceptions, and Misadventures of Security Policy*, 2013.

[24] The debate about when, why and how far coalition partners can and do affect foreign policy making is evolving. See Blarel and van Willigen, 2017, for some comparisons between India's experience and other states in the global South, as well as Mattoo and Jacob, 2010.

[25] For an excellent primer, see Madan, 2015.

[26] The literature on this topic is growing, but see Markey, 2009; Chatterjee Miller, 2013a; or Datta-Ray, 2015.

[27] On this post and the wider apparatus for managing national security, see Ganguly et al., 2018; Gupta, 2018; and Hall 2018.

[28] The literature on this topic is expanding. See especially Sridharan, 2003; Staniland, 2010; Plagemann and Destradi, 2015; Staniland and Narang, 2015; Varadarajan, 2015.

[29] On the involvement of the states in foreign policy, see Hazarika, 2014, and on paradiplomacy by chief ministers, see Wyatt, 2017. On the practice of paradiplomacy by political entities below the level of sovereign states more generally, see Cornago, 2010; and Tavares, 2016.

30 For classic studies of the influence of public opinion and other constituencies, see Bandyopadhyaya, 1991; and Ghosh, 1994.

31 On this topic, see Kochanek, 1996; Kumar, 2015, 2016; and Rothacher, 2016.

32 For a useful and detailed profile of Doval, see Donthi, 2017.

33 On the influence of ideology on Indian foreign policy, see Bandyopadhyaya, 1991, pp. 69–80; and Chatterjee Miller, 2013.

34 On this topic, see Ghosh, 1994, Kapur, 2009 and Kapur, 2015. Scholars are divided about whether foreign policy shapes the choices of voters in democracies. For a helpful overview of the debate, see Aldrich et al., 2006.

35 For a sample of this literature, sceptical as it is about Modi's achievements in foreign policy, see Hall, 2015a, 2016a; Chatterjee Miller and Sullivan de Estrada, 2017; Ganguly, 2017; Mishra, 2017; Pardesi, 2017; Singh, S., 2017; Karnad, 2018; Ogden, 2018.

Chapter 2

1 This chapter deviates a little – for reasons that will hopefully become obvious – from the conventional periodisation of India's foreign policy. Normally, it is split into three phases: the first running from 1947 to the border war with China in 1962, the second covering the rest of the Cold War, and the third being the almost thirty years that have elapsed since the collapse of the Soviet Union (Ganguly and Pardesi, 2013). I argue in what follows that the last phase begins a little later, in the latter half of the 1990s, as earlier economic reforms begin to pay off and New Delhi decides to cross the threshold to become a de facto nuclear weapons state.

2 One measure of Nehru's continued influence is the desire on the part of contemporary analysts and policy makers to appropriate and apply his ideas to present circumstances, including 'nonalignment'; see, for example, Khilnani et al., 2013. On the 'persistence of Nehruvianism' more generally, see Mehta, 2009; and Hall, 2016b.

3 On this topic, see also Edwardes, 1965, p. 50; Singh, 1965, p. 127; Brecher, 2011, p. 564.

4 On the establishment of the MEA and the IFS, see Raghavan, 2015.

5 In general, see Brown, 2003, pp. 247–8.

6 Some observers thought these arrangements, and the concentration of power in Nehru's hands, unhealthy. They generated, as one Australian High Commissioner put it, 'too much eagerness to please the boss', with embassies 'too often sending back to Delhi the kind of reports which they thought congenial to their master' (Crocker, 2008, p. 57).

7 On India's 'post-imperial ideology' and foreign policy, see also Chatterjee Miller, 2013b.

8 On the origins of the term, see Michael Brecher's dialogue with Krishna Menon, Nehru's erstwhile ambassador and Defence Minister (Brecher, 1968, pp. 3–15). The literature on Nehru and nonalignment is vast, but apart from Brecher 1968, see also Rana, 1976; Raghavan, 2010; Bhagavan, 2013; Kennedy, 2015.

9 On the history of Sino-India relations, see especially Garver, 2001.

10 For more exhaustive studies of US-India relations during the conflict, see Chaudhuri, R., 2014; Riedel, 2015.

11 For a short account of Nehru's disagreement with Patel over China, see Dasgupta, 2014.

12 For a contemporary survey of the various positions, see S.C.S., 1959.

[13] For a trenchant account of the attempt by 'Third World' states to reform the international economic order in the 1970s and early 1980s, see Krasner, 1985.

[14] For a useful contemporary account of the financial crisis and this episode, see the essays in Jain, 1992.

[15] Rao's personal and political lives are explored – brilliantly – in Sitapati, 2016. On his politics and the reforms of 1991, see also Baru, 2016.

[16] In 2000, GDP growth dipped to 3.8 per cent according to the World Bank, 2018.

[17] For a useful overview, see Chiriyankandath, 2004.

[18] On the origins and evolution of 'Look East', see also Gordon and Henningham, 1995; and Grare, 2016.

[19] For Gujral's own account of his doctrine and its foundations, see Gujral, 2011.

[20] The literature on the motives for India's tests is large, but see especially Paul, 1998; Ganguly, 1999; Ollapally, 2001; Kennedy, 2011.

[21] This process has been captured in frank memoirs by protagonists on both sides. See Talbott, 2004; and Singh, 2007.

[22] The literature on the US-India nuclear deal is extensive, but see especially Paul, 2007; Pant, 2011; Mistry, 2014.

[23] All figures are adjusted to the 2010 value of the dollar.

[24] The prehistory of China's partnership with Pakistan, prior to the 1965, is explored in Chaudhuri, 2018.

[25] For one useful take on the similarities between nonalignment and strategic autonomy, see Monsonis, 2010.

[26] On the emergence of formal and informal strategic partnerships in the Asian region, see especially Envall and Hall, 2016.

[27] On the evolution of this group, see inter alia, Alden and Vieira, 2005; Flemes, 2009; Taylor, 2009.

[28] The concept of 'multialignment' is discussed in various texts, including Khanna and Mohan, 2006; Tharoor, 2012; Jaffrelot and Singh Sidhu, 2013, p. 319; Hall, 2016a.

[29] On India's conflicted views on democracy promotion and democracy assistance during the 2000s, see especially Mohan, 2007; Muni, 2009; Mishra 2012; and Mazumdar and Statz, 2015.

[30] The literature on India's stance on 'Responsibility to Protect' is now extensive. See especially Virk, 2013; Bloomfield 2015, 2017; and Jaganathan and Kurtz, 2014. For one prominent Indian diplomat-turned-politician's view, see also Singh Puri, 2016.

[31] On the evolution of this partnership, see especially Kapur and Ganguly, 2007; and Schaffer, 2009.

[32] For more broadly positive assessments, see Abhyankar, 2018; Tremblay and Kapur, 2017; and Harsh V. Pant's collected media commentary, in Pant, 2019.

[33] See especially Chatterjee Miller, 2013a; and, more broadly, Ganguly and Thompson, 2017.

Chapter 3

[1] On some of these texts, see Roy, 2012; Rajagopalan, 2014; Singh, U., 2017.

[2] See also Blom Hanson and Jaffrelot, 2001.

[3] There are a number of good short surveys of Indian thinking. See especially Sagar, 2009; Ollapally and Rajagopalan, 2012; and Bajpai, 2014.

[4] For a useful short discussion of Nehru's thinking and the various influences on it, see Das, 1961; for a classic study of nonalignment, see Rana, 1974; and for a provocative revisionist account of how Nehru practised foreign and security policy,

see Raghavan, 2010. His collected speeches are still an excellent introduction to his thought – see Nehru, 1961.

5 On the Hyper-Realists, see Ollapally and Rajagopalan, 2012; and Bajpai, 2014.

6 On the various groups that voted for the BJP in 2014, see especially Nag, 2014; and Jha, 2017. On the influx of military officers and others into the Party since the early 1990s, see Jaffrelot, 1996, pp. 432–6.

7 There was considerable interest in the history and traditions of India among Europeans in the 19th century. Among the Indologists of this period, see especially the work of the German scholar of Sanskrit, Max Müller (1823–1900).

8 The classic biography of Vivekananda is Rolland, 2002, originally published in 1930; see also Radice, 1999.

9 For the best short account of Ramakrishna's beliefs, see Sharma, 2013, pp. 1–116.

10 On the use of Vivekananda by Hindu nationalists, see Radice, 1999 (in particular); Beckerlegge, 2003; Sharma, 2013.

11 To become properly Hindu once more, however, they needed to convert back to that religion.

12 The literature on the RSS is growing, but see especially Kanungo, 2003; and Andersen and Damle, 2018.

13 *We, or Our Nationhood Defined* is often attributed to Golwalkar, and he did lay claim to the book, but Sharma argues the book was written by Ganesh Savarkar (also known as Babarao), V.D. Savarkar's brother. See Sharma, 2010, p. xix, note 21.

14 Jaffrelot finds this claim that Golwalkar and the RSS were apolitical to be unconvincing, calling it 'propaganda' (1996, p. 62).

15 There are a number of studies of Upadhyaya's thinking, but most are sympathetic, verging on hagiographical; see, for example, Sharma, 2009. For a short account of his life and works, see Jaffrelot, 1996, pp. 123–5.

16 The authoritative text on the BJS is Graham, 1990.

17 This section draws on – and expands on – Hall, 2017b, pp. 121–122.

18 Again, this also echoes Golwalkar's organicism. See especially Jaffrelot, 1996, pp. 58–62.

19 Although the volume is undated, the speech from which this quotation comes was made to the Hindu Mahasabha at its 21st Session, in 1939.

20 There are a number of studies of Upadhyaya's thought, mostly written by sympathetic authors; see, for example, Sharma, 2009; and Bakshi, 2018.

21 On the origins and agenda of the BMS, see Jaffrelot, 1996, pp. 127–128; and Andersen and Damle, 2018, pp. 36–37.

Chapter 4

1 See especially Mukhopadhyay's book (2013), which relates some of the obstacles that he encountered when doing his research on Modi's life.

2 These stories appear in various forms in various accounts. See, for example, Kamath and Randeri, 2013, p. 7; Marino, 2014, pp. 6–7; and Verma, 2014, p. 18.

3 A parallel *Rashtriya Sevika Samiti* was created in 1936 to train young women (Andersen and Damle, 2018, pp. 23–5).

4 For more, see also Sharda, 2018, pp. 101–3.

5 For a useful account of the role of *pracharaks* in the RSS written by an insider, see Sharda, 2018, pp. 149–56.

6 See also Price, 2016, p. 101; and Verma 2014, p. 1. Another pro-Modi biography suggests these events took place sometime later, when Modi was in his late teens (Kamath and Randeri, 2013, p. 9).

7   See also Nag, 2013, pp. 38–9.

8   See also Verma, 2014, p. 26.

9   Whether Modi actually enrolled in a degree is unclear. For a discussion of this issue, see Bhattacharya, 2018.

10 See also Marino, 2014, p. 44; Verma, 2014, p. 43.

11 See also Verma, 2014, p. 31.

12 The *Ram Rath Yatra* came to an end before it could reach Ayodhya with the arrest of Advani in Bihar on the orders of its Chief Minister, Lalu Prasad.

13 See also Verma, 2014, pp. 48–51; and Hanson, 1999, p. 160.

14 On the significance of the *yatra* for the Hindu nationalist movement, see Jaffrelot, 1996, pp. 416–19; and on the demolition of the Babri Masjid and its aftermath, see pp. 449–63.

15 For further discussion of this episode, see Marino, 2014, p. 95; and Mukhopadhyay, 2013, pp. 212–13.

16 Among those who advance the former claim are Kamath and Randeri, 2013, pp. 53–4; and Marino, 2014, p. 99. Among those who advance the latter are Mukhopadhyay, 2013, pp. 248–9; Nag, 2013, p. 84; and Dalrymple, 2014.

17 For a still useful set of essays published immediately after the riots, see Varadarajan, 2002. The wider literature is large and growing, but see especially Jaffrelot, 2007; and Mitta, 2014.

18 Modi continues to maintain that the Godhra attack was, as he told Andy Marino (2014, p. 108) 'a terrorist act, a conspiracy, not an act of communal hatred'.

19 On this issue, see Nussbaum, 2007; Spodek, 2010; Jeffrey, 2015.

20 It should be noted that Kodnani's conviction was overturned on appeal in April 2018.

21 See Nag, 2013, p. 11; Menon, 2014, pp. 176–8; and Jagannathan, 2016, p. 84.

22 See also Menon, 2014, pp. 66–7.

23 The literature on Modi's political appropriation of Gujarati identity is extensive. See especially Baxi, 2002; Mehta, 2006; and Jaffrelot, 2013.

24 For different assessments on Modi's populism, see Jaffrelot and Tillin, 2017; and McDonnell and Cabrera, 2019.

25 See also Sridharan, 2014, pp. 27–8.

26 For positive and critical uses of the term *Moditva*, see Bedi et al., 2014; and Tharoor, 2018.

27 Curiously, it seems that Nehru first coined this term; see *Deccan Herald*, 2014. I am grateful to Teesta Prakash for pointing out this earlier usage.

Chapter 5

1   Ravi Shankar styles himself 'Sri Sri Ravi Shankar'.

2   The concept of 'soft power' was invented by Joseph S. Nye, and first appeared in his book *Bound to Lead* in 1990, as well as an accompanying article in *Foreign Policy* (Nye, 1990a, 1990b). It was developed later in another book (Nye, 2004).

3   On Modi's religious diplomacy more generally, see Hall, 2019.

4   Prior to the election, for example, Modi mused about Vivekananda and India as a *vishwa guru* at the Pravasi Bharatiya Divas (Know India Day) held for diaspora businesspeople in Delhi in January 2014 (Modi, 2014c).

5   The Modi government's fascination for soft power has been much commented on. See, for example, Pant, 2015; Chaulia, 2016, pp. 150–60; Tandon, 2016; Hall, 2017; Kugiel, 2017; Palit, P. S., 2017; Tremblay and Kapur, 2017, pp. 53–5; Karnad 2018; and Mazumdar, 2018.

6   For an excellent short account of India's pursuit of soft power, see Mullen, 2015.

7   On the wider context, see Hall and Smith, 2013.

8   See the MEA's so-called 'Detailed Demands for Grants' – effectively its draft budgets – submitted as part of the Union Government budget process. For the 2014–15 budget year, it requested 240 million rupees, and for 2018–19, it requested 219 million rupees (MEA, 2014a, 2018b).

9   On religious diplomacy as a phenomenon in international relations and on its growing salience, see Cox and Philpott 2003; Johnston 2003; Troy 2008.

10   Modi departed from this practice with President Trump, giving him a commemorative stamp and a wooden chest (Glum, 2017).

11   On the wider context, see Jacob, 2015.

12   It should be noted that Indian representatives did not attend the International Buddhist Conference in Lumbini, in Nepal, in May 2016, reportedly because it disapproved of what New Delhi perceived as an attempt by China and Nepal to 'usurp Buddha and Buddhism from India' (Muni, 2017, pp. 126–7).

13   The title of the book alludes, of course, to Al Gore's famous documentary, *An Inconvenient Truth*, released in 2006.

14   The interview is available here: *al Jazeera*, 2016.

15   For a useful discussion of the concept of *Akhand Bharat* and its appeal to Hindu nationalists, see Krishna, 1994.

16   In the language of these gatherings, track 1 is official state-to-state diplomacy; track 1.5 involves both diplomats and non-official representatives, including think-tank professionals, scholars, business groups and others drawn from civil society; and track 2 is meant simply to involve non-officials. In practice, the lines between track 1.5 and track 2 are often blurred.

17   India remains acutely sensitive to issues concerning the funding of such institutions, and indeed non-governmental organisations more broadly. For that reason, Indian think tanks tend to seek funds only from Indian donors.

18   The *India Foundation Journal* was first published in mid-2013. For issues, see http://indiafoundation.in/india-foundation-journal/.

19   On India's diaspora and foreign policy in general, see especially Varadarajan, 2015.

20   These schemes are needed because India's Constitution does not permit dual citizenship, though it does have special arrangements for residents of Jammu and Kashmir.

21   For a fascinating analysis of the diaspora in the US, see Chakravorty et al., 2016.

22   For a useful analysis of Indian evacuation operations, see Xavier, 2016.

Chapter 6

1   Arvind Panagariya is a Princeton-educated economist with extensive experience with the International Monetary Fund (IMF), World Bank, and World Trade Organization, who was Chief Economist at the Asian Development Bank prior to joining NITI Aayog in January 2015 as its Vice-Chairman. He is the author of an important account of India's economic development (Panagariya, 2008). He left his post at NITI Aayog in August 2017.

2   For a useful discussion of these issues, see Chacko, 2019.

3   As a corollary, other analysts argue that the BJS's unwillingness to countenance more liberal policies limited its electoral appeal in the 1960s and 1970s (Graham, 1990, pp. 253–4).

4   Traditionally, a *kar sevak* is someone who devotes themselves to a religious cause. The term is often now used, however, to describe a Hindu nationalist activist.

5   For a useful discussion, see Manor, 2015.
6   There are substantial academic and public debates about the effects of demonetisation. For an early overview, see Ghosh et al., 2017.
7   Of course, a major challenge here is defining 'neoliberalism', which has multiple meanings in different contexts. For an example of the common argument that Modi's approach is neoliberal, see George, 2014; and for a counter-argument, see Ranjan, 2018.
8   On 'nation-branding' as a diplomatic practice, see Dinnie, 2015.
9   On land reform, see Kazmin, 2015; and on all of these issues, see Mehra, 2019.
10 It should be noted that the RSS-affiliated Bharatiya Mazdoor Sangh (BMS), the largest union in India, which expressed its opposition, but did not participate in the action.
11 BIMSTEC's member states are Bangladesh, Bhutan, India, Myanmar, Nepal, Sri Lanka and Thailand.
12 OBOR was outlined in two public speeches made by Xi Jinping – one delivered in Kazakhstan in early September 2013, and the other in Jakarta, a month later (MFAPRC, 2013a, 2013b).
13 By 2017, the value of CPEC had been pushed to $64 billion (Siddiqui, 2017). For a useful short appraisal of CPEC see Small, 2017.
14 For a useful assessment of India's position prior to the Belt and Road Forum in 2017, see Madan, 2016.

Chapter 7

1   See, for example, Burke, 2014; or Miglani and Chalmers, 2014.
2   For a useful corrective to these arguments, see Grare, 2014.
3   On anti-poverty programmes and Maoist violence – particularly the long-term impact of the Mahatma Gandhi National Rural Employment Guarantee Scheme – see Khanna and Zimmermann, 2017. On the settlement with Naga insurgents and the impact of the border deal with Bangladesh, see Singh, M.A., 2016.
4   On these strikes, see especially Gokhale, 2017a.
5   Data compiled for the US State Department show that India experienced a slight increase in the number of terrorist attacks in 2015 (791 incidents, compared with 764 in 2014) but a decrease in deaths (289 compared with 418) (US Department of State, 2016). Recorded attacks increased again in 2016, to 927, and deaths to 337 (US Department of State, 2017), but fell in 2017, to 860, with deaths slightly higher, at 380 (US Department of State, 2018b).
6   Happymon Jacob points out that 2017 saw the highest number of violations of the 2003 ceasefire along the Line of Control in recent years – almost 5,500 in total, leading to the deaths of at least 138 Pakistani soldiers and 28 of their Indian counterparts, according to Indian figures (Jacob, 2018, pp. xi–xii). See also Behera, 2016.
7   On this concept, see especially Cohen and Dasgupta, 2010.
8   On this topic, see Cohen and Dasgupta, 2010; Bitzinger, 2018; Karnad, 2018.
9   Between 2013 and 2017 India was the world's biggest arms importer, according to SIPRI, accounting for 12 per cent of all imports. Russia was its biggest supplier (62 per cent) of the total, followed by the US (15 per cent) and Israel (11 per cent) (Wezeman et al., 2018, p. 6).
10 This section takes its cue from seminal work on this topic by Rahul Sagar, 2009, 2014, 2015, in particular.

11 Recovering Hindu 'manliness' is a common theme – one of the three core concerns of 'beef, biceps and the Bhagavad Gita', as Sharma, 2003, p. 46, puts it.

12 'Moulding Men' is the title of the last part of Golwalkar's *Bunch of Thoughts* (1996, pp. 389–488). As we have seen, the RSS places great emphasis on 'character-building' and physical education for its recruits.

13 This speech, the first Vijayadashami address given by Bhagwat under Modi's government, was also the first televised on the state broadcaster, Doordarshan, prompting protests from political opponents of the BJP and RSS (Press Trust of India, 2014d).

14 On strategic partnerships as a practice in contemporary international relations in the Indo-Pacific, see Envall and Hall, 2016.

15 On the emergence and evolution of the 'Indo-Pacific' idea, see Medcalf, 2013.

16 The relevant part of the statement reads: 'We will support an open and inclusive rules-based global order …'.

17 Modi very rarely used this phrase – which was closely associated with the previous government and with contemporary Nehruvian thinking more broadly – prior to Shangri La; see Ganguly, 2017. It is likely it was included (or allowed to be included) by the Foreign Secretary, V.K. Gokhale, who would have had the final bureaucratic – though not the final political – say on the speech. I am grateful to C. Raja Mohan for sharing his insights into these processes.

18 The Andaman and Nicobar Command is India's first tri-service command, placing army, air force and naval assets in that region under a single Commander-in-Chief. For a comprehensive view of what broader reforms many think are needed, see Kanwal, 2016; Gupta, 2018; Kanwal and Kohli, 2018.

19 On the likely requirements for helicopters, see especially Joshi, M., 2018, p. 7.

20 For a useful account of defence sector reforms under Modi, see also Smith, 2016.

21 For a sympathetic account of the Rebalance by one of its architects, see Campbell, 2016.

22 The literature on India and the Libyan decision is big, but see Hall, 2013; or Virk, 2013.

23 The DTTI is a government-to-government forum for addressing bureaucratic issues standing in the way of deeper cooperation. Under the Singh government, little progress was however made in making the DTTI work as intended (Pant and Joshi, 2017, p. 136). Exercise Malabar also involves the Japanese navy.

24 Obama was not the first to be invited – that honour went to Bill Clinton, who could not attend in 1994 because he could not change the date of his State of Union address.

25 The so-called Logistics Exchange Memorandum of Agreement had been under discussion for more than a decade (Pant and Joshi, 2017, p. 141).

26 This agreement had been announced during Modi's visit to Washington in June 2016, but needed to pass Congress.

27 On Trump and trade, see Chaulia, 2018; and the President's undiplomatic comments, see Gowan, 2018.

28 Pant and Joshi (2017, pp. 143–5) also argue that Modi has himself been crucial to this shift, but they argue that he has simply been more open about the importance of US support for India's rise. They also observe that China has pushed New Delhi to 'bandwagon' (their word) with Washington.

29 On the most important of these – the partnerships with Japan and Singapore – see Ghosh, 2018; and Mohan, 2015b.

30 The first meeting of the new and less provocatively named quadrilateral 'Consultations on the Indo-Pacific' was held on the sidelines of the East Asia Summit meeting in Manila on 12 November 2017.

31 For useful discussions, see Bajpai, 2017; and Panda, 2016.

32 For a description of this incident by an informed Indian analyst, see Gokhale, 2017a, pp. 125–31.

33 For useful analyses of these events, see Bajpai, 2018; Ganguly, 2018; and Ganguly and Scobell, 2018.

34 The attack on Pathankot air base by suspected Jaish-e-Mohammed militants led to the deaths of about 10 Indian personnel and several terrorists.

35 Gokhale, who was close to the Modi government, claims that Pakistani 'radio chatter' suggested up to eighty or so militants died during the raids (2017a, p. 46).

36 For a useful discussion of some of the issues published prior to the strikes in 2016, see Perkovich and Dalton, 2015.

37 See, for example, Ganguly, 2017; Karnad, 2018; or Tharoor, 2018.

Chapter 8

1 By the end of 2018, Modi's travel had cost Indian taxpayers an estimated $280 million (Marlow, 2018).

2 For various sympathetic accounts of a 'Modi doctrine', see Chaulia, 2016; Ganguly et al., 2016; and Tremblay and Kapur, 2017.

3 Modi was far from alone in seeking this kind of role. Nationalist populists like Recep Tayyip Erdoğan, Vladimir Putin or indeed Donald J. Trump, also use foreign policy for domestic political advantage, to isolate opponents, bolster credentials or mobilise a base, casting themselves as defenders of national values and pride. On the argument that the BJP under Modi should be seen as a populist party, see Kenny, 2017; McDonnell and Cabrera, 2019; and Plagemann and Destradi, 2019. On populists and foreign policy more broadly, see Carpenter, 2017; Drezner, 2017; Leslie, 2017; Verbeek and Zaslove, 2017; Karnad 2018, pp. 1–36.

4 See Hall, 2015; but also Mohan, 2015; Panda, 2016; and Pant 2015.

5 See, for example, Karnad, 2017; or Tharoor, 2018. I do not deny, of course, that ego played a part in this behaviour.

6 To emphasise this rebranding, the BJP released a slick online campaign advert, *Main Bhi Chowkidar* ('I am a watchman too') (BJP, 2019a); see also Kawade, 2019.

7 See also Karnad, 2005, pp. 392–3.

8 See especially Kapur, 2009.

9 Although I do not agree with all of it, this argument is well made by Karnad, 2018, especially pp. 17–21.

10 I have already noted that a rumour that a national security strategy might be produced circulated in 2018, but a paper did not emerge; see Gokhale, 2018.

11 Take, for example, the SPMRF-sponsored publication on *The Modi Doctrine* (Ganguly et al., 2016). More than half the authors who contributed chapters (13 out of 23) were foreigners; only two (Shakti Sinha, a Director of the India Foundation, and Mukul Asher, a Fellow of SPMRF) had any association with a Hindu nationalist think tank. On this point, I am very grateful to a diplomat who served in New Delhi during Modi's time in office.

12 On this point, see especially Ganguly, 2017, p. 142; and Plagemann and Destradi, 2019, p. 13.

¹³ The membership of the NSAB announced in July 2018 including P.S. Raghavan, a former ambassador to Russia, A.B. Mathur, a former RAW officer, Lieutenant General (retired) S.L. Narasimhan and Professor Bimal N. Patel of the Gujarat National Law University. In its previous incarnation, the NSAB had 17 members.

¹⁴ See, for example, United States Commission on International Religious Freedom, 2016; or Human Rights Watch, 2017.

¹⁵ More broadly, see Crabtree, 2017.

References

Abhyankar, R. M. (2018) *Indian Diplomacy: Beyond Strategic Autonomy*, New Delhi: Oxford University Press.

Acharya, A. (2015) 'India's "Look East" policy', in Malone, D., Mohan, C. R. and Raghavan, S. (eds) *The Oxford Handbook of Indian Foreign Policy*, Oxford: Oxford University Press, 452–465.

Adeney, K. and Sáez, L. (eds) (2005) *Coalition Politics and Hindu Nationalism*, London and New York: Routledge.

Advani, L. K. (2010) *My Country, My Life*, New Delhi: Rupa.

AIUMB (All India Ulama and Mashaikh Board) (2017) *Vision*, www.aiumb.org/about-us/vision/.

Alden, C. and Vieira, M. A. (2005) 'The new diplomacy of the South: South Africa, Brazil, India and trilateralism', *Third World Quarterly* 26(7): 1077–1095.

Aldrich, J. H., Gelpi, C., Feaver, P., Reifler, J. and Sharp, K. T. (2006) 'Foreign policy and the electoral connection', *Annual Review of Political Science* 9: 477–502.

al Jazeera (2016) 'Transcript: Ram Madhav on Hindu nationalism', 7 June, www.aljazeera.com/programmes/headtohead/2016/02/transcript-ram-madhav-hindu-nationalism-160201131633738.html.

Almonte, J. T. (1997) 'Ensuring security the "ASEAN way"', *Survival* 39(4): 80–92.

Andersen, W. K. (1983) 'The domestic roots of Indian foreign policy' *Asian Affairs: An American Review* 10(3): 45–53.

Andersen, W. K. and Damle, S. D. (2018) *The RSS: A View to the Inside*, New Delhi: Penguin Viking.

Appadorai, A. (1969) *Essays in Politics and International Relations*, Bombay: Asia Publishing House.

Art of Living (2016) *The World Culture Festival*, www.artofliving.org/world-culture-festival#/.

Asian Development Bank (2018) *Updating and Enhancement of the BIMSTEC Transport Infrastructure and Logistics Study: Final Report*, July, www.adb.org/sites/default/files/publication/439106/updating-bimstec-transport-logistics-study.pdf

Ayres, A. (2015) 'How Americans See India as a Power', *Forbes*, 16 September, www.forbes.com/sites/alyssaayres/2015/09/16/how-americans-see-india-as-a-power/#5c358359313d.

Ayres, A. (2018) *Our Time Has Come: How India Is Making Its Place in the World*, New York: Oxford University Press.

Bajpaee, C. (2016) 'Modi, India and the emerging global economic order', *Journal of Asian Public Policy* 9(2): 198–210.

Bajpai, K. (2005) 'Where are India and the US heading?', *Economic and Political Weekly* 40(32): 3577–3581.

Bajpai, K. (2009) 'The BJP and the bomb', in S. D. Sagan (ed.) *Inside Nuclear South Asia*, Stanford, CA: Stanford University Press, 25–67.

Bajpai, K. (2014) 'Indian grand strategy: six schools of thought', in K. Bajpai, S. Basit and V. Krishnappa (eds) *India's Grand Strategy: History, Theory, Cases*, London, New York and New Delhi: Routledge, 127–164.

Bajpai, K. (2017) 'Narendra Modi's Pakistan and China policy: assertive bilateral diplomacy, active coalition diplomacy', *International Affairs* 93(1): 69–92.

Bajpai, K. (2018) 'Modi's China policy and the road to confrontation', *Pacific Affairs* 91(2): 245–260.

Bakshi, S. S. N. (2018) *Deendayal Upadhyaya: Life of an Ideologue Politician*, New Delhi: Rupa.

Bana, N. and Yhome, K. (2017) 'The road to Mekong: The India-Myanmar-Thailand trilateral highway project', *ORF Issue Brief*, 7 February, www.orfonline.org/research/the-road-to-mekong-the-india-myanmar-thailand-trilateral-highway-project/.

Bandyopadhyaya, J. (1982) *North over South: A Non-Western Perspective of International Relations*, New Delhi and Madras: South Asian Publishers.

Bandyopadhyaya, J. (1991) *The Making of India's Foreign Policy: Determinants, Institutions, Processes and Personalities*, revised edn, Calcutta: Allied Publishers.

Banerjee, A. (2018) 'FDI in defence since 2014 mere Rs 1.17 cr', *The Tribune*, 8 March, www.tribuneindia.com/news/nation/fdi-in-defence-since-2014-mere-rs-1-17-cr/554635.html.

Baru, S. (2015) *The Accidental Prime Minister: The Making and Unmaking of Manmohan Singh*, New Delhi: Penguin.

Baru, S. (2016) *1991: How P. V. Narasimha Rao Made History*, New Delhi: Aleph.

Basrur, R. (2017) 'Modi's foreign policy fundamentals: trajectory unchanged', *International Affairs* 93(1): 7–26.

Basrur, R. (2018) 'Modi, *Hindutva* and foreign policy', *International Studies Perspectives* 20(1): 7–11.

Basu, D. and Misra, K. (2015) 'BJP's youth vote dividend', *Economic and Political Weekly* 50(3): 69–73.

Baxi, U. (2002) 'The second Gujarat catastrophe', *Economic and Political Weekly* 37(34): 3519–3531.

BBC (2018) 'India's Ayodhya site: masses gather as Hindu-Muslim dispute simmers', 25 November, www.bbc.com/news/world-asia-india-46318505.

Beckerlegge, G. (2003) 'Saffron and seva: the Rashtriya Swayamsevak Sangh's appropriation of Swami Vivekananda', in Copley, A. (ed.) *Hinduism in Public and Private: Reform, Hindutva, Gender and Sampraday*, New Delhi: Oxford University Press, 31–65.

Bedi, K., Singh, J. and Swamy, S. (2014) *Moditva: The Idea Behind the Man*, Ahmedabad: Navbharat.

Bedi, R. (2018) 'India's defence budget rises marginally', *Janes*, 1 February, www.janes.com/article/77536/india-s-defence-budget-rises-marginally.

Behera, N. C. (2016) 'The Kashmir conflict: multiple fault lines', *Journal of Asian Security and International Affairs* 3(1): 41–63.

Bevir, M. (1994) 'The west turns eastward: Madame Blavatsky and the transformation of the occult tradition', *Journal of the American Academy of Religion* 62(3): 747–767.

Bhagavan, M. (2013) *India and the Quest for One World: The Peacemakers*, New York: Palgrave.

Bhagwat, M. (2014) 'Full text of speech by RSS Sarasanghchalak Mohan Bhagwat on Vijaya Dashmi – 2014, Nagpur', *Samvada*, 3 October, https://samvada.org/2014/news/full-text-of-speech-by-rss-sarasanghchalak-mohan-bhagwat-on-vijaya-dashmi-2014-nagpur/.

Bhagwat, M. (2015) 'Full text of speech by RSS Sarasanghachalak Mohan Bhagwat's #RSSVijayadashami Speech – 2015', *Samvada*, 22 October, https://samvada.org/2015/news/mohan-bhagwats-rssvijayadashami-speech-2015/.

Bhagwat, M. (2016) 'Full speech of Sarsanghachalak Dr. Mohan Bhagwat Ji at Vijaya Dashami Utsav, Reshimbagh Nagpur', *Vishwa Samvad Kendra Bharat*, 11 October, http://vskbharat.com/full-speech-of-sarsanghachalak-dr-mohan-bhagwat-ji-at-vijaya-dashami-utsav-reshimbagh-nagpur/?lang=en.

Bhagwat, M. (2017) 'Summary of the address of Sarsanghchalak Dr Mohan Bhagwat Ji on the occasion of Vijayadashami Utsav – 2017', *Vishwa Samvad Kendra Bharat*, 1 October, http://vskbharat.com/summary-of-the-address-of-sarsanghchalak-dr-mohan-bhagwat-ji-on-the-occasion-of-vijayadashami-utsav-2017/?lang=en.

Bhagwat, M. (2018) 'Mohan Bhagwat Vijayadashami 2018 speech FULL TEXT: RSS chief discusses 2019 elections, Ramjanmabhoomi and "Urban Naxals"', *FirstPost*, 18 October, www.firstpost.com/politics/mohan-bhagwat-vijayadashami-2018-speech-full-text-rss-chief-discusses-2019-elections-ramjanmabhoomi-and-urban-naxals-5401441.html.

Bhatnagar, A. and Passi, R. (eds) (2016) *Neighbourhood First: Navigating Ties under Modi*, London: Global Policy and Observer Research Foundation.

Bhatt, C. (2001) *Hindu Nationalism: Origins, Ideologies and Modern Myths*, Oxford and New York: Berg.

Bhattacharya, T. (2018) 'The curious case of Prime Minister Narendra Modi's degree', *National Herald*, 16 June, www.nationalheraldindia.com/india/the-curious-case-of-prime-minister-narendra-modis-degree.

Bhattacherjee, K. (2016) 'Overseas Indian Affairs Ministry, MEA merged', *The Hindu*, 7 January, www.thehindu.com/news/national/Overseas-Indian-Affairs-Ministry-MEA-merged/article13986483.ece.

Bhattercherjee, K. (2018) 'PIOs make a "mini-world parliament"', *The Hindu*, 9 January, www.thehindu.com/news/national/pio-parliamentarian-conference-you-have-preserved-indian-culture-says-narendra-modi/article22403108.ece.

Bhaumik, A. (2019) 'EC rejects Yogi's explanation for 'Modi ki Sena' remark', *Deccan Herald*, 6 April, www.deccanherald.com/national/ec-rejects-yogis-explanation-for-modi-ki-sena-remark-727248.html.

Biswas, A. (2018) 'Will more countries join Indo-Japanese "Asia Africa growth corridor"?', *Dhaka Tribune*, 22 February, www.dhakatribune.com/bangladesh/foreign-affairs/2018/02/21/will-countries-join-indo-japanese-asia-africa-growth-corridor/.

Bitzinger, R. A. (2015) 'Comparing defense industry reforms in China and India', *Asian Politics and Policy* 7(4): 531–553.

Bitzinger, R. A. (2018) 'India's defence industrial base: decay and reform', in S. Ganguly, N. Blarel and M. S. Pardesi (eds) *The Oxford Handbook of India's National Security*, New Delhi: Oxford University Press, 132–148.

BJP (Bharatiya Janata Party) (2014a) *Ek Bharat, Shreshtha Bharat: Sabka Saath, Sabka Vikas* – Election Manifesto 2014, New Delhi: BJP.

BJP (2014b) 'BJP delegation to visit China to study their political structure', 15 November, www.bjp.org/en/media-resources/press-releases/press-bjp-delegation-to-visit-china-to-study-their-political-structure.

BJP (2014c) 'Modi's Gujarat model: the vision India awaits', www.bjp.org/images/pdf_2014/the_gujarat_model.pdf.

BJP (2015) 'Resolution on foreign policy passed in BJP national executive meeting at Bengaluru (Karnataka)', 3 April, www.bjp.org/en/media-resources/press-releases/resolution-on-foreign-policy-passed-in-bjp-national-executive-meeting-at-bengaluru-karnataka.

BJP (2019a) *Main Bhi Chowkidar*, 15 March, www.youtube.com/watch?v=Eaqslt6lrfE.

BJP (2019b) *Sankalpit Bharat, Sashakt Bharat: BJP Manifesto 2019*, www.bjp.org/en/manifesto2019.

Blarel, N. and van Willigen, N. (2017) 'Coalitions and foreign-policy-making: insights from the global South', *European Political Science* 16(4): 502–514.

Blom Hansen, T. (1999) *The Saffron Wave: Democracy and Hindu Nationalism in Modern India*, Princeton and Oxford: Princeton University Press.

Blom Hansen, T. (2001) 'The ethics of Hindutva and the spirit of capitalism', in T. B. Hansen and C. Jaffrelot (eds), *The BJP and the Compulsions of Politics in India*, 2nd edn, New Delhi: Oxford University Press, 291–314.

Blom Hansen, T. and Jaffrelot, C. (eds) (2001) *The BJP and the Compulsions of Politics in India*, 2nd edn, New Delhi: Oxford University Press.

Bloomfield, A. (2015) 'India and the Libyan crisis: flirting with the responsibility to protect, retreating to the sovereignty norm', *Contemporary Security Policy* 36(1): 27–55.

Bloomfield, A. (2017) *India and the Responsibility to Protect*, New York and London: Routledge.

Bobbio, T. (2012) 'Making Gujarat vibrant: Hindutva, development and the rise of subnationalism in India', *Third World Quarterly* 33(4): 657–672.

Bommakanti, K. (2017) 'India's evolving views on responsibility to protect (R2P) and humanitarian interventions: the significance of legitimacy', *Rising Powers Quarterly* 2(3): 99–123.

Brecher, M. (1968) *India and World Politics: Krishna Menon's View of the World*, New York and Washington: Frederick A. Praeger.

Brecher, M. (2011) *Nehru: A Political Biography*, New Delhi: Oxford University Press.

Brewster, D. (2018) 'The expansion of India's security sphere', in S. Ganguly, N. Blarel and M. S. Pardesi (eds) *The Oxford Handbook of India's National Security*, New Delhi: Oxford University Press, 495–514.

BRICS Post (2013) 'China, India conclude "very positive" talks', 12 February, http://thebricspost.com/china-india-conclude-very-positive-talks/.

Brown, J. M. (2003) *Nehru: A Political Life*, New Haven and London: Yale University Press.

Burke, J. (2014) 'Indian election alarm as BJP raises prospect of nuclear weapons rethink', *The Guardian* (UK), 7 April, www.theguardian.com/world/2014/apr/07/indian-election-bjp-manifesto-nuclear-weapons.

Burns, J. F. (1998) 'India sets 3 nuclear blasts, defying a worldwide ban; tests bring a sharp outcry', *New York Times*, 12 May, www.nytimes.com/1998/05/12/world/india-sets-3-nuclear-blasts-defying-a-worldwide-ban-tests-bring-a-sharp-outcry.html.

Burns, J. M. (1978) *Leadership*, New York: Harper and Row.

Campbell, K. M. (2016) *The Pivot: The Future of American Statecraft in Asia*, New York: Twelve.

Carpenter, T. G. (2017) 'The populist surge and the rebirth of foreign policy nationalism', *SAIS Review of International Affairs* 37(1): 33–46.

Chacko, P. (2018) 'The right turn in India: authoritarianism, populism and neoliberalisation', *Journal of Contemporary Asia* 48(4): 541–565.

Chacko, P. (2019) 'Marketizing *Hindutva*: the state, society, and markets in Hindu nationalism', *Modern Asian Studies* 53(2): 377–410.

Chacko, P. and Mayer, P. (2014) 'The Modi *lahar* (wave) in the 2014 Indian national election: a critical realignment?' *Australian Journal of Political Science* 49(3): 518–528.

Chakraborty, S. (2018) 'India jumps 23 spots to 77 in World Bank's ease-of-doing-business rankings', *Business Standard*, 1 November, www.business-standard.com/article/economy-policy/india-jumps-23-spots-to-77-in-world-bank-s-ease-of-doing-business-rankings-118103101238_1.html.

Chakravorty, S., Kapur, D. and Singh, N. (2016) *The Other One Percent: Indians in America*, New York: Oxford University Press.

Challagalla, S. (2018) 'The diaspora and India's growth story', *ORF Issue Brief* 232, March, www.orfonline.org/wp-content/uploads/2018/03/ORF_Issue_Brief_232_Diaspora.pdf.

Chand, B. (2017) 'Disaster relief as a political tool: analysing Indian and Chinese responses after the Nepal earthquakes' *Strategic Analysis* 41(6): 535–545.

Chandra, S. (2014) 'The style and substance of Modi's foreign policy', *Indian Foreign Affairs Journal* 9(3): 213–218.

Chatterjee Miller, M. (2013a) 'India's feeble foreign policy', *Foreign Affairs* 92(3): 14–19.

Chatterjee Miller, M. (2013b) *Wronged by Empire: Post-Imperial Ideology and Foreign Policy in India and China*, Stanford, CA: Stanford University Press.

Chatterjee Miller, M. and Sullivan de Estrada, K. (2017) 'Pragmatism in Indian foreign policy: how ideas constrain Modi', *International Affairs* 93(1): 27–50.

Chaturvedy, R. R. (2017) 'The Indian Ocean policy of the Modi government', in S. Singh (ed.) *Modi and the World: (Re)Constructing Indian Foreign Policy*, Singapore: World Scientific, 163–184.

Chaudhary, A. and Pandya, D. (2017) 'India builds highway to Thailand to counter China's Silk Road', *Bloomberg*, 9 August, www.bloomberg. com/news/articles/2017-08-08/china-s-silk-road-lends-urgency-to-india-s-regional-ambitions.

Chaudhuri, P. P. (2014) '$100bn to $20bn: what missing billions say about Sino-India ties', *Hindustan Times*, 19 September, www.hindustantimes. com/india/100bn-to-20bn-what-missing-billions-say-about-sino-india-ties/story-SWW1JXnBzXCcLLLTco5DTK.html.

Chaudhuri, R. (2014) *Forged in Crisis: India and the United States since 1947*, London: C. Hurst and Co.

Chaudhuri, R. (2018) 'The making of an "all weather friendship" Pakistan, China and the history of a border agreement: 1949–1963', *International History Review* 40(1): 41–64.

Chaulia, S. (2016) *Modi Doctrine: The Foreign Policy of India's Prime Minister*, New Delhi: Bloomsbury.

Chaulia, S. (2018) 'India is the latest front in Trump's endless trade war', *Foreign Policy*, 21 June, https://foreignpolicy.com/2018/06/21/india-is-the-latest-front-in-trumps-endless-trade-war/.

Chhibber, P. K. and Jassal, N. (2017) 'India in 2017: the BJP, economic reform, and contentious politics', *Asian Survey* 58(1): 86–99.

Chhibber, P. K. and Verma, R. (2018) *Ideology and Identity: The Changing Party Systems of India*, New York: Oxford University Press.

Chiriyankandath, J. (2004) 'Realigning India: Indian foreign policy after the cold war', *The Round Table: The Commonwealth Journal of International Affairs* 93(374): 199–211.

Cohen, S. P. (2001) *India: Emerging Power*, Washington, DC: Brookings Institution Press.

Cohen, S. P. and Dasgupta, S. (2010) *Arming without Aiming: India's Military Modernization*, Washington, DC: Brookings Institution Press.

Cohen, S. P. and Dasgupta, S. (2011) 'Arms sales for India: how military trade could energize US-Indian relations', *Foreign Affairs* 90(2): 22–26.

Cook, M. and B. Das (2019) 'RCEP's strategic opportunity', *ISEAS Yusof Ishak Institute Perspective* 76, 16 October, www.think-asia.org/bitstream/handle/11540/7546/ISEAS_Perspective_2017_76.pdf?sequence=1.

Corbridge, S. and Harriss, J. (2000) *Reinventing India: Liberalization, Hindu Nationalism and Popular Democracy*, Cambridge: Polity.

Cornago, N. (2010) 'On the normalization of sub-state diplomacy', *The Hague Journal of Diplomacy* 5(1–2): 11–36.

Cox, B. and Philpott, D. (2003) 'Faith-based diplomacy: an ancient idea newly emergent', *The Brandywine Review of Faith & International Affairs* 1(2): 31–40.

Crabtree, J. (2017) '"If they kill even one Hindu, we will kill 100!"', *The Diplomat*, 30 March, https://foreignpolicy.com/2017/03/30/if-they-kill-even-one-hindu-we-will-kill-100-india-muslims-nationalism-modi/.

Crocker, W. (2008) *Nehru: A Contemporary's Estimate*, Noida: RandomHouse India.

Cronk, T. M. (2017) 'Mattis: meeting with Indian defense minister comes at time of strategic convergence', US Department of Defense, 26 September, https://dod.defense.gov/News/Article/Article/1325107/mattis-meeting-with-indian-defense-minister-comes-at-time-of-strategic-converge/.

Curtis, L. (2014) 'India and Pakistan under Modi', The Heritage Foundation, 2 April, www.heritage.org/asia/commentary/india-and-pakistan-under-modi.

Dalrymple, W. (2014) 'Narendra Modi: man of the masses', *New Statesman*, 12 May 2014, www.newstatesman.com/politics/2014/05/narendra-modi-man-masses.

Das, M. N. (1961) *The Political Philosophy of Jawaharlal Nehru*, London: George Allen and Unwin.

Dasgupta, C. (2014) 'Nehru, Patel and China', *Strategic Analysis* 38(5): 717–724.

Das Gupta, M. (2018) 'Bureaucrats wary of lateral entry in govt service as deadline for applications looms', *Hindustan Times*, 30 June, www.hindustantimes.com/india-news/unease-among-bureaucrats-over-lateral-entry-as-deadline-for-govt-s-ad-for-joint-secretary-looms/story-WApB0BSVGoPpOWqiZIwazI.html.

Dashi, D. K. (2017) 'Imphal-Moreh highway expansion likely to get cabinet nod', *Times of India*, 11 July, https://timesofindia.indiatimes.com/india/imphal-moreh-highway-expansion-likely-to-get-cabinet-nod/articleshow/59550183.cms.

Datta-Ray, D. K. (2015) *The Making of Indian Diplomacy: A Critique of Eurocentrism*, New Delhi: Oxford University Press.

Deccan Chronicle (2014) 'Flashback Friday: old pictures of PM Modi's US visit', 25 September, www.deccanchronicle.com/140925/nation-current-affairs/gallery/eve-pm-modis-us-visit-old-pictures-surface.

Deccan Herald (2014) 'Nehru was first to declare himself "pradhan sevak", says Siddaramaiah', 15 November, www.deccanherald.com/content/441653/nehru-first-declare-himself-pradhan.html.

Deccan Herald (2015) 'Modi to use "mosque diplomacy" in UAE', 14 August, www.deccanherald.com/content/495112/modi-use-mosque-diplomacy-uae.html.

Department of Commerce (2018) *Annual Report 2017–18: India's Trade Back on Track*, https://commerce.gov.in/writereaddata/uploadedfile/MOC_636626711232248483_Annual%20Report%20%202017-18%20English.pdf.

Department of Prime Minister and Cabinet (2018) 'Joint statement of the ASEAN-Australia Special Summit: the Sydney Declaration', 18 March, https://aseanaustralia.pmc.gov.au/Declaration.

Dhume, S. (2019) 'India's Government Considers a "Muslim Ban"', *The Wall Street Journal*, 18 April, www.wsj.com/articles/indias-government-considers-a-muslim-ban-11555629051.

Dinnie, K. (2015) *Nation Branding: Concepts, Issues, Practice*, London and New York: Routledge.

Dixit, J. N. (2004) *Makers of India's Foreign Policy: Raja Ram Mohan Roy to Yashwant Sinha*, New Delhi: HarperCollins.

Donthi, P. (2017) 'Undercover: Ajit Doval in theory and practice', *The Caravan: A Journal of Politics and Culture*, 1 September, www.caravanmagazine.in/reportage/ajit-doval-theory-practice.

Drezner, D. W. (2017) 'The angry populist as foreign policy leader: real change or just hot air?', *The Fletcher Forum of World Affairs* 41(2): 23–43.

Dutta, S. (2018) 'Indian Army puts Mountain Strike Corps aimed at China in cold storage', *The Print*, 12 July, https://theprint.in/security/indian-army-puts-mountain-strike-corps-aimed-at-china-in-cold-storage/82319/.

Duttagupta, I. (2018) 'How the matrix of remittances is changing for Indians', *Economic Times*, 1 July, https://economictimes.indiatimes.com/nri/visa-and-immigration/how-the-matrix-of-remittances-is-changing-for-indians/articleshow/64809196.cms.

The Economist (2015) 'High visibility', 21 May, www.economist.com/special-report/2015/05/21/high-visibility.

Edwardes, M. (1965) 'Illusion and reality in India's foreign policy', *International Affairs* 41(1): 48–58.

Envall, H. D. P. (2014) 'Japan's India engagement: from different worlds to strategic partners', in Hall, I. (2014) *The Engagement of India: Strategies and Responses*, Washington, DC: Georgetown University Press, 39–59.

Envall, H. D. P. and Hall, I. (2016) 'Asian strategic partnerships: new practices and regional security governance', *Asian Politics and Policy* 8(1): 87–105.

Fair, C. C. (2007) 'India and Iran: New Delhi's Balancing Act', *The Washington Quarterly* 30(3): 145–159.

Fernandes, V. (2014) *Modi: Making of a Prime Minister: Leadership, Governance and Performance*, Delhi: Orient.

Flåten, L. T. (2017) 'Spreading Hindutva through education: still a priority for the BJP?', *India Review* 16(4): 377–400.

Flemes, D. (2009) 'India–Brazil–South Africa (IBSA) in the new global order: interests, strategies and values of the emerging coalition', *International Studies* 46(4): 401–421.

Friedlander, P. (2016) 'Hinduism and politics', in Haynes, J. (ed.), *The Routledge Handbook of Religion and Politics*, 2nd edn, New York and London: Routledge, 70–82.

Gady, F. S. (2018) 'India's defense ministry approves procurement of 135 helicopters for navy', *The Diplomat*, 28 August, https://thediplomat.com/2018/08/indias-defense-ministry-approves-procurement-of-135-helicopters-for-navy/.

Gahilote, P. (2015) 'All the PM's men and women', *Outlook*, 28 September, www.outlookindia.com/magazine/story/all-the-pms-men-women/295335.

Gahilote, P. and Sengupta, U. (2014) 'The Pracharak is going places', *Outlook India*, 8 December, www.outlookindia.com/magazine/story/the-pracharak-is-going-places/292726.

Ganguly, A., Chauthaiwale, V. and Sinha, V.K. (eds) (2016) *The Modi Doctrine: New Paradigms in Indian Foreign Policy*, revised edn, New Delhi: Wisdom Tree.

Ganguly, S. (1994) 'The role of the prime minister in the making of foreign and defense policy in India', in J Manor (ed.), *From Nehru to the Nineties: The Chief Executive in India*, London: Hurst and Company, 138–160.

Ganguly, S. (1999) 'India's pathway to Pokhran II: the prospects and sources of New Delhi's nuclear weapons program', *International Security* 23(4): 148–177.

Ganguly, S. (2002) *Conflict Unending: India-Pakistan Tensions since 1947*, New York: Columbia University Press.

Ganguly, S. (2004) 'India and China: border issues, domestic integration, and international security', in F. R. Frankel and H. Harding (eds), *The India-China Relationship: What the United States Needs to Know*, New York: Columbia University Press and Woodrow Wilson Center Press, 103–133.

Ganguly, S. (2014) 'What will Narendra Modi's foreign policy be like?', *BBC News*, 21 May, www.bbc.com/news/world-asia-india-27482166.

Ganguly, S. (2016) 'India's emerging security policy', *Brown Journal of World Affairs* 23(1): 253–266.

Ganguly, S. (2017) 'Has Modi truly changed India's foreign policy?', *The Washington Quarterly* 40(2): 131–143.

Ganguly, S. (2018) 'India and China: on a collision course?', *Pacific Affairs* 91(2): 231–244.

Ganguly, S., Blarel, N. and Pardesi, M. S. (eds) (2018) *The Oxford Handbook of India's National Security*, New Delhi: Oxford University Press.

Ganguly, S. and Pardesi, M. S. (2013) 'Explaining sixty years of Indian foreign policy', *India Review* 8(1): 4–19.

Ganguly, S. and Scobell, A. (2018) 'The Himalayan impasse: Sino-Indian rivalry in the wake of Doklam', *The Washington Quarterly* 41(3): 177–190.

Ganguly, S. and Thompson, W. (2017) *Ascending India and Its State Capacity*, New Haven: Yale University Press.

Garver, J. W. (2001) *Protracted Contest: Sino-Indian Rivalry in the Twentieth Century*, Seattle and London: University of Washington Press.

George, V. K. (2014) 'A Hindutva variant of neo-liberalism', *The Hindu*, 4 April, www.thehindu.com/opinion/lead/a-hindutva-variant-of-neoliberalism/article5868196.ece.

George, V. K. (2018) 'The 'Acharya envoys' who propagate Indian culture', *The Hindu*, 11 March, www.thehindu.com/news/international/the-acharya-envoys-who-propagate-indian-culture/article23042016.ece.

Ghatak, M. and Roy, S. (2014) 'Did Gujarat's growth rate accelerate under Modi?', *Economic and Political Weekly* 44(15): 12–15.

Ghosh, A. (2016) 'PMO pushes for 360-degree feedback on top officials', *Indian Express*, 29 June, https://indianexpress.com/article/india/india-news-india/pmo-pushes-for-360-degree-feedback-on-top-officials-2882557/.

Ghosh, J., Chandrasekhar, C. P. and Patnaik, P. (2017) *Demonetisation Decoded: A Critique of India's Currency Experiment*, New Delhi: Routledge India.

Ghosh, M. (2018) 'The Indian perspective on the security partnership with Japan', in W. Vosse and P. Midford (eds) *Japan's New Security Partnerships: Beyond the Security Alliance*, Manchester: Manchester University Press.

Ghosh, P. S. (1994) 'Foreign policy and electoral politics in India: inconsequential connection', *Asian Survey* 34(9): 807–817.

Globescan (2017) 'Sharp drop in world views of US, UK: global poll', 7 April, https://globescan.com/sharp-drop-in-world-views-of-us-uk-global-poll/.

Glum, J. (2017) 'Presents for the President: Modi's Lincoln-themed gift tells Trump to believe in people's "basic goodness"', *Newsweek*, 27 June, www.newsweek.com/gifts-president-trump-narendra-modi-629469.

Goel, V. (2015) 'Narendra Modi, Indian Premier, courts Silicon Valley to try to ease nation's poverty', *New York Times*, 27 September, www.nytimes.com/2015/09/28/technology/narendra-modi-prime-minister-of-india-visits-silicon-valley.html.

Gokhale, N. (2017a) *Securing India the Modi Way: Pathankot, Surgical Strikes and More*, New Delhi: Bloomsbury.

Gokhale, N. (2017b) 'Ministry of Defence on the cusp of change: needs efficient follow up', in Debroy, B. and Malik, A. (eds) *India @70, Modi @3.5: Capturing India's Transformation under Narendra Modi*, New Delhi: Wisdom Tree, 157–162.

Gokhale, N. (2018) 'Indian national security strategy crystallising at a fast pace', *Bharat Shakti*, 16 August, https://bharatshakti.in/indian-national-security-strategy-crystallising-at-a-fast-pace/.

Golwalkar, M. S. (1996) *Bunch of Thoughts*, 3rd edn, Bangalore: Sahitya Sindhu Prakashana.

Gopalan, S. T. (2016) 'Withering regulation? An interim review of Modi government's labour reforms', *Journal of Asian Public Policy* 9(2): 170–184.

Gordon, S. and Henningham, S. (eds) (1995) 'India looks East: an emerging power and its Asia-Pacific neighbours', *Canberra Papers on Strategy and Defence* 111, Canberra: Strategic and Defence Studies Centre, The Australian National University.

Gowan, A. (2018) 'Trump joked he could play matchmaker for India's prime minister, report says', *The Washington Post*, 13 August, www.washingtonpost.com/world/2018/08/13/trump-joked-he-could-play-matchmaker-indias-bachelor-prime-minister-report-says/?utm_term=.9ac8746853a8.

Graham, B. (1990) *Hindu Nationalism and Indian Politics: The Origins and Development of the Bharatiya Jana Sangh*, Cambridge: Cambridge University Press.

Grare, F. (2014) 'India-Pakistan relations: does Modi matter?' *The Washington Quarterly* 37(4): 101–114.

Grare, F. (2016) *India Turns East: International Engagement and US-China Rivalry*, London: C. Hurst and Co.

Guha, R. (2014) 'How the Congress lost the diaspora', *Hindustan Times*, 28 September, www.hindustantimes.com/columns/how-the-congress-lost-the-diaspora/story-K8hIXsz1D7dzZFFjr41fbO.html.

Gujral, I. K. (2011) *Matters of Discretion: An Autobiography*, New Delhi: Hay House.

Gupta, A. (2018) *How India Manages Its National Security*, New Delhi: Penguin.

Gupta, B. S. (1997) 'India in the twenty-first century', *International Affairs* 73(2): 297–314.

Gupta, G. (2008) '"Welcome" SMS was all it took to get Tata: Modi', *Indian Express*, 13 October, http://archive.indianexpress.com/news/-welcome--sms-was-all-it-took-to-get-tata-modi/372943/.

Gupta, S. (2015) 'PM Narendra Modi to cut down foreign trips in 2016', *Hindustan Times*, 31 December, www.hindustantimes.com/india/narendra-modi-to-cut-down-foreign-trips-in-2016/story-aiZ2P1Wcsw1lnmpKJBdblO.html.

Gupta, S. (2019) 'India's trade engagement: the more things change, the more they remain the same', *International Studies Perspectives* 20(1): 14–19.

Hagerty, D. (1991) 'India's regional security doctrine', *Asian Survey* 31(4): 351–363.

Haidar, S. (2015) 'Jaishankar takes charge as foreign secretary', *The Hindu*, 29 January, www.thehindu.com/news/national/jaishankar-takes-charge-as-indias-foreign-secretary/article6833477.ece.

Hall, I. 'India's New Public Diplomacy: Soft Power and the Limits of Government Action', *Asian Survey* 42(6): 1089–1110.

Hall, I (2013) 'Tilting at windmills? The Indian debate on responsibility to protect after UNSC 1973', *Global Responsibility to Protect* 5(1): 84–108.

Hall, I. (2015a) 'Is a "Modi doctrine" emerging in Indian foreign policy?', *Australian Journal of International Affairs* 69(3): 247–252.

Hall, I. (2015b) 'Normative power India?', in J. Gaskarth (ed.), *China, India and the Future of International Society*, Lanham, MD: Rowman and Littlefield, 89–104.

Hall, I. (2016a) 'Multialignment and Indian foreign policy under Narendra Modi', *The Round Table: The Commonwealth Journal of International Affairs* 105(3): 271–286.

Hall, I. (2016b) 'The persistence of Nehruvianism in Indian strategic culture', in A. J. Tellis, A. Szalwinski and M. Weiss (eds) *Strategic Asia 2016–17: Understanding Strategic Cultures in the Asia-Pacific*, Seattle and Washington, DC: National Bureau of Asian Research, 141–168.

Hall, I. (2017a) 'Not promoting, not exporting: India's democracy assistance', *Rising Powers Quarterly* 2(3): 51–69.

Hall, I. (2017b) 'Narendra Modi and India's normative power', *International Affairs* 93(1): 113–131.

Hall, I. (2018) 'India's national security: a liberal account', in S. Ganguly, N. Blarel and M. S. Pardesi (eds) *The Oxford Handbook of India's National Security*, New Delhi: Oxford University Press, 42–59.

Hall, I. (2019) 'Narendra Modi's New Religious Diplomacy', *International Studies Perspectives* 20(1): 11–14.

Hall, I. and Smith, F. (2013) 'The struggle for soft power in Asia: public diplomacy and regional competition' *Asian Security* 9(1): 1–18.

Hazarika, O. B. (2014) 'Evolving dynamics of federalism and foreign policy: engagement of Indian states in external affairs', *Indian Foreign Affairs Journal* 9(1): 33–45.

Heath, O. (2015) 'The BJP's return to power: mobilisation, conversion and vote swing in the 2014 Indian elections', *Contemporary South Asia* 23(2): 123–135.

Hopewell, K. (2016) *Breaking the WTO: How Emerging Powers Disrupted the Neoliberal Project*, Stanford, CA: Stanford University Press.

Houreld, K. (2015) 'China and Pakistan launch economic corridor plan worth $46 billion', *Reuters*, 20 April, www.reuters.com/article/us-pakistan-china/china-and-pakistan-launch-economic-corridor-plan-worth-46-billion-idUSKBN0NA12T20150420.

HT Correspondent (2019) 'Full text of PM Modi's exclusive interview', *Hindustan Times*, 6 April, www.hindustantimes.com/india-news/full-text-of-pm-modi-s-exclusive-interview/story-7OqHvrn88TQhqfKutNqF5I.html.

Human Rights Watch (2017) 'India: "cow protection" spurs vigilante violence', 27 April, www.hrw.org/news/2017/04/27/india-cow-protection-spurs-vigilante-violence.

Hurrell, A. and Sengupta, S. (2012) 'Emerging powers, North–South relations and global climate politics', *International Affairs* 88(3): 463–484.

India TV News Desk (2013) 'RSS sets four Hindutva conditions for supporting Modi as PM', *India TV*, 10 September, www.indiatvnews.com/politics/national/rss-sets-four-hindutva-conditions-for-supporting-modi-as-pm-12457.html.

Indian Express (2012) "We are not the HR manager for the BJP. Everyone has to run their own organisation", 9 September, http://archive.indianexpress.com/news/anna-has-a-standing-of-his-own.-why-should-the-sangh-take-credit-for-his-planning/999881/0#.

International Energy Agency (2018) 'Renewables 2018: Market analysis and forecast from 2018 to 2023', www.iea.org/renewables2018/power/.

Ireland, J. (2014) 'How Narendra Modi turned Parliament House into a rock star's stage', *Sydney Morning Herald*, 19 November, www.smh.com.au/politics/federal/how-narendra-modi-turned-parliament-house-into-a-rock-stars-stage-20141118-11p4qn.html.

Jacob, H. (2018) *The Line of Control*, New Delhi: Penguin Viking.

Jacob, J. and Giri, A. (2016) 'Saarc summit collapses after India and three other members pull out', *Hindustan Times*, 29 September, www.hindustantimes.com/world-news/saarc-summit-collapses-after-india-and-3-other-members-pull-out/story-kIMWfSqirGLzB6MEfuS3CN.html.

Jacob, J. T. (2015) 'Thinking East Asia, acting local: constraints, challenges, and contradictions in Indian public diplomacy', in J. Melissen and Y. Sohn (eds), *Understanding Public Diplomacy in East Asia: Middle Powers in a Troubled Region*, New York: Palgrave, 155–178.

Jaffrelot, C. (1996) *The Hindu Nationalist Movement in India,* New York: Columbia University Press.

Jaffrelot, C. (2007) 'The 2002 pogrom in Gujarat: the post 9/11 face of Hindu nationalist anti-Muslim violence', in J. R. Hinnells and R. King (eds) *Religion and Violence in South Asia: Theory and Practice*, London and New York: Routledge, 164–182.

Jaffrelot, C. (2008) 'Gujarat: the meaning of Modi's victory', *Economic and Political Weekly* 43(15): 13–14.

Jaffrelot, C. (2012) 'Gujarat 2002: what justice for the victims? The Supreme Court, the SIT, the police and the state judiciary', *Economic and Political Weekly* 47(8): 77–89.

Jaffrelot, C. (2013) 'Gujarat elections: the sub-text of Modi's "hattrick" – High tech populism and the "neo-middle class"'. *Studies in Indian Politics* 1(1): 79–95.

Jaffrelot, C. (2015a) 'The Modi-centric BJP 2014 election campaign: new techniques and old tactics', *Contemporary South Asia* 23(2): 151–166.

Jaffrelot, C. (2015b) 'What 'Gujarat model'? – Growth without development – and with socio-political polarisation', *South Asia: Journal of South Asian Studies* 38(4): 820–838.

Jaffrelot, C. (2015c) 'Narendra Modi and the power of television in Gujarat', *Television and New Media* 16(4): 346–353.

Jaffrelot, C. (2016) 'Narendra Modi between Hindutva and subnationalism: the Gujarati *asmita* of a Hindu Hriday Samrat', *India Review* 15(2): 196–217.

Jaffrelot, C. (2017) 'India in 2016: assessing Modi mid-term', *Asian Survey* 57(1): 21–32.

Jaffrelot, C. and Singh Sidhu, W. P. (2013) 'From Plurilateralism to Multilateralism? G20, IBSA, BRICS, and BASIC', in Singh Sidhu, W. P., Mehta, P. B. and Jones, B. (eds) (2013) *Shaping the Emerging World: India and the Multilateral Order*, Washington, DC: Brookings, 319–340.

Jaffrelot, C. and Tillin, L. (2017) 'Populism in India', in C. Rovira Kaltwasser, P. A. Taggart, P. Ochoa Espejo and P. Ostiguy (eds), *The Oxford Handbook of Populism*, Oxford: Oxford University Press, 179–194.

Jaganathan, M. M. and Kurtz, G. (2014) 'Singing the tune of sovereignty? India and the responsibility to protect', *Conflict, Security & Development* 14(4): 461–487.

Jagannathan, R. (2016) 'Who is the real Narendra Modi: a "communal czar" or an "inclusive icon"?', in *Making Sense of Modi's India*, New Delhi: HarperCollins, 80–88.

Jain, P. C. (ed.) (1992) *India's Economic Crisis: Diagnosis and Treatment*, New Delhi: Concept Publishing.

Jain, S. (2016) 'For Sri Sri Event, Union Government Gave Rs. 2.25-Crore Grant' *NDTV*, 11 March, www.ndtv.com/india-news/for-sri-sri-event-union-government-gave-rs-2-5-crore-grant-1285381.

Jaishankar, D. (2014) 'Eeny, Meeny, Miney, Modi: Does India's prime minister actually have a foreign policy?', *Foreign Policy*, 19 May, https://foreignpolicy.com/2014/05/19/eeny-meeny-miney-modi/.

Jaishankar, S. (2015a) Comments after 'India, the United States and China' Fullerton Lecture (International Institute for Strategic Studies), 19 July, www.youtube.com/watch?v=et2ihw8jHaY&feature=youtu.be&t=46m27s.

Jaishankar, S. (2015b) 'India, the United States and China', Fullerton Lecture (International Institute for Strategic Studies), 19 July, www.mea.gov.in/Speeches-Statements.htm?dtl/25493/iiss+fullerton+lecture+by+dr+s+jaishankar+foreign+secretary+in+singapore.

Jeffrey, R. (2015) 'The rise and rise of Narendra Modi', *Inside Story*, 10 June, https://insidestory.org.au/the-rise-and-rise-of-narendra-modi.

Jha, P. (2015) 'India's most influential think-tanks', *Hindustan Times*, 16 August, www.hindustantimes.com/india/india-s-most-influential-think-tanks/story-emb0db2lmqltL8pKeYuZiL.html.

Jha, P. (2017) *How the BJP Wins: Inside India's Greatest Election Machine*, New Delhi: Juggernaut.

Johnston, A. I. (2008) *Social States: China in International Institutions, 1980–2000*, Princeton, NJ and Oxford: Princeton University Press.

Johnston, D. (ed.) (2003) *Faith-based Diplomacy: Trumping Realpolitik*, Oxford: Oxford University Press.

Joseph, J. (2016) *A Feast of Vultures: The Hidden Business of Democracy in India*, New Delhi: HarperCollins.

Joshi, M. (2018) *Scraping the Bottom of the Barrel: Budgets, Organisation and Leadership in the Indian Defence System*, ORF Special Report 74, August, www.orfonline.org/wp-content/uploads/2018/08/ORF_Special_Report_74_Defence_1.pdf.

Joshi, S. (2015a) *Indian Power Projection: Ambition, Arms and Influence*, Whitehall Paper 85, London: Royal United Services Institute.

Joshi, S. (2015b) 'Indian defence policy', *RUSI Commentary*, 11 May, https://rusi.org/commentary/indian-defence-policy.

Joshi, S. (2018) 'Indian military modernization', in S. Ganguly, N. Blarel and M. S. Pardesi (eds) *The Oxford Handbook of India's National Security*, New Delhi: Oxford University Press, 389–416.

Kamath, M. V. and Randeri, K. (2013) *The Man of the Moment: Narendra Modi*, New Delhi: Times Group Books.

Kang, B. (2004) 'RSS eyes change, seeks to involve young blood, modern ideology', *India Today*, 20 December, www.indiatoday.in/magazine/nation/story/20041220-gennext-in-rashtriya-swayamsevak-sangh-rss-leadership-tries-to-do-sangh-makeover-by-reviving-sanghs-medieval-ideas-about-india-and-indian-culture-788936-2004-12-20.

Kang, B. (2018) 'How PM Modi's "Party of Muslims" Remark Exposes Congress' Never-Ending Identity Crisis', *News18*, 17 July, www.news18.com/news/opinion/opinion-does-pm-modis-party-of-muslims-remark-exposes-congress-never-ending-identity-crisis-1814137.html.

Kanungo, P. (2003) *RSS's Tryst with Politics: From Hedgewar to Sudarshan*, New Delhi: Manohar.

Kanungo, P. and Farooqui, A. (2008) 'Tracking Moditva: an analysis of the 2007 Gujarat elections campaign', *Contemporary Perspectives* 2(2): 222–245.

Kant, A. (2009) *Branding India: An Incredible Story*, New Delhi: HarperCollins.

Kanwal, G (ed) (2016) *The New Arthashastra: A Security Strategy for India*, New Delhi: HarperCollins.

Kanwal, G. and Kohli, N. (eds) (2018) *Defence Reforms: A National Imperative*, New Delhi: Institute for Defence Studies and Analyses and Pentagon Press.

Kapur, D. (2009) 'Public opinion and Indian foreign policy' *India Review* 8(3): 286–305.

Kapur, D. (2015) 'Public Opinion', in D. M. Malone, C. R. Mohan and S. Raghavan (eds), *The Oxford Handbook of Indian Foreign Policy*, Oxford: Oxford University Press, 298–311.

Kapur, D. and Vaishnav, M. (2018) 'Introduction', in D. Kapur and M. Vaishnav (eds) *Costs of Democracy: Political Finance in India*, New Delhi: Oxford University Press, 1–14.

Kapur, S. P. and Ganguly, S. (2007) 'The transformation of US-India relations: an explanation for the rapprochement and prospects for the future', *Asian Survey* 47(4): 642–656.

Karmakar, R. (2014) 'Modi advises China to shed its "expansionist" attitude', *Hindustan Times*, 23 February, www.hindustantimes.com/india/modi-advises-china-to-shed-its-expansionist-attitude/story-wF4wevDFm2v01rDNOgBmgK.html.

Karnad, B. (2005) *Nuclear Weapons and Indian Security: The Realist Foundations of Strategy*, 2nd edn, New Delhi: Macmillan.

Karnad, B. (2015) *Why India is not a Great Power (yet)*, New Delhi: Penguin Viking.

Karnad, B. (2018) *Staggering Forward: Narendra Modi and India's Global Ambition*, New Delhi: Penguin Viking.

Kartha, T. (2018) 'The rejig of India's national security architecture has been a long time coming', *The Wire*, 17 October, https://thewire.in/security/ajit-doval-national-security-council-secretariat.

Kawade, A. (2019) 'What Are the Political Implications of Narendra Modi's #MainBhiChowkidar Campaign?', *Economic and Political Weekly* 54(20), 15 May, www.epw.in/engage/article/what-are-political-implications-narendra-modis.

Kautilya (2000) *The Arthashastra*, New Delhi: Penguin India.

Kazmin, A. (2015) 'India's Narendra Modi stumbles on land reform', *Financial Times*, 10 August, www.ft.com/content/ee2fb6ec-3e55-11e5-9abe-5b335da3a90e.

Kennedy, A. B. (2011) 'India's nuclear odyssey: implicit umbrellas, diplomatic disappointments, and the bomb', *International Security* 36(2): 120–153.

Kennedy, A. B. (2015) 'Nehru's foreign policy: realism and idealism conjoined', in D. M. Malone, C. R. Mohan and S. Raghavan (eds), *The Oxford Handbook of Indian Foreign Policy*, Oxford: Oxford University Press, 92–103.

Kenny, P. (2017) *Populism and Patronage: Why Populists Win Elections in India, Asia, and Beyond*, Oxford: Oxford University Press.

Khanna, G. and Zimmermann, L. (2017) 'Guns and butter? Fighting violence with the promise of development', *Journal of Development Economics* 124: 120–141.

Khanna, P. and Mohan, C. R. (2006) 'Getting Asia right', *Policy Review*, www.hoover.org/research/getting-india-right.

Khilnani, S. (2012) *The Idea of India*, new edn, New Delhi: Penguin.

Khilnani, S., Kumar, R. Bhanu Mehta, P., Menon, P., Nilekani, N., Raghavan, S. Saran, S. and Varadarajan, S. (2013) *NonAlignment 2.0: A Foreign and Strategic Policy for India in the 21st Century*, New Delhi: Centre for Policy Research.

Kochanek, S. A. (1996) 'Liberalisation and business lobbying in India', *Journal of Commonwealth and Comparative Politics* 34(3): 155–173.

Kohli, A. (1990) *Democracy and Discontent: India's Growing Crisis of Governability*, Cambridge: Cambridge University Press.

Kohli, N. S. (2019) 'TsuNamo 2.0: How BJP won a landslide, and the big messages coming out of its resounding victory', *Times of India*, 28 May, https://timesofindia.indiatimes.com/blogs/toi-edit-page/tsunamo-2-0-how-bjp-won-a-landslide-and-the-big-messages-coming-out-of-its-resounding-victory/.

Krasner, S. (1985) *Structural Conflict: The Third World against Global Liberalism*, Berkeley and Los Angeles, CA: University of California Press.

Kripalani, A. J. B. (1959) 'For principled neutrality: a new appraisal of Indian foreign policy', *Foreign Affairs* 38: 46–60.

Krishna, S. (1994) 'Cartographic anxiety: mapping the body politic in India', *Alternatives: Global, Local, Political* 19: 507–521.

Krishnan, A. (2014) 'China wants India to play key role in "Silk Road" plan', *The Hindu*, 10 August, www.thehindu.com/news/international/world/china-wants-india-to-play-key-role-in-silk-road-plan/article6301227.ece.

Kugiel, P. (2017) *India's Soft Power: A New Foreign Policy Strategy*, London and New York: Routledge.

Kulkarni, S. (2016) 'India under Modi: will the turning point be followed by a point of return?', in *Making Sense of Modi's India*, New Delhi: HarperCollins, 120–137.

Kumar, R. (2015) 'The private sector', in in D. Malone, C. R. Mohan and S. Raghavan (eds) *The Oxford Handbook of Indian Foreign Policy*, Oxford: Oxford University Press, 247–258.

Kumar, R. (2016) 'Role of business in India's foreign policy', *India Review* 15(1): 98–111.

Kumar, S. (2002) 'Gujarat assembly elections 2002', *Economic and Political Weekly* 38(4): 270–275.

Kux, D. (1992) *India and the United States: Estranged Democracies, 1947–1991*, Washington, DC: National Defense University Press.

Langa, M. (2015) 'Gautam Adani, PM Modi's constant companion on overseas trips', *Hindustan Times*, 16 April, www.hindustantimes.com/india/gautam-adani-pm-modi-s-constant-companion-on-overseas-trips/story-CMDqyMTSNxoewGpQVqEeDK.html.

Leslie, J. G. (2017) 'Netanyahu's populism: an overlooked explanation for Israeli foreign policy', *SAIS Review* 37(1): 75–82.

Leveillant, M. (2017) 'Diplomacy as diaspora management: the case of India and the Gulf States', *Asie Visions* 95, November, www.ifri.org/sites/default/files/atoms/files/levaillant_diplomacy_diaspora_management_2017.pdf.

Lucas, G. (2014) 'Narendra Modi's foreign policy challenges', *Deutsche Welle*, 26 May, www.dw.com/en/narendra-modis-foreign-policy-challenges/a-17662599.

Madan, T. (2014) 'A Modi foreign policy: the knowns and unknowns', Brookings Institution, 16 May, www.brookings.edu/blog/up-front/2014/05/16/a-modi-foreign-policy-the-knowns-and-unknowns/.

Madan, T. (2015) 'Officialdom: South block and beyond', in D. Malone, C. R. Mohan and S. Raghavan (eds) *The Oxford Handbook of Indian Foreign Policy*, Oxford: Oxford University Press, 232–246.

Madan, T. (2016) 'What India thinks about China's One Belt, One Road initiative (but does not explicitly say)', *Order from Chaos* blog, Brookings Institution, 14 March, www.brookings.edu/blog/order-from-chaos/2016/03/14/whatindia-thinks-about-chinas-one-belt-one-road-initiative-but-doesnt-explicitly-say/.

Madhav, R. (2011) 'Chinese aggression – Indian response', India Foundation online, www.indiafoundation.in/chinese-aggression-indias-response/.

Madhav, R. (2014a) *Uneasy Neighbours: India and China after 50 Years of the War*, New Delhi: Har Anand.

Madhav, R. (2014b) 'Moving beyond the Panchsheel deception', *Indian Express*, 28 June, https://indianexpress.com/article/opinion/columns/moving-beyond-the-panchsheel-deception/.

Madhav, R. (2017) 'Address at the BRICS political parties forum', 15 June, www.rammadhav.in/speeches/address-at-the-brics-political-parties-forum-10-06-2017-fuzhou-china/.

Madhukalya, A. (2019) 'PM speech asking voters to dedicate ballot to Balakot not violation: EC', *Hindustan Times*, 2 May, www.hindustantimes.com/lok-sabha-elections/pm-modi-s-speech-asking-youngsters-to-dedicate-vote-to-soldiers-for-balakot-strikes-didn-t-violate-poll-code-ec/story-X0pHp70FHAWSL5hVvrMi8J.html.

Mail Today Bureau (2015) 'India Today-Cicero Mood of the Nation Poll: 300 days after storming into Delhi durbar, PM Modi's popularity has slid due to ghar wapsi', *India Today*, 14 February, www.indiatoday.in/mail-today/story/modi-popularity-hit-by-ghar-wapsi-church-issue-hindutva-mood-of-the-nation-poll-246952-2015-02-14.

Maini, T. S. (2015) 'The center is not all: how india's states are luring foreign investors', *Global Asia* 10(2): 94–99.

Malik, J. M. (1991) 'India's response to the Gulf Crisis: implications for indian foreign policy', *Asian Survey* 31(9): 847–861.

Mallet, V. (2014) 'China-India border stand-off overshadows Xi Jinping's deals', *Financial Times*, 19 September, www.ft.com/content/28c61aae-3f0f-11e4-a861-00144feabdc0.

Malone, D. M. (2011) *Does the Elephant Dance? Contemporary Indian Foreign Policy*, Oxford: Oxford University Press.

Malone, D., Mohan, C. R and Raghavan, S. (eds) (2015) *The Oxford Handbook of Indian Foreign Policy*, Oxford: Oxford University Press.

Mankoff, J. (2015) 'Russia's Asia pivot: confrontation or cooperation?' *Asia Policy* 19: 65–88.

Mann, J. (2014) 'Why Narendra Modi was banned from the US', *The Wall Street Journal*, 2 May, www.wsj.com/articles/why-narendra-modi-was-banned-from-the-u-s-1399062010.

Manor, J. (2015) 'A precarious enterprise? Multiple antagonisms during year one of the Modi government', *South Asia: Journal of South Asian Studies* 38(4): 736–754.

Mansingh, S. (2015) 'Indira Gandhi's foreign policy: hard realism?', in D. Malone, C. R. Mohan and S. Raghavan (eds) *The Oxford Handbook of Indian Foreign Policy*, Oxford: Oxford University Press, 104–116.

Mantri, R. and Gupta, H. (2013) 'Narendra Modi as the anti-Nehru', *LiveMint*, 2 September, www.livemint.com/Opinion/DCrr6B9v1MvR6QTEMGDcJM/Narendra-Modi-as-the-antiNehru.html.

Marino, A. (2014) *Narendra Modi: A Political Biography*, New Delhi: HarperCollins.

Markey, D. (2009) 'Developing India's foreign policy "software"', *Asia Policy* 8: 75–96.

Marlow, I. (2018) 'Modi's trips around the world cost Indian taxpayers $280 million', *Bloomberg*, 13 December, www.bloomberg.com/news/articles/2018-12-13/here-s-what-modi-spent-to-sell-the-india-story-around-the-world.

Mattoo, A. and Jacob H. (eds) *Shaping India's Foreign Policy: People, Politics and Places*, New Delhi: Har Anand.

Maxwell, N. (2015) *India's China War*, revised and updated edn, New Delhi and Dehradun: Natraj Publishers.

Mazumdar, A. and Statz, E. (2015) 'Democracy promotion in India's foreign policy: emerging trends and developments', *Asian Affairs: An American Review* 42(2): 77–98.

Mazumdar, A. (2018) 'India's Soft Power under the Modi Administration: Buddhism, Diaspora and Yoga', *Asian Affairs* 49(3): 468–491.

McCarthy, J. (2015) 'In India, Obama speeches spark debate on religious tolerance', *National Public Radio*, 6 February, www.npr.org/sections/thetwo-way/2015/02/06/384345012/in-india-obama-speeches-spark-debate-on-religious-tolerance.

McDonnell, D. and Cabrera, L. (2019) 'The right-wing populism of India's Bharatiya Janata Party (and why comparativists should care)', *Democratization* 26(3): 484–509.

McGarr, P. (2013) *The Cold War in South Asia: Britain, the United States and the Indian Subcontinent, 1945–1965*, Cambridge: Cambridge University Press.

MEA (Ministry of External Affairs) (2008) *Annual Report 2007–08*, www.mea.gov.in/Uploads/PublicationDocs/168_Annual-Report-2006-2007.pdf.

MEA (2009) *Annual Report 2008–09*, www.mea.gov.in/Uploads/PublicationDocs/170_Annual-Report-2008-2009.pdf.

MEA (2014a) 'Detailed demands for grants 2014–15', 1 August, www. mea.gov.in/Uploads/PublicationDocs/23803_Detailed_Demands_for_ Grants_2014_15.pdf.

MEA (2014b) *Breakthrough Diplomacy: New Vision, New Vigour*, 11 December, http://mea.gov.in/Images/pdf/Breakthroughdiplomacy. pdf.

MEA (2014c) 'Joint statement between the Republic of India and the People's Republic of China on building a closer developmental partnership', 19 September, http://mea.gov.in/bilateral-documents. htm?dtl/24022.

MEA (2014d) 'Vision statement for the US-India Strategic Partnership – "Chalein saath saath: Forward together we go"', 29 September, www. mea.gov.in/bilateral-documents.htm?dtl/24048/vision+statement+for +the+usindia+strategic+partnershipchalein+saath+saath+forward+ together+we+go.

MEA (2015a) 'US-India joint strategic vision for the Asia-Pacific and Indian Ocean region', 25 January, www.mea.gov.in/bilateral-documents. htm?dtl/24728/USIndia_Joint_Strategic_Vision_for_the_AsiaPacific_ and_Indian_Ocean_Region.

MEA (2015b) 'Remarks by Foreign Secretary at the release of Dr C. Raja Mohan's book "Modi's World-Expanding India's Sphere of Influence"' (July 17, 2015)', 18 July, http://mea.gov.in/Speeches-Statements. htm?dtl/25491/Remarks+by+Foreign+Secretary+at+the+release+ of+Dr+C+Raja+Mohans+book+Modis+WorldExpanding+Indias+ Sphere+of+InfuencequotJuly+17+2015.

MEA (2015c) 'IISS Fullerton Lecture by Dr S. Jaishankar, Foreign Secretary in Singapore', 20 July, www.mea.gov.in/Speeches-Statements. htm?dtl/25493/iiss+fullerton+lecture+by+dr+s+jaishankar+foreign+ secretary+in+singapore.

MEA (2016) 'Speech by Foreign Secretary at Raisina Dialogue in New Delhi', 2 March, http://mea.gov.in/Speeches-Statements. htm?dtl/26433/Speech_by_Foreign_Secretary_at_Raisina_Dialogue_ in_New_Delhi_March_2_2015.

MEA (2017a) 'Inaugural address by Prime Minister at second Raisina Dialogue, New Delhi', 17 January, https://mea.gov.in/Speeches-Statements.htm?dtl/27948/Inaugural_Address_by_Prime_Minister_at_ Second_Raisina_Dialogue_New_Delhi_January_17_2017.

MEA (2017b) 'Official spokesperson's response to a query on participation of India in OBOR/BRI Forum', 13 May, www.mea.gov.in/media-briefings.htm?dtl/28463/Official+Spokespersons+response+to+a+ query+on+participation+of+India+in+OBORBRI+Forum.

MEA (2017c) 'India-Australia-Japan-US consultations on Indo-Pacific (November 12, 2017)', https://mea.gov.in/press-releases. htm?dtl/29110/IndiaAustraliaJapanUS_Consultations_on_IndoPacific_ November_12_2017.

MEA (2018a) Overseas Citizenship of India Scheme, https://mea.gov.in/ overseas-citizenship-of-india-scheme.htm.

MEA (2018b) 'Detailed demands for grants 2014–15', 13 April, www. mea.gov.in/Uploads/PublicationDocs/29813_DDG_2018-19.pdf.

MEA (2018c) 'Prime Minister's keynote address at Shangri La Dialogue', 1 June, www.mea.gov.in/Speeches-Statements.htm?dtl/29943/ Prime+Ministers+Keynote+Address+at+Shangri+La+Dialogue+ June+01+2018.

MEA (2018d) 'India-China informal summit at Wuhan', 28 April, https://mea.gov.in/press-releases.htm?dtl/29853/IndiaChina_Informal_ Summit_at_Wuhan.

Medcalf, R. (2013) 'The Indo-Pacific: what's in a name?' *The American Interest* 9(2): 58–66.

Mehra, P. (2019) *The Lost Decade, 2008–2018: How India's Growth Story Devolved into Growth Without a Story*, Gurgaon: Penguin.

Mehta, J. S. (2010) *The Tryst Betrayed: Reflections on Diplomacy and Development*, New Delhi: Penguin Viking.

Mehta, N. (2006) 'Modi and the camera: the politics of television in the 2002 Gujarat riots', *South Asia: Journal of South Asian Studies* 29(3): 395–414.

Mehta, P. B. (2009) 'Still under Nehru's shadow? The absence of foreign policy frameworks in India', *India Review* 8(3): 209–233.

Menon, A. (2015) 'Rise of Ram Madhav: Modi's outreach man', *DailyO*, 26 June, www.dailyo.in/politics/meet-ram-madhav-modis-outreach-man/story/1/690.html.

Menon, R. (2014) *Modi Demystified: The Making of a Prime Minister*, New Delhi: HarperCollins.

Miglani, S. and Chalmers, J. (2014) 'BJP puts "no first use" nuclear policy in doubt', *Reuters*, 7 April, https://in.reuters.com/article/india-election-bjp-manifesto/bjp-puts-no-first-use-nuclear-policy-in-doubt-idINDEEA3605820140407.

Ministry of Commerce and Industry (2015) Foreign Trade Policy, 1st April, 2015–31st March, 2020, http://dgft.gov.in/sites/default/files/ Updated_FTP_2015-2020.pdf.

MFAPRC (Ministry of Foreign Affairs of the People's Republic of China) (2013a) 'President Xi Jinping delivers important speech and proposes to build a Silk Road economic belt with Central Asian countries', 7 September, www.fmprc.gov.cn/mfa_eng/topics_665678/xjpfwzysiesgjtfhshzzfh_665686/t1076334.shtml.

MFAPRC (2013b) 'Xi Jinping: let the sense of community of common destiny take deep root in neighbouring countries', 25 October, www.fmprc.gov.cn/mfa_eng/wjb_663304/wjbz_663308/activities_663312/t1093870.shtml

Ministry of Foreign Affairs of Japan (2016) 'Japan-India joint statement,' 11 November, www.mofa.go.jp/files/000202950.pdf.

Mishra, A. (2012) 'India's non-liberal democracy and the discourse of democracy promotion', *South Asian Survey* 19(1): 33–59.

Mishra, A. R. (2015) 'NDA govt scraps plan to set up Saarc development bank', *LiveMint*, 3 February, www.livemint.com/Politics/vGeDRynVJ7ziAcgEHA6QNN/NDA-govt-scraps-plan-to-set-up-Saarc-development-bank.html.

Mishra, S. (2017) 'Modi and America: great expectations and enduring constraints', in S. Singh, (ed.) *Modi and the World: (Re)Constructing Indian Foreign Policy*, Singapore: World Scientific, 43–68.

Mistry, D. (2014) *The US-India Nuclear Agreement: Diplomacy and Domestic Politics*, New Delhi: Cambridge University Press.

Mitra, S. K. (2009) 'Nuclear, engaged, and non-aligned: contradiction and coherence in India's foreign policy', *India Quarterly* 65(1): 15–35.

Mitta, M. (2014) *The Fiction of Fact-Finding: Modi and Godhra*, New Delhi: HarperCollins.

MoD (Ministry of Defence) (2018) Defence Procurement Procedure, https://mod.gov.in/defence-procurement-procedure.

Modi, N. (2011) *Convenient Action: Gujarat's Response to the Challenge of Climate Change*, New Delhi: Macmillan.

Modi, N. (2014a) 'Full text: Prime Minister Narendra Modi's speech on 68th Independence Day', *Indian Express*, 16 August, https://indianexpress.com/article/india/india-others/full-text-prime-minister-narendra-modis-speech-on-68th-independence-day/.

Modi, N. (2014b) 'Address to the 69th session of the General Assembly', 27 September, www.narendramodi.in/text-of-the-pms-statement-at-the-united-nations-general-assembly-6660.

Modi, N. (2014c) 'I assure all our NRIs that India will never let you down: Narendra Modi speaks at Pravasi Bharatiya Divas 2014', 9 January, www.narendramodi.in/shri-modis-speech-at-pravasi-bharatiya-divas-2014-5863

Modi, N. (2014d) 'PM's address to Indian community at Allphones Arena, Sydney', 17 November, www.narendramodi.in/pms-address-to-indian-community-at-allphones-arena-sydney-6904.

Modi, N. (2014e) 'Red carpet, not red tape', 10 May, www.narendramodi.in/red-carpet-not-red-tape-3160.

Modi, N. (2014f) 'Text of Prime Minister's speech at 2014 SAARC Summit in Nepal', 26 November, www.narendramodi.in/text-of-prime-ministers-speech-at-2014-saarc-summit-in-nepal-6941.

Modi, N. (2014g) 'PM's address at the Combined Commanders Conference', 17 October, www.narendramodi.in/pms-address-at-the-combined-commanders-conference-6766.

Modi, N. (2015a) *Jyotipunj*, New Delhi: Prabhat Prakashan.

Modi, N. (2015b) 'PM to IAS probationers', 16 February, www.narendramodi.in/pm-to-ias-probationers-7261.

Modi, N. (2015c) 'Prime Minister Narendra Modi: full speech in Toronto, Canada', 15 April, www.youtube.com/watch?v=vNd8RZG4j-c.

Modi, N. (2015d) 'PM Modi's address at "Samvad"', http://samvadebook.narendramodi.in.

Modi, N. (2015e) 'India doesn't want favours from the world, India wants equality': PM Modi at Wembley, 13 November, www.narendramodi.in/india-doesn-t-want-favours-from-the-world-india-wants-equality-pm-modi-at-wembley-375884.

Modi, N. (2015f) 'Text of the PM's remarks on the commissioning of the coast ship Barracuda', 12 March, www.narendramodi.in/text-of-the-pms-remarks-on-the-commissioning-of-coast-ship-barracuda-2954.

Modi, N. (2016a) 'World Culture Festival is a Kumbh Mela of culture: PM Modi', 11 March, www.narendramodi.in/pm-modi-at-the-inaguration-of-2016-world-culture-festival-by-art-of-living-in-new-delhi-428085.

Modi, N. (2016b) 'Sufism is the voice of peace, co-existence, compassion and equality; a call to universal brotherhood: PM Modi', 17 March, www.narendramodi.in/pm-modi-at-the-world-islamic-sufi-conference-in-new-delhi-428276.

Modi, N. (2018a) 'Our aim is to generate 175GW of renewable energy by 2022: PM Modi', 11 March, www.narendramodi.in/text-of-pms-address-at-the-inaugural-session-of-the-founding-conference-of-international-solar-alliance-539272.

Modi, N. (2018b) 'Every Indian is working to realize the vision of a "New India": PM Modi in Muscat', 11 February, www.narendramodi.in/excerpts-from-pm-s-address-at-community-event-in-muscat-oman-538904.

Modi, N. (2018c) 'Impatient to take the country to new heights: PM Modi on Independence Day', 15 August, www.narendramodi.in/english-rendering-of-prime-minister-shri-narendra-modi-s-address-to-the-nation-from-the-ramparts-of-the-red-fort-on-the-72nd-independence-day-august-15-2018-541147.

Modi, N. and Obama, B. H. (2014) 'A renewed US-India partnership for the 21st century', *The Washington Post*, 30 September, www.washingtonpost.com/opinions/narendra-modi-and-barack-obama-a-us-india-partnership-for-the-21st-century/2014/09/29/dac66812-4824-11e4-891d-713f052086a0_story.html.

Mohammed, N. (2018) 'Once FDI-averse, Modi opens doors at a time when global investment flows are shrinking', *The Wire*, 11 January, https://thewire.in/economy/fdi-averse-modi-opens-doors-time-global-investment-flows-shrinking.

Mohan, A. (2014) 'Ram Madhav: Modi's ambassador at large', *Business Standard*, 29 November, www.business-standard.com/article/specials/ram-madhav-modi-s-ambassador-at-large-114112800875_1.html.

Mohan, C. R. (2003) *Crossing the Rubicon: The Shaping of India's New Foreign Policy*, New York: Palgrave.

Mohan, C. R. (2005) 'Rethinking India's grand strategy', in N. S. Sisodia and C. U. Bhaskar (eds), *Emerging India: Security and Foreign Policy Perspectives*, New Delhi: Institute for Defence Studies and Analyses and Promilla and Co., 32–42.

Mohan, C. R. (2007) 'Balancing interests and values: India's struggle with democracy promotion', *The Washington Quarterly* 30(3): 99–115.

Mohan, C. R. (2013) 'The changing dynamics of India's multilateralism', in Singh Sidhu, W. P., Mehta, P. B. and Jones, B. (eds) *Shaping the Emerging World: India and the Multilateral Order*, Washington, DC: Brookings, 25–42.

Mohan, C. R. (2014a) 'Modi and the Middle East: towards a Link West policy', *Indian Express*, 21 August, https://indianexpress.com/article/opinion/columns/modi-and-the-middle-east-towards-a-link-west-policy/.

Mohan, C. R. (2014b) 'Indian military diplomacy: humanitarian assistance and disaster relief', *ISAS Working Paper* 185, March, www.files.ethz.ch/isn/178456/ISAS_Working_Paper__184_-_Indian_Military_Diplomacy__Humanitarian_Assistance_26032014162545.pdf.

Mohan, C. R. (2015a) *Modi's World: Expanding India's Sphere of Influence*, New Delhi: HarperCollins.

Mohan, C. R. (2015b) 'Restoring the Eastern anchor: India's strategic partnership with Singapore', in A. Mukherjee (ed.) *The Merlion and the Ashoka: Singapore-India Strategic Ties*, Singapore: World Scientific, 23–43.

Mohan, C. R. and Chauhan, R. (2015) 'Focus on the diaspora', *Seminar*, 665, www.india-seminar.com/2015/665/665_raja_mohan_&_rishika.htm.

Monsonis, G. (2010) 'India's strategic autonomy and rapprochement with the US', *Strategic Analysis* 34(4): 611–624.

MRTH (Ministry of Road Transport and Highways) (2018) 'BBIN motor vehicles agreement regains momentum', 15 January, http://pib.nic.in/newsite/PrintRelease.aspx?relid=175638.

Mukerji, S. (2017) 'Land acquisition in contemporary India: the growth agenda, legislation, and resistance', *Indian Journal of Public Administration* 63(1): 85–103.

Mukherjee, A. (2014) 'India as a net security provider: concept and impediments', RSIS Policy Brief, August, www.rsis.edu.sg/wp-content/uploads/2014/09/PB_140903_India-Net-Security.pdf.

Mukhopadhyay, N. (2013) *Narendra Modi: The Man, The Times*, New Delhi: Tranquebar.

Mukhopadhyay, N. (2017) 'Past continuous: what lies behind BJP's deification of Deen Dayal Upadhyaya', *The Wire*, 26 September, https://thewire.in/history/bjp-deen-dayal-upadhyaya.

Mullen, R. D. (2015) 'India's soft power', in D. Malone, C. R. Mohan and S. Raghavan (eds) (2015) *The Oxford Handbook of Indian Foreign Policy*, Oxford: Oxford University Press, 188–201.

Muni, S. D. (2009) *India's Foreign Policy: The Democracy Dimension*, New Delhi: Foundation.

Muni, S. D. (2017) 'Modi's "neighbourhood first" policy', in S. Singh (ed.) *Modi and the World: (Re)Constructing Indian Foreign Policy*, Singapore: World Scientific, 117–138.

Murphy, C. N. (1983) 'What the Third World wants: an interpretation of the development and meaning of the New International Economic Order ideology', *International Studies Quarterly* 27(1): 55–76.

Nag, K. (2013) *The NaMo Story: A Political Life*, New Delhi: Roli Books.

Nag, K. (2014) *The Saffron Tide: The Rise of the BJP*, New Delhi: Rainlight.

Nag, K. (2016) 'The one-man government in New Delhi', *Economic and Political Weekly* 51(52), www.epw.in/journal/2016/52/web-exclusives/one-man-government-new-delhi.html.

Nag, K. (2017) *Atal Bihari Vajpayee: A Man for All Seasons*, New Delhi: Rupa.

Naidu, M. V. (2018) 'Key note address by Shri M. Venkaiah Naidu, Honourable Vice President of India at the Valedictory Session of the first ever PIO Parliamentarians Conference, in New Delhi', 9 January, http://vicepresidentofindia.nic.in/speechesinterviews/key-note-address-shri-m-venkaiah-naidu-honourable-vice-president-india.

Nair, R. (2016) 'India has a new law on bankruptcy', *LiveMint*, 12 May, www.livemint.com/Politics/mQNm3XHXSqFVFoSCGsn3bO/ Parliament-clears-Insolvency-and-Bankruptcy-Code-2016.html.

Nandy, A. (2002) 'Obituary of a culture', *Seminar* 513, www.india-seminar. com/2002/513/513%20ashis%20nandy.htm.

Narang, V. (2018) 'India's nuclear strategy twenty years later: from reluctance to maturation', *India Review* 17(1): 159–179.

Narlikar, A. (2017) 'India's role in global governance: a modi-fication?', *International Affairs* 93(1): 93–112.

Nayak, N. R. (2018) 'Nepal-China transit agreement: an evaluation', *IDSA Issue Brief*, 27 September, https://idsa.in/issuebrief/nepal-china-transit-agreement-nnayak-270918.

Nayyar, D. (2018) 'India's Asian trade strategy', in S. Armstrong and T. Westland (eds) *Asian Economic Integration in an Age of Global Uncertainty*, Canberra: Australian National University Press, 217–234.

Nehru, J. (1961) *India's Foreign Policy: Selected Speeches*, September 1946-April 1961, New Delhi: Government of India.

Nussbaum, M. C. (2007) *The Clash Within: Democracy, Religious Violence and India's Future*, Cambridge, Mass: Harvard University Press.

Nye, J. S. (1990a) *Bound to Lead: The Changing Nature of American Power*, New York: Basic Books.

Nye, J. S. (1990b) 'Soft power', *Foreign Policy* 80: 153–171.

Nye, J. S. (2004) *Soft Power: The Means to Success in World Politics*, New York: PublicAffairs.

O'Donnell, F. and Ghoshal, D. (2019) 'Commitment traps make Kashmir de-escalation tricky', *East Asia Forum* online, 3 March, www. eastasiaforum.org/2019/03/03/commitment-traps-make-kashmir-de-escalation-tricky/.

Office of the United Nations High Commissioner for Human Rights (2018) *Report on the situation of human rights in Kashmir: developments in the Indian state of Jammu and Kashmir from June 2016 to April 2018, and general human rights concerns in Azad Jammu and Kashmir and Gilgit-Baltistan*, 14 June, www.ohchr.org/Documents/Countries/IN/ DevelopmentsInKashmirJune2016ToApril2018.pdf.

Ogden, C. (2014) *Hindu Nationalism and the Evolution of Contemporary Indian Security: Portents of Power*, New Delhi: Oxford University Press.

Ogden, C. (2018) 'Tone shift: India's dominant foreign policy aims under Modi', *Indian Politics and Policy* 1(1): 2–23.

Ollapally, D. M. (2001) 'Mixed motives in India's search for nuclear status', *Asian Survey* 41(6): 925–942.

Ollapally, D. M. and Rajagopalan, R. (2012) 'India: Foreign Policy Perspectives of an Ambiguous Power', in H. R. Nau and D. M. Ollapally (eds) *Worldviews of Aspiring Powers: Domestic Foreign Policy Debates in China, India, Iran, Japan, and Russia*, New York: Oxford University Press, 73–113.

Pal, D. (2014) 'Decoding Modi's foreign policy', *Foreign Policy*, 6 March, https://foreignpolicy.com/2014/03/06/decoding-modis-foreign-policy/.

Palit, A. (2015) 'Economics in Narendra Modi's foreign policy', Asie Visions 77, Paris and Brussels: Institut français des relations internationals, www.ifri.org/sites/default/files/atoms/files/asie_visions77_0.pdf/.

Palit, P. S. (2017) *Analysing China's Soft Power Strategy and Comparative Indian Initiatives*, New Delhi: Sage.

Paliwal, A. (2017) *My Enemy's Enemy: India in Afghanistan from the Soviet Invasion to the US*, London: Hurst and Co.

Panagariya, A. (2008) *India: The Emerging Giant*, New York: Oxford University Press.

Panda, A. (2013) 'Narendra Modi's foreign policy', *The Diplomat*, 5 November, https://thediplomat.com/2013/11/narendra-modis-foreign-policy/.

Panda, A. (2014) 'Narendra Modi gets tough on China', *The Diplomat*, 25 February https://thediplomat.com/2014/02/narendra-modi-gets-tough-on-china/.

Panda, J. (2016) 'Narendra Modi's China policy: between pragmatism and power parity', *Journal of Asian Public Policy* 9(2): 185–197.

Pant, H. V. (2011) *The US-India Nuclear Pact: Policy, Process, and Great Power Politics*, New Delhi: Oxford University Press.

Pant, H. V. (2012) 'The Pakistan thorn in China-India-US relations', *The Washington Quarterly* 35(1): 83–95.

Pant, H. V. (2014) 'Modi's muscle team: flexing a new national security?', *Foreign Policy*, 24 June, https://foreignpolicy.com/2014/06/24/modis-muscle-team-flexing-a-new-national-security/.

Pant, H. V. (2015) 'Is India developing a strategy for power?', *The Washington Quarterly* 38(4): 99–113.

Pant, H. V. (2019) *India Foreign Policy: The Modi Era*, New Delhi: Har Anand.

Pant, H. V. and Joshi, Y. (2017) 'Indo-US relations under Modi: the strategic logic underlying the embrace', *International Affairs* 93(1): 133–146.

Parashar, U. (2014) 'PM Narendra Modi visits Pashupatinath temple, offers 2,500 kg of sandalwood', *Hindustan Times*, 4 August, www.hindustantimes.com/india/pm-narendra-modi-visits-pashupatinath-temple-offers-2-500-kg-of-sandalwood/story-ygxo9wPUPA6Q6wOfrqv8DL.html.

Pardesi, M. S. (2017) 'Modi's China policy – change or continuity', in S. Singh, (ed.) *Modi and the World: (Re)Constructing Indian Foreign Policy*, Singapore: World Scientific, 3–24.

Parthasarathy, M. (2000) 'India, US natural allies: Vajpayee', *The Hindu*, 8 September, www.thehindu.com/2000/09/09/stories/01090005.htm.

Pathak, M. (2017) India-Japan partnership to play key role in Asia–Africa corridor," *LiveMint*, 25 May, www.livemint.com/Politics/gfSbaVJjfHuoUKPTMxrU8L/IndiaJapan-partnership-to-play-key-role-in-AsiaAfrica-corr.html.

Patnaik, P. (2015) 'From the planning commission to the NITI Aayog', *Economic and Political Weekly* 50(4): 10–12.

Paul, T. V. (1998) 'The systemic bases of India's challenge to the global nuclear order', *The Nonproliferation Review* 6(1): 1–11.

Paul, T.V. (2007) 'The US-India nuclear accord: implications for the nonproliferation regime' *International Journal* 62(4): 845–865.

Perkovich, G. (2004) 'The nuclear and security balance', in F. R. Frankel and H. Harding (eds), *The India-China Relationship: What the United States Needs to Know*, New York: Columbia University Press and Woodrow Wilson Center Press, 178–218.

Perkovich, G. and Dalton, T. (2015) 'Modi's strategic choice: how to respond to terrorism from Pakistan', *The Washington Quarterly* 38(1): 23–45.

Pethiyagoda, K. (2017) 'Supporting Indian workers in the Gulf: what Delhi can do', *Brookings*, 21 November, www.brookings.edu/research/supporting-indian-workers-in-the-gulf-what-delhi-can-do/.

Piccone, T. (2016) *Five Rising Democracies and the Fate of the International Liberal Order*, Washington, DC: Brookings Institution Press.

Plagemann, J. and Destradi, S. (2015) 'Soft sovereignty, rising powers, and subnational foreign policy-making: the case of India', *Globalizations* 12(5): 728–743.

Plagemann, J. and Destradi, S. (2019) 'Populism and foreign policy: the case of India', *Foreign Policy Analysis* 15: 283–301.

Power, P. (1964) 'Indian foreign policy: the age of Nehru', *Review of Politics* 26(2): 257–286.

Prakash, P. and Ahuja, J. (2019) 'Rahul Gandhi in Wayanad and Amethi: What's There to Lose?', *The Diplomat*, 5 April, https://thediplomat.com/2019/04/rahul-gandhi-in-wayanad-and-amethi-whats-there-to-lose/.

Press Information Bureau (2015) 'Review of Foreign Direct Investment (FDI) Policy on investments by Non-Resident Indians (NRIs), Persons of Indian Origin (PIOs) and Overseas Citizens of India (OCIs)', 25 May, http://pib.nic.in/newsite/printrelease.aspx?relid=121914.

Price, L. (2015) *The Modi Effect: Inside Narendra Modi's Campaign to Transform India*, London: Hodder and Stoughton.

Press Trust of India (2014a) 'I'm your "pradhan sewak": Modi tells nation', *The Hindu*, 15 August, www.thehindu.com/news/national/im-your-pradhan-sewak-and-not-pradhan-mantri-modi/article6321514.ece.

Press Trust of India (2014b) 'BJP President Amit Shah dissolves all the national cells', *DNA India*, 3 November, www.dnaindia.com/india/report-bjp-president-amit-shah-dissolves-all-the-national-cells-2031841.

Press Trust of India (2014c) '"Want India to break into top 50 nations on ease of doing business": PM', *NDTV*, 19 November, www.ndtv.com/india-news/pm-modi-wants-india-to-break-into-top-50-nations-on-ease-of-doing-business-ranking-1950055.

Press Trust of India (2014d) 'Opposition targets govt over Bhagwat's speech on Doordarshan', *The Hindu*, 3 October, www.thehindu.com/news/national/congress-left-parties-target-bjp-over-rss-chief-mohan-bhagwats-speech-on-doordarshan/article6468846.ece.

Press Trust of India (2015a) 'Senior Chinese Communist Party official meets BJP President Amit Shah', *NDTV*, 15 February, www.ndtv.com/india-news/senior-chinese-communist-party-official-meets-bjp-president-amit-shah-739768.

Press Trust of India (2015b) 'We need a vision of "Made by India": Swadeshi Jagran Manch', *Economic Times*, 25 December, https://economictimes.indiatimes.com/news/politics-and-nation/we-need-a-vision-of-made-by-india-swadeshi-jagran-manch/articleshow/50327326.cms.

Press Trust of India (2015c) 'RSS-affiliated outfit holds protest against land bill', *IndiaTV*, 6 May, www.indiatvnews.com/politics/national/rss-affiliated-outfit-holds-protest-against-land-bill-28921.html.

Press Trust of India (2016) 'India slams Pakistan at UN rights council after Uri attack, rakes up human rights violations in Balochistan', *India Today*, 20 September, www.indiatoday.in/india/story/un-rights-council-india-pakistan-uri-balochistan-human-rights-violation-342007-2016-09-20.

Press Trust of India (2018a) 'International Solar Alliance: $1 trillion needed to achieve 1TW solar power capacity by 2030, says Emmanuel Macron' *Economic Times*, 11 March, https://economictimes.indiatimes.com/industry/energy/power/international-solar-alliance-emmanuel-macron-announces-additional-700-million-euros-for-solar-energy/articleshow/63255044.cms.

Press Trust of India (2018b) 'Ram Madhav: US India bilateral relationship independent of its ties with Russia and China', *Indian Express*, 22 May, https://indianexpress.com/article/india/ram-madhav-us-india-bilateral-relationship-independent-of-its-ties-with-russia-and-china-5186481/.

Pubby, M. (2018) 'Pensions overtake modernisation, modest 7.8 % hike in defence budget', *The Print*, 1 February, https://theprint.in/economy/pensions-overtake-modernisation-modest-7-8-hike-in-defence-budget/32880/.

Puri, H. S. (2017) *India's Trade Policy Dilemma and the Role of Domestic Reform*, Washington, DC: Carnegie Endowment for International Peace, http://carnegieendowment.org/files/CP_298_Puri_Trade_A5_Web.pdf.

Purie, A. (2006) 'Davos 2006: India showcases contemporary face at World Economic Forum', *India Today*, 13 February, www.indiatoday.in/magazine/cover-story/story/20060213-davos-2006-india-showcases-contemporary-face-at-world-economic-forum-783700-2006-02-13.

Radice, W. (1999) *Swami Vivekananda and the Modernisation of Hinduism*, New Delhi: Oxford University Press.

Raghavan, P. (2015) 'Establishing the Ministry of External Affairs', in D. M. Malone, C. R. Mohan and S. Raghavan (eds) *The Oxford Handbook of Indian Foreign Policy*, Oxford: Oxford University Press, 80–91.

Raghavan, S. (2010) *War and Peace in Modern India*, New York: Palgrave.

Raghavan, S. (2013) *1971: A Global History of the Creation of Bangladesh*, Ranikhet: Permanent Black.

Rajagopalan, S. (2014) '"Grand strategic thought" in the Ramayana and the Mahabharata', in K. Bajpai, S. Basir and V. Krishnappa (eds) *India's Grand Strategy: History, Theory, Cases*, New Delhi: Routledge, 31–62.

Rajendram, D. (2014) *India's new Asia-Pacific strategy: Modi acts East*, Sydney: Lowy Institute, www.lowyinstitute.org/sites/default/files/indias-new-asia-pacific-strategy-modi-acts-east.pdf.

Ramachandaran, S. (2015) 'Religion in diplomacy makes South Block uneasy', *DNA India*, 16 September, www.dnaindia.com/analysis/column-religion-in-diplomacy-makes-south-block-uneasy-2125511.

Ramachandran, S. K. (2016) 'What we were waiting for has happened: Bhagwat on surgical strikes', *Hindustan Times*, 29 September, www.hindustantimes.com/india-news/what-we-were-waiting-for-has-happened-bhagwat-on-surgical-strikes/story-LTLAaAA6sxuVnwzAu4A7hM.html.

Ramchandran, S. K. (2018) 'I&B ministry and MEA at odds over All India Radio external service', *Hindustan Times*, 6 August, www.hindustantimes.com/india-news/i-b-ministry-and-mea-at-odds-over-all-india-radio-external-service/story-k8CDvm9gmYSJ4gDzuYrHiK.html.

Ramaseshan, R. (2014) 'Key posts for Shah boys', *The Telegraph*, 4 November, www.telegraphindia.com/1141104/jsp/nation/story_18996983.jsp.

Ramesh, J. (2005) *Making Sense of Chindia: Reflections on China and India*, New Delhi: India Research Press.

Ramesh, J. (2018) *Intertwined Lives: P.N. Haksar and Indira Gandhi*, New Delhi: Simon and Schuster.

Rana, A. P. (1976) *The Imperatives of Nonalignment: A Conceptual Study of India's Foreign Policy Strategy in the Nehru Period*, Delhi: Macmillan.

Rana, K. S. (2009) 'India's diaspora diplomacy', *Hague Journal of Diplomacy* 4(3): 361–372.

Ranjan, P. (2018) 'What's so neoliberal about Narendra Modi's India anyway?', *The Wire*, 28 July, https://thewire.in/political-economy/neoliberalism-modi-bjp-congress-india.

Rej, A. and Sagar, R. (2019) The BJP and Indian Grand Strategy, in M. Vaishnav (ed), *Return to the BJP in Power: Indian Democracy and Religious Nationalism*, Washington DC: Carnegie Endowment for International Peace, https://carnegieendowment.org/2019/04/04/bjp-and-indian-grand-strategy-pub-78686.

Riedel, B. (2015) *JFK's Forgotten Crisis: Tibet, the CIA, and the Sino-Indian War*, Washington, DC: Brookings.

RIS / ERIA / IDE (Research and Information System for Developing Countries, Economic Research Institute for ASEAN and East Asia and Institute of Developing Economies) (2017) *Asia Africa Growth Corridor: Partnership for Sustainable and Innovative Development: A Vision Document*, www.eria.org/Asia-Africa-Growth-Corridor-Document.pdf.

Roche, E. (2015) 'India protests China's plans for $46 billion PoK investments', *LiveMint*, 14 May, www.livemint.com/Politics/NX9251BYbqEXgIBM9Ch55L/India-protests-Chinas-plans-for-PoK-investments.html.

Roggenveen, S. (2015) 'Jaishankar: India become a leading power', *The Interpreter*, 17 March, www.lowyinstitute.org/the-interpreter/jaishankar-india-becoming-leading-power.

Rolland, R. ([1930] 2002) *The Life of Vivekananda: The Universal Gospel*, trans. Macolm-Smith, E. F., Hollywood, CA: Vedanta.

Rothacher, J. U. (2016) 'The ambivalent influence of the domestic industries on India's meandering foreign economic policies', *India Review* 15(1): 61–97.

Roy, K. (2012) *Hinduism and the Ethics of Warfare in South Asia: From Antiquity to the Present*, Cambridge: Cambridge University Press.

Roy, S. (2014a) 'Focus on issues, not protocol, Modi tells young diplomats', *Indian Express*, 13 June, https://indianexpress.com/article/india/india-others/focus-on-issues-not-protocol-modi-tells-young-diplomats/.

Roy, S. (2014b) 'Prettiest Gita of them all? PM Modi's khadi covered gift to Obama was extra special', *FirstPost*, 1 October, www.firstpost.com/world/prettiest-gita-of-them-all-pm-modis-khadi-covered-gift-to-obama-was-extra-special-1737273.html.

RSS (Rastriya Swayamsevak Sangh) (2018) 'Mohanji Bhagwat at World Hindu Congress', 8 September, www.youtube.com/watch?v=Of1PqfJpsIg.

Sagar, P. R. (2018) 'Military not happy with Modi govt's "surgical strike" celebrations', *The Week*, 28 September, www.theweek.in/news/india/2018/09/28/military-not-happy-with-modi-govt-surgical-strike-celebrations.html.

Sagar, R. (2009) 'State of mind: what kind of power will India become?', *International Affairs* 85(4): 801–816.

Sagar, R. (2014) '"Jiski lathi, uski bains": the Hindu nationalist view of international politics', in K. Bajpai, S. Basit and V. Krishnappa (eds) *India's Grand Strategy: History, Theory, Cases*, London, New York and New Delhi: Routledge, 234–257.

Sagar, R. (2015) 'Before midnight: views on international relations, 1857–1947', in Malone, D., Mohan, C. R. and Raghavan, S. (eds) *The Oxford Handbook of Indian Foreign Policy*, Oxford: Oxford University Press, 65–79.

Sagar, R. (2018) 'A malnourished Bismarck astride the Indo-Pacific', *LiveMint*, 5 April, www.livemint.com/Opinion/1f5LedQUsZ4NM8Vs8xyBVO/A-malnourished-Bismarck-astride-the-IndoPacific.html.

Sagar, R. and Panda, A. (2015) 'Pledges and pious wishes: the constituent assembly debates and the myth of a "Nehruvian consensus"', *India Review* 14(2): 203–220.

Saran, S. (2012) India and Africa: Development Partnership, Discussion Paper # 180, New Delhi: RIS, www.ris.org.in/india-and-africa-development-partnership.

Sardesai, R. (2015) *2014: The Election that Changed India*, New Delhi: Penguin.

SASEC/ADB (South Asia Subregional Economic Cooperation, with the Asian Development Bank) (2016), *South Asia Sub-Regional Economic Cooperation Operational Plan*, www.adb.org/sites/default/files/institutional-document/193351/sasec-operational-plan2016-2025.pdf.

Sasikumar, K. (2007) 'India's emergence as a "responsible" nuclear power', *International Journal* 62(4): 825–844.

Sasikumar, K. (2010) 'State agency in the time of the global war on terror: India and the counter-terrorism regime', *Review of International Studies* 36(3): 615–638.

Savarkar, V. D. (n.d.) *Hindu Rashtra Darshan*, Poona: Maharashtra Prantik Hindusabha.

Savarkar, V. D. (writing as 'An Indian Nationalist') (1909) *The Indian War of Independence of 1857*, London: no publisher.

Savarkar, V. D. (writing as 'A Maratha') (1923) *Hindutva*, Nagpur: V. V. Kelkar.

Schaffer, T. C. (2009) *India and the United States in the 21st Century: Reinventing Partnership*, Washington, DC: The CSIS Press.

Schaffer, H. and Schaffer, T. C. (2013) 'India: Modi's international profile', *Brookings*, 12 December, www.brookings.edu/opinions/india-modis-international-profile/.

Schaffer, T. C. and Schaffer, H. B. (2016) *India at the Global High Table: The Quest for Regional Primacy and Strategic Autonomy*, Washington, DC: Brookings.

Schaus, J. (2017) 'US offer of Sea Guardian drones to India signals converging strategic interests', *Hindustan Times*, 5 July, www.hindustantimes.com/opinion/us-offer-of-sea-guardian-drones-to-india-signals-converging-strategic-interests/story-kQxzxKe2fj6KrcGWE5IEBN.html.

S. C. S. [pseudonym] (1959) 'Indian reactions to the crisis in Tibet', *The World Today* 15(6): 236–246.

Sen, R. (2016) 'Narendra Modi's makeover and the politics of symbolism', *Journal of Asian Public Policy* 9(2): 98–111.

Shah, G. (2001) 'The BJP's riddle in Gujarat: caste, factionalism and Hindutva', in T. B. Hansen and C. Jaffrelot (eds) *The BJP and the Compulsions of Politics in India*, 2nd edn, New Delhi: Oxford University Press, 243–266.

Shani, O. (2007) *Communalism, Caste and Hindu Nationalism: The Violence in Gujarat*, Cambridge: Cambridge University Press.

Sharda, R. (2018) *RSS 360°: Demystifying Rashtriya Swayamsevak Sangh*, New Delhi: Bloomsbury.

Sharma, J. (n.d.) *Economic Philosophy of Deendayal Upadhyaya*, New Delhi: BJP, http://library.bjp.org/jspui/bitstream/123456789/435/1/Economic%20Philosphy%20of%20Dcendayal%20Upadhayay.pdf.

Sharma, J. (2003) *Hindutva: Exploring the Idea of Hindu Nationalism*, New Delhi: Penguin.

Sharma, J. (2007) *Terrifying Vision: M. S. Golwalkar, the RSS, and India*, New Delhi: Viking.

Sharma, J. (2013) *A Restatement of Religion: Swami Vivekananda and the Making of Hindu Nationalism*, New Haven and London: Yale University Press.

Sharma, J. N. (2009) *The Political Thought of Pandit Deendayal Upadhyaya*, Encyclopaedia of Eminent Thinkers 23, New Delhi: Concept Publishing Company.

Siddiqui, S. (2017) 'CPEC investment pushed from $46b to $62b', *The Express Tribune* (Pakistan), 12 April, https://tribune.com.pk/story/1381733/cpec-investment-pushed-55b-62b/.

Sikri, V. (2017) 'Soft power as a strategic asset', in Debroy, B. and Malik, A. (eds) *India @70, Modi @3.5: Capturing India's Transformation under Narendra Modi*, New Delhi: Wisdom Tree, 183–194.

Singh, A. (2014) 'China's maritime Silk Route: implications for India', *IDSA Comment*, Institute for Defence Studies and Analyses, New Delhi, 16 July, www.idsa.in/idsacomments/ChinasMaritimeSilkRoute_AbhijitSingh_160714.

Singh, B. (1965) 'Pundits and Panchsheela: Indian intellectuals and their foreign policy', *Background* 9(2): 127–136.

Singh, J. (1995) 'An Indian perspective', in Gordon, S. and Henningham, S. (eds) *India Looks East: An Emerging Power and its Asia-Pacific Neighbours*, Canberra Papers on Strategy and Defence 111, Canberra: Strategic and Defence Studies Centre, The Australian National University, 45–57.

Singh, J. (1998) 'Against nuclear apartheid', *Foreign Affairs* 77(5): 41–52.

Singh, J. (2007) *In Service of Emergent India: A Call to Honor*, Bloomington and Indianapolis, IN: Indiana University Press.

Singh, J. (2013) *India at Risk: Mistakes, Misconceptions, and Misadventures of Security Policy*, New Delhi: Rainlight Rupa.

Singh, M. (2013) 'PM's speech at the foundation stone laying ceremony for the Indian National Defence University at Gurgaon', Press Information Bureau, Government of India, 23 May, http://pib.nic.in/newsite/mbErel.aspx?relid=96146.

Singh, M. A. (2016) 'Narendra Modi and Northeast India: development, insurgency and illegal migration', *Journal of Asian Public Policy* 9(2): 112–127.

Singh, R. (2018) 'Air Force struggles to create Tejas fleet as HAL misses delivery targets', *Hindustan Times*, 16 March, www.hindustantimes.com/india-news/air-force-struggles-to-create-tejas-fleet-as-hal-misses-delivery-targets/story-ykR7EYqmvu0HdzUnzsU4FP.html.

Singh, S. (2017) 'Introduction', in S. Singh, (ed.) *Modi and the World: (Re)Constructing Indian Foreign Policy*, Singapore: World Scientific, xv–xxiv.

Singh, S. (2018) 'Washington lets Delhi know: buy our F-16s, can give Russia deal waiver', *Indian Express*, 20 October, https://indianexpress.com/article/india/washington-lets-delhi-know-buy-our-f-16s-can-give-russia-deal-waiver-5409894/.

Singh, T. (2013) 'Gandhi and Modi: foreign policy enigmas', *The Diplomat*, 16 October, https://thediplomat.com/2013/10/gandhi-and-modi-foreign-policy-enigmas/.

Singh, U. (2017) *Political Violence in Ancient India*, Cambridge, Mass: Harvard University Press.

Singh Puri, H. (2016) *Perilous Interventions: The Security Council and the Politics of Chaos*, New Delhi: HarperCollins.

Singh Sidhu, W. P., Mehta, P. B. and Jones, B. (eds) (2013) *Shaping the Emerging World: India and the Multilateral Order*, Washington, DC: Brookings.

Sitapati, V. (2016) *Half Lion: How P. V. Narasimha Rao Transformed India*, New Delhi: Penguin Viking.

Small, A. (2017) 'First movement: Pakistan and the Belt and Road Initiative', *Asia Policy* 24 (2017): 80–87.

Small, A. (2018) 'Fair winds, heavy burdens: the limitations of India's turn East', *Asia Policy* 25(2): 150–153.

Smith, J. M. (2016) 'Waking the beast: India's defense reforms under Modi', *The Diplomat*, 16 December, https://thediplomat.com/2016/12/waking-the-beast-indias-defense-reforms-under-modi/.

Soz, S. A. (2019) *The Great Disappointment: How Narendra Modi Squandered a Unique Opportunity to Transform the Indian Economy*, Gurgaon: Penguin Random House.

Spodek, H. (2010) 'In the Hindutva laboratory: pogroms and programs in Gujarat, 2002', *Modern Asian Studies* 44(2): 349–399.

Sridharan, E. (2014) 'Behind Modi's victory', *Journal of Democracy* 25(4): 20–33.

Sridharan, E. (2017) 'Where is India headed? Possible future directions in Indian foreign policy', *International Affairs* 93(1): 51–68.

Sridharan, K. (2003) 'Federalism and foreign relations: the nascent role of the Indian states', *Asian Studies Review* 27(4): 463–489.

Staniland, P. (2010) 'Foreign policy making in India in the pre-liberalization and coalition era: unit level variables as determinants', in A. Mattoo and H. Jacob (eds) *Shaping India's Foreign Policy: People, Politics and Places*, New Delhi: Har Anand, 255–274.

Staniland, P. and Narang, V. (2015) 'State and politics', in D. Malone, C. R. Mohan and S. Raghavan (eds) *The Oxford Handbook of Indian Foreign Policy*, Oxford: Oxford University Press, 205–218.

Stobdan, P. (2016) 'Asia's Buddhist connectivity and India's role', *IDSA Issue Brief*, 19 February, www.idsa.in/system/files/issuebrief/ib_asia's-buddhist-connectivity-and-india_pstobdan_190216.pdf.

Suhrud, T. (2008) 'Modi and Gujarati "asmita"', *Economic and Political Weekly* 43(1): 11–13.

Suri, N. (2011) 'Public diplomacy in India's foreign policy', *Strategic Analysis* 35(2): 297–303.

Swamy, S. (2007) *Hindus under Siege: The Way Out*, New Delhi: Har-Anand.

Swamy, S. (2013) *Virat Hindu Identity: Concept and Its Power*, New Delhi: Har-Anand.

Talbott, S. (2004) *Engaging India: Diplomacy, Democracy, and the Bomb*, Washington, DC: Brookings.

Tandon, A. (2016) 'Transforming the unbound elephant to the lovable Asian hulk: why is Modi leveraging India's soft power?', *The Round Table: The Commonwealth Journal of International Affairs* 105(1): 57–65.

Tapasyananda, S. (1990) 'Swami Vivekananda's theory of Indian nationalism', in S. Vivekananda, *The Nationalistic and Religious Lectures of Swami Vivekananda*, Calcutta: Advaita Ashrama, v–xv.

Tavares, R. (2016) *Paradiplomacy: Cities and States as Global Players*, New York: Oxford University Press.

Taylor, I. (2009) '"The South will rise again"? New alliances and global governance: the India-Brazil-South Africa dialogue forum', *Politikon* 36(1): 45–58.

Tellis, A. J. (2001) *India's Emerging Nuclear Posture: Between Recessed Deterrent and Ready Arsenal*, Santa Monica, CA: RAND.

Tellis, A. J. (2005) *India as a New Global Power: An Action Agenda for the United States*, New Delhi: Carnegie Endowment for International Peace and India Research Press.

Tellis, A. J. (2008) 'The merits of dehyphenation: explaining US success in engaging India and Pakistan', *The Washington Quarterly* 31(4): 21–42.

Tellis, A. J. (2015) 'US-India relations: the struggle for an enduring partnership', in D. Malone, C. R. Mohan and S. Raghavan (eds) *The Oxford Handbook of Indian Foreign Policy*, Oxford: Oxford University Press, 481–494.

Tharoor, S. (2003) *Nehru: The Invention of India*, New York: Arcade.

Tharoor, S. (2012) *Pax Indica: India and the World of the 21st Century*, New Delhi: Allen Lane.

Tharoor, S. (2018) The *Paradoxical Prime Minister: Narendra Modi and His India*, New Delhi: Aleph.

Thussu, D. K. (2016) *Communicating India's Soft Power: Buddha to Bollywood*, New Delhi: Sage.

Times of India (2007) '"Maut ke saudagar" may have hurt Congress', 24 December, https://timesofindia.indiatimes.com/india/Maut-ke-saudagar-may-have-hurt-Congress/articleshow/2646136.cms.

Times of India (2015) 'India, Pakistan and Bangladesh will reunite to form 'Akhand Bharat': Ram Madhav', 26 December, https://timesofindia.indiatimes.com/india/India-Pakistan-and-Bangladesh-will-reunite-to-form-Akhand-Bharat-Ram-Madhav/articleshow/50333856.cms.

Times of India (2018) 'Mega Times Group poll: 71.9% of Indians say they will vote for Narendra Modi as PM again in 2019', 26 May, https://timesofindia.indiatimes.com/india/mega-times-group-poll-71-9-of-indians-say-they-will-vote-for-narendra-modi-as-pm-again-in-2019/articleshow/64324490.cms.

Torri, M. (2015) 'The "Modi wave": behind the results of the 2014 general elections in India', *The International Spectator* 50(2): 56–74.

Tremblay, R. C. and Kapur, A. (2017) *Modi's Foreign Policy*, New Delhi: Sage.

Troy, J. (2008) 'Faith-based diplomacy under examination', *The Hague Journal of Diplomacy* 3(3): 209–231.

Twining, D. (2014) 'The US engagement of India after 1991: transformation', in Hall, I. (ed.) *The Engagement of India: Strategies and Responses*, Washington, DC: Georgetown University Press, 19–38.

Uberoi, P (2016) 'Problems and prospects of the BCIM economic corridor', *China Report* 52(1): 19–44.

Unnithan, S. (2016a) 'India signs Rs 5000 crore M777 howitzer contract with US', *India Today*, 30 November, www.indiatoday.in/india/story/m777-howitzer-india-america-bae-systems-354924-2016-11-30.

Unnithan, S. (2016b) 'Man of the world', *India Today*, 17 August, www.indiatoday.in/magazine/cover-story/story/20160829-mood-of-the-nation-survey-foreign-policy-829436-2016-08-17.

Upadhaya, D. (1958) *The Two Plans: Promises, Performance and Prospects*, Lucknow: Rashtradharma Prakashan.

Upadhaya, D. (1968) *Political Diary*, Bombay: Jaico Publishing House, www.readwhere.com/read/673138/Political-Diary-English/Wed-Dec-23,-2015#page/1/1.

Upadhyaya, D. (1992) *Integral Humanism*, Noida: Jagriti Prakashan, www.bjp.org/about-the-party/philosophy.

USCIRF (United States Commission on International Religious Freedom) (2016) *2016 Annual Report*. www.uscirf.gov/sites/default/files/USCIRF%202016%20Annual%20Report.pdf.

US Department of State (2016) 'Annex of Statistical Information: Country Reports on Terrorism 2015', June, www.state.gov/documents/organization/257738.pdf.

US Department of State (2017) 'Annex of Statistical Information: country reports on terrorism 2016', July, www.state.gov/documents/organization/272485.pdf.

US Department of State (2018a) 'Joint statement on the Inaugural US-India 2+2 Ministerial Dialogue', 6 September, www.state.gov/r/pa/prs/ps/2018/09/285729.htm.

US Department of State (2018b) 'Annex of Statistical Information: Country Reports on Terrorism 2017', July, www.state.gov/documents/organization/283097.pdf.

US Embassy, New Delhi (2015) 'US-India joint working group for aircraft carrier technology cooperation holds first meeting', 15 August, https://in.usembassy.gov/u-s-india-joint-working-group-for-aircraft-carrier-technology-cooperation-holds-first-meeting/.

Vaishnav, M. (2015) 'Modi's reform agenda: change you can believe in?', *Asia Policy Brief* 2015/04, Bertelsmann Stiftung, http://aei.pitt.edu/73889/1/2015.4.pdf.

Vaishnav, M. (2017) *When Crime Pays: Money and Muscle in Indian Politics*, New Haven and Oxford: Yale University Press.

Vaishnav, M. (2018) *From Cakewalk to Contest: India's 2019 General Election*, Carnegie Endowment for International Peace, 16 April, https://carnegieendowment.org/2018/04/16/from-cakewalk-to-contest-india-s-2019-general-election-pub-76084.

Varadarajan, L. (2015) 'Mother India and her children abroad: the role of diaspora in India's foreign policy', in D. Malone, C. R. Mohan and S. Raghavan (eds) *The Oxford Handbook of Indian Foreign Policy*, Oxford: Oxford University Press, 285–297.

Varadarajan, S. (ed.) (2002) *Gujarat: The Making of a Tragedy*, New Delhi: Penguin.

Varadarajan, S. (2015) 'How PM has sidelined Sushma Swaraj again', *NDTV*, 29 January, www.ndtv.com/opinion/how-pm-has-sidelined-sushma-swaraj-again-735521.

Venugopal, V. (2016) 'Demonetisation: RSS reaches out to public, preaches Modi's money mantra', *Economic Times*, 24 November, https://economictimes.indiatimes.com/news/politics-and-nation/demonetisation-rss-reaches-out-to-public-preaches-modis-money-mantra/articleshow/55590031.cms.

Verbeek, B. and Zaslove, A. (2017) 'Populism and foreign policy', in C. Rovira Kaltwasser, P. A. Taggart, P. Ochoa Espejo and P. Ostiguy (eds) *The Oxford Handbook of Populism*, Oxford: Oxford University Press, 384–405.

Verma, H. (2018) 'Diaspora for development: Modi's global envoy Vijay Chauthaiwale spells out the importance of outreach', *Connected to India*, 24 May, www.connectedtoindia.com/diaspora-for-development-modis-global-envoy-vijay-chauthaiwale-spells-out-the-importance-of-4087.html.

Verma, S. (2014) *Narendra Modi: The GameChanger*, New Delhi: Vitasta.

Vivekananda International Foundation (2018) *Global Hindu Buddhist Initiative*, http://samvad.vifindia.org.

Vijaykumar, N. (2016) 'How Sushma Swaraj means hope for Indians around the world', *The Week*, 17 October, www.theweek.in/webworld/features/society/sushma-swaraj-helpful-minister-twitter.html.

Virk, A. (2018) 'For the First Time, Modi's Popularity Rating Slips Below 50%', *The Quint*, 21 August, www.thequint.com/news/politics/india-today-mood-of-nation-poll-narendra-modi-declining-popularity.

Virk, K. (2013) 'India and the responsibility to protect: a tale of ambiguity', *Global Responsibility to Protect* 5(1): 56–83.

Vivekananda, S. (1990) *The Nationalistic and Religious Lectures of Swami Vivekananda*, Calcutta: Advaita Ashrama.

Vivekananda, S. (2010) *The East and the West*, Kolkata: Advaita Ashrama.

Vivekananda, S. (2015) *Karma Yoga: The Yoga of Action*, Kolkata: Advaita Ashrama.

Wagner, C. (2005) 'From hard power to soft power? Ideas, interactions, institutions, and images in India's South Asia policy', *Heidelberg Papers in South Asian and Comparative Politics* 26, http://archiv.ub.uni-heidelberg.de/volltextserver/5436/1/hpsacp26.pdf.

Weerakoon, D. and Thennakoon, J. (2006) 'SAFTA: myth of free trade', *Economic and Political Weekly*, 41(37): 3920–3923

Wei Wei (2014) 'Reviving the Silk Road: connecting India, China and Central Asia', *Economic Times*, 14 April, www.fmprc.gov.cn/mfa_eng/wjb_663304/zwjg_665342/zwbd_665378/t1146648.shtml.

Wezeman, P. D., Fleurant, A., Kuimova, A., Tian, N. and Wezeman, S. T. (2018) *Trends in International Arms Transfers, 2017*, SIPRI Fact Sheet, March, www.sipri.org/sites/default/files/2018-03/fssipri_at2017_0.pdf.

White House (2001) 'Joint statement between US and India', 9 November, https://georgewbush-whitehouse.archives.gov/news/releases/2001/11/20011109-10.html.

White House (2014) 'US-India joint statement', 30 September, https://obamawhitehouse.archives.gov/the-press-office/2014/09/30/us-india-joint-statement.

White House (2017) 'United States and India: prosperity through partnership', 26 June, www.whitehouse.gov/briefings-statements/united-states-india-prosperity-partnership/.

Wilson, W. T. and Curtis, L. (2014) 'India's big WTO mistake', *The National Interest*, 25 August, https://nationalinterest.org/feature/indias-big-wto-mistake-11141.

The Wire (2017) 'Sri Sri Ravi Shankar's World Culture Festival destroyed Yamuna floodplain: NGT panel', 12 April, https://thewire.in/environment/sri-sri-ravi-shankars-world-culture-festival-destroyed-yamuna-floodplain-ngt-panel.

World Bank (2018) GDP growth (annual%), https://data.worldbank.org/indicator/NY.GDP.MKTP.KD.ZG?locations=IN

World Bank (2019) 'Doing Business: Measuring Business Regulations', www.doingbusiness.org/en/rankings.

Wyatt, A. (2017) 'Paradiplomacy of India's chief ministers', *India Review* 16(1): 106–124.

Xavier, C. (2016) *India's Expatriate Evacuation Operations: Bringing the Diaspora Back Home*, Carnegie India paper, December 2016, https://carnegieendowment.org/files/CP_299_Xavier_India_Diaspora_Final.pdf.

Xavier, C. (2018) *Bridging the Bay of Bengal: Toward a Stronger BIMSTEC*, Carnegie India paper, February, https://carnegieendowment.org/files/CP_325_Xavier_Bay_of_Bengal_INLINE.pdf.

Yadav, A. (2014) 'Modi rolls out labour reforms', *The Hindu*, 16 October, www.thehindu.com/news/national/narendra-modi-launches-host-of-schemes-at-labour-meet/article6506570.ece.

Zinkin, T. (1955) 'Indian foreign policy: an interpretation of attitudes', *World Politics* 7(2): 179–208.

Index

Quadrilateral Security Dialogue
121, 140
renewing strategic partnerships 127,
136–40
Shangri-La Dialogue 78, 96, 133–4,
145
self-reliance (*swadeshi*) 23, 29, 57, 59,
107, 109
Shah, Amit 78, 79, 89, 97
Shangri-La Dialogue 78, 96, 133–4,
135
Shankar, Ravi 81
Singapore 28, 29, 90, 96, 97, 140
Singh doctrine 34, 35, 37
Singh, Jaswant 31, 133, 136
Singh, Manmohan 7, 14, 15, 28
government 33–7
Public Diplomacy Division 87–8
reaching out to diaspora 99
relations with US 37, 137, 140–1
religious diplomacy 90–1
response to China's BRI 118–19
similarities between policies of Modi
and 38–9
US-India Nuclear Deal 12–13, 137
Singh, Rajnath 15
Singh, Sujatha 16, 143
Singh, Vijay Kumar 15
Sino-Indian war 1962 25, 32, 58
Sitaraman, Nirmala 15, 98
SJM (Swadeshi Jagran Manch) 57, 107,
108, 109
social contract theory 54
Social Darwinism 45, 49
soft power
in BJP election manifesto 2014 84
measuring success of 102–3
under Modi 9, 39, 88–9, 92, 93,
149
prior to Modi 87–8
South Asian Association for Regional
Cooperation (SAARC) 115–16,
144
South Asian Free Trade Agreement
(SAFTA) 116
South Asian Subregional Economic
Cooperation (SASEC) 117–18
sovereignty issues 36–7
Soviet Union
collapse and impact on India 27,
28
India tilts towards 26–7

Nehru's policy on 23–4
Treaty of Peace, Friendship and
Cooperation with India 27
Spencer, Herbert 45, 49
Sri Lanka 90, 92, 132
states, 'paradiplomacy' of 13–14
strategic autonomy 33–5, 134
Swadeshi Jagran Manch (SJM) 57, 107,
108, 109
swadeshi (self-reliance) 23, 29, 57, 59,
107, 109
Swamy, Subramanian 108–9
Swaraj, Sushma 14–15, 89, 94, 101,
119, 120

T

Taiwan 5, 32
Talbott-Singh talks 31, 133, 136
Tata Group 73
terrorism 126, 143–4, 166n5
Pulwama attack 39–40, 40, 79, 126,
145, 152
Uri attack 39, 126, 143–4, 145
Thailand 28, 118
the Emergency 66
think tanks and track 1.5 and track 2.0
conferences 97–8, 155
Tibet
China's suzerainty over 24, 25, 26,
58
Chinese invasion of 24–5
Deng, Gandhi and ongoing talks on
border 32–3
invitation to Sangay 5
Panchsheel agreement 24
Times of India poll 153
trade deficit 114, 141
trade liberalisation
resistance to 107–10, 111–12,
122–3
slow pace of change on 105–6
Trade Policy, 2015 113
trade, seaborne 133
trade unions 115
transcendentalism 46, 52, 58
Treaty of Peace, Friendship and
Cooperation, 1971 27
Trump, Donald 122, 127, 136, 138–9,
156